# The Preservation of the Village

## New Mexico's Hispanics and the New Deal

Suzanne Forrest

*New Mexico Land Grant Series*

John R. Van Ness, Series Editor

University of New Mexico

Albuquerque

Library of Congress Cataloging-in-Publication Data

Forrest, Suzanne, 1926–
    The preservation of the village : New Mexico's Hispanics and the New
Deal / Suzanne Forrest. — 1st ed.
    p.  cm. — (New Mexico land grant series)
    Bibliography: p.
    Includes index.
    ISBN 0–8263–1135–0. — ISBN 0–8263–1147–4 (pbk.)
    1. Hispanic Americans—Government policy—New Mexico—History—
20th century. 2. New Deal, 1933–1939. 3. New Mexico—Politics and
government—1848–1950. 4. Villages—New Mexico—History—20th
century. I. Title. II. Series.
F805.S75F67    1989
978.9'052—dc19
88–30310
        CIP

# Contents

**Maps**

# Foreword

This fourth volume in the New Mexico Land Grant Series is a departure from the earlier volumes because it is not devoted specifically to the Hispanic land grants. The previous volumes in the series have provided an up-to-date synthesis of the scholarship on the Hispanic land grants in the northern Rio Grande region and treated a variety of special aspects of land grant issues. *The Preservation of the Village,* however, is devoted to a study of a crucial period in the history of the Hispanic land grant villages, the depression years of the 1930s.

For the Hispanic villages in northern New Mexico, this was when the consequences of grant land alienation, environmental degradation, and the drastic contraction of wage labor opportunities created a crisis of life-threatening proportions. This period saw the full weight of the long-standing social and economic injustices, inequities, and governmental neglect of the Hispanic villagers come to a head. Emergency relief in the form of various Roosevelt New Deal programs saved the Hispanic villages from outright starvation; much-needed programs for social and economic modernization were also initiated, leading to improved health, nutrition, and standard of living. Thus, as the reader will learn, the New Deal programs set in motion social and economic changes that shaped the villages as we know them today. Rural northern New Mexico cannot be understood properly without knowledge of this important transitional era. Indeed, this study was long overdue.

A principal strength of this marvelous book by Suzanne Forrest is its breadth. It successfully places northern New Mexico of the 1930s in a broad regional and national perspective. The reader learns of the major currents of social and political thought in American society that influenced Hispanic New Deal programs. The national political arena where federal New Deal policies and programs were conceived and administered is also described. The study is successful in revealing the philosophical and social backgrounds of the Anglo Americans who, by and large, administered the New Deal programs. The reader is able to understand these bureaucrats as real human beings motivated by ideals that can be understood readily, even if at times we judge them to have been misguided. The book is first-rate American regional history; it is also ethnic history that defines the distinctive experience setting New Mexican Hispanos apart from other Chicanos. Furthermore, it sheds light on aspects of Anglo-American ethnicity. As intellectual history, this study brings into focus the first period when substantial social and cultural data on the Hispanic villages were gathered and analyzed. Many seminal studies were completed at this time, including those by George Sanchez, Charles Loomis, Paul Walter, and Florence Kluckhohn.

The study may hold greatest benefits for aspiring agents of change and development. This work is virtually a case study of George Santayana's admonition that "Those who cannot remember the past are condemned to repeat it." Beyond the immediate relief of villagers in dire straits, the New Deal programs sought to restore the cultural and economic integrity of an old and distinctive rural population. This ambitious goal was pursued through efforts to modernize small-scale agriculture and stock raising and to augment the economy by reviving native arts and crafts and developing cottage industries. It also sought to raise the standard of living generally through educational programs directed at modernizing all phases of domestic life. Finally, efforts to document and preserve Hispanic traditions—music, folklore, art, and social customs—were meant to inject new life into village culture.

As Forrest cogently argues, however, this agenda was doomed to failure from the beginning, for it embodied conflicting goals. New Deal agents sought to preserve the cooperative communitarian values of the villages while attempting to transform the backward and inefficient economy. As has frequently been the case, these agents of change failed to realize that a new technology cannot be instituted in agriculture, animal husbandry, homemaking, and child care without transforming many other aspects of the social life and culture. They failed to grasp the organic whole that was Hispanic village culture; that is, the fact that the means of gaining a livelihood, general patterns of social life, community beliefs, and values were all closely interrelated and interdependent. Hispanos must have been struck by the tremendous incongruities in thought and action displayed by the agents of the New Deal programs. As Forrest points out, the New Deal agents praised the virtues of Hispanic art, crafts, music, and folklore, and at the same time they vowed to eradicate what were deemed to be undesirable "superstitions" and "irrational" economic behavior that placed family and village solidarity above monetary gain. It is not difficult to understand why these federal agents were received with suspicion nor why villagers were often reluctant to participate in New Deal programs.

*The Preservation of the Village* makes an important contribution to Hispanic land grant history in describing the substantial New Deal effort at land reform. This program envisioned restoring large sections of New Mexico's grant lands to exclusive village use as well as reclaiming eroded lands and restoring fertility. To facilitate this effort the government studied the history of New Mexico land titles, which demonstrated that the Hispanic villages had rightful claims to much of the vast grazing lands controlled by the federal government. As the reader will learn, however, the land reform program fell far short of its goal due to its controversial nature (it emphasized communal tenure and common land use); it also threatened the large ranchers and created friction with the Indian communities.

As Forrest convincingly demonstrates, the New Deal programs ultimately failed because they did not change any of the existing economic realities in northern New Mexico. When the programs terminated, the villagers still lacked the basic land and water resources to subsist, and local sources of wage labor were not created to replace the old agropastoral economy. Of course, northern New Mexico merely reflected the way American rural life in general was changing, with the development of postwar technology, the decline of the small farm, and the growth of corporate agribusiness.

In conclusion, this carefully researched and extremely well-written book will certainly find a wide audience. It is an important contribution to the study of the Hispanic land grant villages and the disastrous consequences of their dwindling resources. More broadly, it successfully chronicles a tumultuous and complex period of twentieth-century New Mexico history. The book will be a valuable contribution to Chicano studies and, more generally, ethnic studies in America. For many of us who came to know and love northern New Mexico during the most recent period of social upheaval and economic change and the Johnson-era War on Poverty that followed it, the New Deal story has a familiar resonance. One feels he has experienced similar times and cannot help wondering when the next cycle of social unrest and reform will begin in this unique region of the country.

John R. Van Ness
Series Editor
Ursinus College

# Preface

The idea for this study first occurred to me during the late 1970s when, as director of the Albuquerque Museum, I became aware of the great importance of traditional Hispanic crafts to the then current Chicano cultural revival. Through personal discussions with many of the artist-craftsmen involved in the movement, as well as through more formal oral histories, I learned that most had either learned their craft in New Deal WPA classes or been influenced and taught by others who had. Since I know that the recording and revival of Hispanic folk crafts, along with similar efforts to record and preserve traditional Hispanic music, drama, folk medicine, legends and, tales, had been an important emphasis of New Mexico's New Deal, I was led to wonder how this period fit into the scheme of Spanish Borderlands history, Chicano history, and the history of American ethnic relationships. Thus, while this study may appear at first glance to be a case study of the New Deal on the state level, it is really much more, and much less. It does not purport to cover all the New Deal programs in New Mexico or to compare them with those of other state programs. Neither does it attempt to relate these programs, except in a very specific way, to the philosophy and politics of the national New Deal. What it does is attempt to place what I have chosen to call the New Mexican Hispanic New Deal within the context of Anglo American ethnic history, and to explore the significance of this little-known and rather divergent chapter of Mexican American history on the subsequent history of New Mexico's Hispanos.

Because my first exposure to the New Mexico New Deal programs was through the crafts revival, my first question was why crafts, along with other aspects of traditional Hispanic culture, had played such an important role in the Anglo-dominated New Deal. The fact that a similar, and generally better known, effort to preserve the historic crafts of Appalachia had stimulated similar WPA programs suggested a broader Anglo American concern with traditional cultures than would have applied had the crafts programs been confined to New Mexico alone. In both cases the crafts revivals had their immediate origins in a romantic regionalism that was an expression of American nationalism. This observation led to my first area of research; an inquiry into the relation of the New Deal crafts revival to the broader history of American nationalism and romantic thought.

The New Mexico crafts revival differed from the similar one in Appalachia in a vitally important respect. Whereas the inhabitants of Appalachia are poor relations of Anglo-Saxon America, the Hispanos of New Mexico are both culturally and, to a lesser degree, racially different. Thus the concern of Anglo-Saxon America for the preservation of Hispanic cultural distinctiveness took on ethnic overtones, with the closest historical parallel being the 1920s progressive effort to preserve elements of immigrant culture in the nation's eastern slums. This observation led me to my next question, which was how the cultural revival related to American ethnic history. Here I found John Higham's landmark studies of American immigrants and interethnic relations, *Strangers in the Land: Patterns of American Nativism, 1860–1925* and *Send These to Me: Jews and Other Immigrants in Urban America* to be a useful point of departure.[1]

Several related questions concerned the specifics of the New Mexican New Deal. How was the Hispanic cultural revival incorporated into the New Deal guidelines? Was there, as I suspected, a continuity of personnel and motivation between the 1920s Spanish-Colonial revival and the 1930s New Deal? If so, did this fact imply a stronger continuation of both romantic thought and progressive idealism in the New Deal than many historians have heretofore recognized?

As it turned out, the crafts revival was no more than the tip of the iceberg. A cursory review of the literature produced during the period suggested a much further reaching program of land reform and cultural revival than could reasonably have been motivated by romantic, nationalistic concerns alone. Strong economic and political motives had to have existed as well. I determined to discover what they were, who served to benefit, who to lose, and how these motives had influenced the directions taken by the programs.

As for the long term effect of the New Deal on New Mexico's Hispanic communities, contemporary writers considered the programs to have been effective yet few traces remain today of their successes. Most historians, in fact, blame the New Deal for much of the area's present day poverty and dependence. Since the programs clearly failed to do what they had intended; that is, restore the cultural and economic integrity of this rural population, I wanted to know how and why they had failed. Whatever the assessment, I knew that it would be an interesting chapter in the history of Anglo-Hispanic relations—one more characterized by cooperation than by conflict, and more driven by humanitarian concerns than by economic exploitation. Only after I was well into the study did I realize that it would be a revealing chapter in the history of Hispanic-Indian relations, as well.

It is an odd fact that, although much has been written about the history of American immigrants, our oldest immigrant group and second largest ethnic minority, Americans of Mexican descent, has been virtually ignored in the historical literature. In part this can be explained by the predominantly east coast, urban perspective of most historians of the immigrant experience. Mexican Americans have, however, differed from other immigrants in several respects. Like the American Indians, the Hispanos who settled the Southwest decades before the Anglo Americans annexed it in 1846 were forcibly incorporated into the United States under terms that colored their future history in many ways. They did not choose assimilation and, for the most part, refused to leave their homeland in the interests of economic betterment. Instead, they fought desperately to retain their ancestral lands and their traditional values. While the imposition of colonial status upon both Hispanos and Indians put these people in a distinctly unfavorable social and economic situation, it enabled some Anglo Americans to establish a special protective relationship over them—one that assuaged their guilt even as it enhanced their sense of themselves as socially and intellectually superior human beings. This special relationship, which reached its zenith during the 1930s New Deal, is the subject of this study. As much as anything, it highlights what Higham has called the essential American dilemma— the problem of reconciling integration with pluralism; of protecting the rights of individuals while preserving the rights of minorities.[2]

Though Mexican American history came into its own during the 1960s it is still a relatively new field of inquiry. Much of what has been written has focused around themes of exploitation, discrimination, resistance, and liberation. These matters, which have been universally a part of the Mexican American experience, have been explained according to two prevailing models. One model relates them to the historical perspective of colonialism; the other relates them to the dynamics of economic and social class structure. It is significant, therefore, that the first important sociocultural study of Hispanos by a native born Mexican American, George Sanchez's classic *Forgotten People: A Study of New Mexicans*, not only emerged in New Mexico during the 1930s but traced Hispanic problems to their nineteenth-century colonial origins.[3] Though primarily concerned with problems of assimilation, Sanchez called attention to the many inequities faced by his people and was a pioneer in noting that group pride mediates the assimilative process. By calling attention to the fact that the arousal of nationalist and racial sentiments is an essential phase in the mingling of peoples he paved the way for the new Chicano historiography which stresses community survival, the development of a dynamic, syncretic culture, and resistance to the homogenizing forces of total assimilation. The wide and popular acceptance of his work advanced the cause of cultural pluralism and contributed to a new mind-set within the emerging Hispanic middle class.

This study which, among other things, explores the theme of community survival, should help to fill the need recently expressed by Chicano historian, Carlos E. Cortés, for more comprehensive state-level histories of the Chicano experience.[4] It should also fill the need expressed by Otis L. Graham for more histories of American minority groups during the 1930s and for another look at New Deal successes and failures.[5] Some historians may regret that I have not been more assiduous in apportioning credit and blame. To this complaint I readily confess a greater concern with social processes—the dynamics of social forces and barriers to change—than with politics. While this orientation may derive in part from the fact that I have not personally suffered "the slings and arrows" of my Mexican American colleagues, I would argue, like Otis Graham, that "there cannot be good political history without knowledge of the full social setting within which men attempted social management."[6] This study of Anglo-Hispanic relations in northern New Mexico during the depression will, I hope, further this understanding.

No study of this sort can be complete without a full and appreciative acknowledgment of all the individuals and institutions that made it possible. First among these are my professors at the University of Wyoming, and in particular the members of my doctoral committee: Lawrence Cardoso, Chair; Deborah Hardy; William Howard Moore and Robert Righter in the Department of History; and Audrey Shalinsky in the Department of Anthropology. All have encouraged my efforts and helped in the production of this manuscript in ways too numerous to mention. I am deeply appreciative to the History Department collectively for awarding me a graduate research grant, and to the anonymous donor of that grant. I wish to express my appreciation as well to other teachers who, over the years, stimulated my curiosity and encouraged my desire to learn. Primary among these, in more ways than one, are my mother and my late father.

I am grateful to the staff of the National Archives in Washington, D.C., and in particular to Robert Kvasnicka and Richard Crawford of the Scientific, Economic, and Natural Resources Division. They provided me with the materials I needed with admirable efficiency and in record time. I am grateful as well to Richard Salazar and Donald Padilla of the New Mexico State Records Center and Archives, and to Orlando Romero of the Museum of New Mexico History Library for their help in locating elusive documents. Peter Iverson, originally on my doctoral committee, left it when he joined the faculty at Arizona State University West. Before he left he read portions of the manuscript and besides offering many excellent criticisms, was most helpful in offering suggestions for further research. Donald Parman of Purdue University and Lawrence Kelly of North Texas State University were both helpful in providing me with information and suggestions concerning John Collier and the Indian New Deal. G. Emlyn Hall, an Albuquerque attorney and a professor in the University of New Mexico School of Law, provided me with some interesting information concerning the Pueblo Lands controversy; and Rick Hanks, manager of the Rio Puerco Resource Area of the Bureau of Land Management in Albuquerque, New Mexico, helped me trace the final disposition of the New Mexico lands acquired for dependent populations through the New Deal land program. John Van Ness of Ursinus College, Sarah Deutsch of the Massachusetts Institute of Technology, and Malcolm Ebright, Director of the Center for Land Grant Studies in Santa Fe read portions of the manuscript and offered much appreciated criticism and information. Jerie Owens of Laramie, Wyoming, typed the manuscript with letter perfect accuracy and in record time. The Extension Service and Inter-Library Loan staffs of the University of Wyoming could not have been more helpful.

I have come to understand and appreciate Hispanic village culture over the years through a number of people and experiences. David and Jeannine Ortega of Chimayo, New Mexico, first introduced me to it years ago. I learned more about it from the many contemporary Hispanic craftspersons whom I met during the planning and preparation of the exhibit "One Space—Three Visions" which opened the new Albuquerque Museum building in August, 1979.

The greatest appreciation must go to my husband without whose support and encouragement this study could never have been accomplished. It was he who read each chapter and reminded me, when I got too close and involved with my subject matter, that I had to keep pointing a finger—a long, bony literary finger—to guide my readers through the ideas to the final conclusion. It is to him that this manuscript is affectionately dedicated.

# Abbreviations

The following abbreviations are commonly used throughout the text and footnotes:

| | |
|---|---|
| AAA | Agricultural Adjustment Administration |
| CCC | Civilian Conservation Corps |
| CWA | Civil Works Administration |
| ECW | Emergency Conservation Works (also known as CCC) |
| FERA | Federal Emergency Relief Administration |
| FSA | Farm Security Administration |
| FDRL | Franklin D. Roosevelt Library |
| MNM-HL | Museum of New Mexico—History Library |
| MNM-LA | Museum of New Mexico—Laboratory of Anthropology |
| NARG | National Archives Record Group |
| NMHR | *New Mexico Historical Review* |
| NMSRCA | New Mexico State Records Center and Archives |
| NRA | National Relief Administration |
| POUR | President's Organization for Unemployment Relief |
| RA | Resettlement Administration |
| RFC | Reconstruction Finance Corporation |
| SCS | Soil Conservation Service |
| SES | Soil Erosion Service |
| WPA | Works Progress Administration (later Work Projects Administration) |

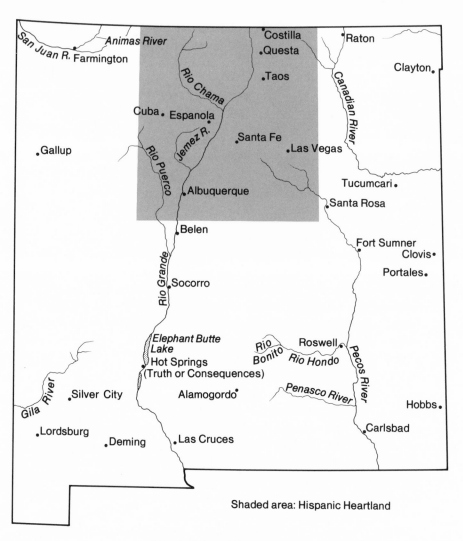

Shaded area: Hispanic Heartland

Map 1. Map of New Mexico.

ONE

# The New Mexico Difference

A scenic but lesser traveled road leading north from Santa Fe to Taos departs from the main highway near the village of Nambé and passes through the heart of Hispanic New Mexico. For a few miles it follows a well watered valley lush with cottonwoods and lined with the adobe homes of Santa Fe and Los Alamos exurbanites. Then, passing the village of Nambé, it climbs up onto a broken, eroded landscape of juniper and piñon covered hills. The land here is stark and empty. The only sign of human occupation as far as the eye can see is a slim white cross atop one of the rolling hills. Far to the west lie the purple shadowed Jemez peaks, remnants of a vast extinct volcano. Closer to the east are the pine covered slopes of the Sangre de Cristo range. The road twists and climbs, dips and climbs again, then descends into the Santa Cruz valley, wider than the last, scattered with small garden plots, orchards and homes. The green of cottonwoods and irrigated fields, sharply contrasting with the dun brown hillsides, attests to the ingenuity of man and the life-giving run-off from the neighboring snow capped peaks.

Settlers from Mexico, or New Spain as it was called then, began to trek north to this picturesque land in the closing decade of the sixteenth century. By 1609, just two years after the founding of Jamestown, Virginia, the Spanish Colonial bureaucracy was established in its capital city of Santa Fe—the city of the Holy Faith. The site was deliberately located in the midst of the Pueblo Indian population, since "civilizing" and Christianizing the Indian natives was an official goal of settlement. Other goals were the establishment of a military outpost to protect this far northern frontier of Spanish empire from foreign invasion and the enrichment of the Spanish Crown through the presumed riches of the province.

The riches proved illusory, and the Spanish Colonials failed to dominate either the sedentary Pueblo Indians or the nomadic Navajos, Apaches,
Comanches, and Utes. The Pueblo Indians did adopt Christianity, but
they soon became frustrated with the heavy handed efforts of the Spanish
authorities to put them to the service of the Crown and change their
traditional way of life. In 1680, in a rare show of unity, they united in
a bloody rebellion and drove the Spanish settlers out of New Mexico.[1]

The Spanish returned in 1692. Chastened by their earlier experience,
they announced to the Pueblos that they came in peace, and not to avenge
past wrongs. The reconquest, though far from bloodless, was soon accomplished and, with dreams of riches now long gone, the colonists
settled into a simple and stable agricultural life-style. Most settled in
villages made up of extended family units along the Rio Grande and in
the sheltered intermountain river valleys to the east and west. Here they
diverted water from the river or streams for farming and grazed flocks
of goats and hardy sheep called *churros* on the nearby hillsides.

The Spanish colonists occupied irrigable bottom lands adjacent to the
Indian pueblos. Some of these lands had never been cultivated, but most
had been abandoned earlier in the century as a result of the severe decline
in the Indian population following its first exposure to European dis-
eases.[2] Numbers of both groups were relatively small, but despite the
lack of population pressure disputes arose over the use of land, and even
more so, over the land's all-important source of water. The Spanish
penchant for town life, private ownership of agricultural land, and the
introduction of domestic animals put a strain on water resources every-
where. Spanish water law permitted most disputes to be settled relatively
equitably, however, and the two populations learned to live together in
considerable harmony.[3] They frequently cooperated in fighting off at-
tacks from other Indian groups, notably the nomadic Navajos, Apaches,
and Comanches; and, when not fighting, traded with them and with
each other. Over the years many Hispanic farmers intermarried with
their Indian neighbors, adding to the Indian heritage most had brought
with them from Mexico. Even so, the villagers retained a distinctively
Hispanic cast to their culture and retained, virtually intact, their Roman
Catholic faith and Spanish language.

New Mexico's Hispanic heartland encompasses the upper and middle
valleys of the Rio Grande watershed from the Colorado–New Mexico
border southward to the Elephant Butte dam below Socorro. (See Maps

2 and 3) It comprises, in rough fashion, the counties of Taos, Rio Arriba, Santa Fe, Sandoval, Bernalillo, Socorro, and Valencia. A diverse area of pine and aspen clad mountains, deep canyons, intermountain river valleys, grassy plateaus, and flat-topped mesas, the area is commonly acknowledged to be one of the most picturesque regions in the United States and is the source and inspiration of New Mexico's renown as "the Land of Enchantment." It is also one of the oldest areas of human habitation in the Western Hemisphere. The present population includes three distinct ethnic groups: native Indian, Hispanic American, and Anglo American, who occupied the area in the order named. For the bulk of its history the population has been rural and concentrated in small settlements along the rivers adjacent to irrigated lands. The lands surrounding the watershed are largely semiarid and offer only limited possibilities for dry farming. Since the arrival of the Spanish in the sixteenth century with their domesticated cattle and sheep, they have been used as rangeland. Until late in the nineteenth century herds of buffalo roamed the plains providing the inhabitants of the Rio Grande Valley with a source of meat to supplement their largely vegetarian diet of corn, beans, squash, and chile peppers.

The land is high and dry, with elevations ranging from 4,200 feet at Elephant Butte to over 8,000 feet in the upper valley. The surrounding mountains range in altitude from 10,000 to 14,000 feet.[4] Because of the elevation, winters are cold and snowy with temperature readings of fifty degrees below zero (Fahrenheit) not unknown in some mountain communities. Fortunately, the abundant winter sunshine brings milder temperatures in the daytime. Spring, summer, and fall are pleasant and mild but early and late frosts are common, shortening the growing season.

The villages established by these Spanish pioneers survive today, anachronisms in a twentieth-century America devoted to industrial technology and commercial agriculture. These villages are unlike any other communities in the country. Although several different village types exist, all have certain features in common. There is first and foremost the impression of great antiquity—the sense that the twentieth century with its electricity, television aerials, and pick-up trucks has intruded very recently upon a basic structure centuries old. Most villages are very small, consisting of a few hundred residents. There are no paved streets and no centers of business activity. Often there is a filling station and a

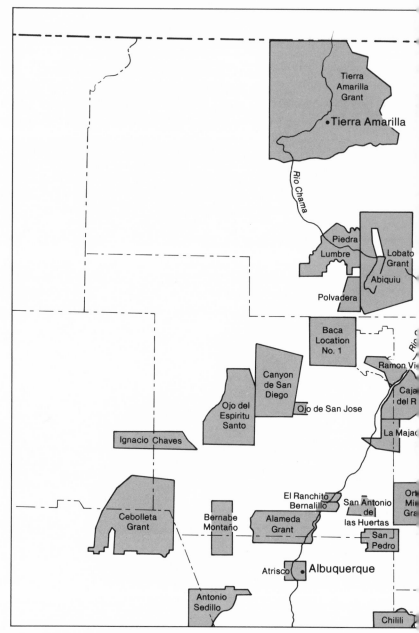

## Principal Land Grants of North Central New Mexico

Map 2. New Mexico land grants.

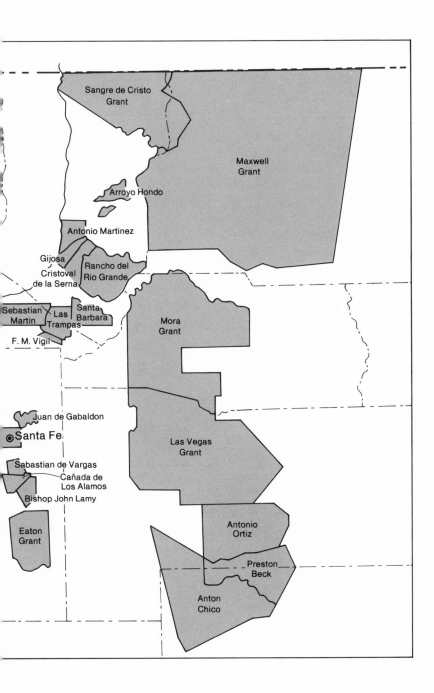

Sangre de Cristo
Grant

Maxwell
Grant

Arroyo Hondo

Antonio Martinez

Gijosa

Cristoval
de la Serna

Rancho del
Rio Grande

Sebastian
Martin

Las
Trampas

Santa
Barbara

Mora
Grant

F. M. Vigil

Juan de Gabaldon

Santa Fe

Sabastian de Vargas

Cañada de
Los Alamos

Las Vegas
Grant

Bishop John Lamy

Eaton
Grant

Antonio
Ortiz

Preston
Beck

Anton
Chico

5

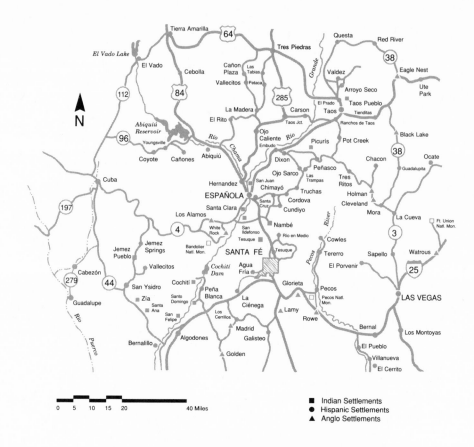

Map 3. New Mexico's Hispanic heartland.

6

general store, sometimes combined with a post office and package liquor store. Occasionally a shingle hung on the side of a house or on a gatepost announces a service or a trade for sale. In the mountain villages the houses are clustered around and near a central plaza. In the valleys the houses tend to string out along the river and its feeder irrigation ditches. The dominant, and invariably the best kept, structure in the community is the Catholic Church, quite often a massive adobe building flanked by a small graveyard and encircled by an adobe wall or picket fence. The irrigated fields, which give the village its reason for being, extend beyond it in long, narrow strips, like fingers of land reaching for the source of water.

A visitor to the area may well wonder what keeps the villages alive. The deficiencies can be read in the face of the land. The irrigated patches of corn, beans, and chile peppers are too small for efficient farming and many patches of land are weed choked and abandoned. Beyond them the eroded hillsides, cut with gullies, show the telltale scars of chronic overgrazing. Many orchards are old and scraggly; the few head of live-stock are of poor quality. Although not immediately apparent, the fact is that the poverty would be much worse were it not for government aid and money sent by family members who have left the villages to seek employment elsewhere.[5] Yet the villages persist despite their apparent lack of economic viability.[6]

The Hispanos of New Mexico, along with other Spanish-speaking inhabitants of the vast Southwestern area acquired by the United States from Mexico between 1845 and 1854, share a unique position with the American Indians as a people annexed against their will. Unlike the Indians, they have had no special government agency to protect them and look after their rights. The Treaty of Guadalupe-Hidalgo, signed in 1848 between the United States and Mexico when the territory was acquired, included specific provisions concerning the Mexicans who re-mained in the conquered territory. Those who wished to return to Mexico were permitted to do so. Those who wished to remain, yet retain their Mexican citizenship, could do so by making a public declaration of their intent within the year. Those who chose to become new Americans were guaranteed "all the rights of citizens of the United States."[7] Three arti-cles, VIII, IX, and X, spelled out these rights. Article VIII assured the new Mexican Americans the "enjoyment of all the rights of citizens of the United States according to the principles of the Constitution," in-cluding the free enjoyment of their liberty and property, and the free exercise of their religion. Article IX made them politically equal to the inhabitants of all other territories of the United States. Article X declared that "all grants of land made by the Mexican government or by competent authorities in territories previously appertaining to Mexico . . . shall be respected as valid, to the same extent . . . as if the said territories had remained within the limits of Mexico." Although the United States Senate eliminated Article X before it ratified the treaty, a protocol appended to the treaty assured Mexico that the rights of Mexican Americans would be fully guaranteed because "these invaluable blessings, under our form of Government, do not result from Treaty stipulations, but from the very nature and character of our institutions."

The United States did not regard the protocol as legally binding, but the Mexicans, under duress to sign, took it seriously.[8] That the United States, in retrospect, did not provide the guarantees it promised lay not with the treaty but with the failure of the Congress and its appointed officials to assure its prompt and equitable implementation.[9] It lay as well with the enormous impact of Anglo immigration into the newly opened territories.

Texas was already overwhelmingly Anglo American when it achieved its independence in 1836. The next decade saw its population quadruple, with most of the increase coming from Anglo immigration. The Texas constitution solidified Anglo political power by denying all rights of citizenship and land ownership to persons who had refused to participate in the revolution or who had aided the enemy. While not all Texas Mexicans had sided with Mexico, Anglo Texans tended to paint them all with the same brush. Subject to intimidation and fearful of the anti-Mexican hatred and reprisals that followed the Texas Revolution, many Texas Mexicans abandoned their lands and fled across the Rio Grande. In 1860 only 12,000 native Mexicans remained in Texas out of a population which, by mid-decade numbered about half a million, a third of which were black slaves. Although the state upheld the validity of most of the Spanish and Mexican grants, lower-class Mexicans lost their lands through force and intimidation, while the upper class lost theirs through litigation, chicanery, and high taxes.[10] Meanwhile, the continued presence of large contingents of U.S. troops along the Texan border was such a stimulant to the Texan economy that by 1860 it was dominated by Anglo Americans. Not until the 1890s, when irrigation agriculture displaced the open range cattle industry, did a demand for Mexican labor bring large numbers of Mexicans back to Texas.[11]

In California the Anglo-American population grew even faster than it had in Texas as thousands of gold seekers flooded the state in 1848. By the end of 1849, 115,000 people lived in California, only 13,000 of whom were Mexican. By 1850 the state had a population of 380,000, enough to qualify the territory for statehood. Mexican economic competition undoubtedly prompted Anglos to make them a despised minority unable to obtain equal protection of the law and subject to intimidation and violence. The new state legislature passed a rash of laws discriminatory to Mexican labor and culture. Other laws gave Anglo Americans an advantage in taking over Mexican lands.[12] A series of natural disasters in the 1860s completed the process of land loss by devastating the native Californio ranching industry. By the 1870s the native Californios had lost three-quarters of their land, and along with it, their remaining economic and political power. Only after the arrival of the railroads, and the full development of the California industrial and agricultural economy, did Mexicans from Mexico enter the state in significant numbers to become the dominant laboring class.[13]

Arizona Mexicans constituted the majority of the population through the 1870s but, unlike the Hispanos of New Mexico, with whom they shared the New Mexico Territory, most were newly arrived immigrants from Sonora. They held transient jobs on ranches and farms and, by the 1880s, in mines, smelters and railroad yards. Few were American citizens. As the lower class of manual laborers on a lawless frontier where peonage not only existed, but was protected by law, the Arizona Mexicans were exploited and brutalized. In the 1870s, with the mechanization of mining and agriculture, they became the most vulnerable element in Arizona's developing market economy.[14]

In contrast to Texas, California, and Arizona, Anglo economic domination in New Mexico developed slowly. In 1850 the area contained a population of approximately 54,000, of which approximately 47,000 or 86 percent were Hispanos, 6400 or 12 percent were Indians, and 1000 to 1500 or 2 percent were Anglo Americans, most of the latter having come into the area in the preceding decade. Outside of this area there were only about seven thousand persons in all of what is now the state of New Mexico, most of them in the area surrounding Las Vegas.[15]

Between 1850 and 1930 the population in the upper and middle Rio Grande valleys outside the two major cities of Santa Fe and Albuquerque grew by a modest 44 percent, while the population of the rest of the state grew by an amazing 3,953 percent. By 1930 the population within the northern valleys, numbered at 137,713, represented only 33 percent of the population of the state. Within this rural population Hispanos made up 76 percent of the total, Indians 10 percent, and Anglo Americans 14 percent. Though the Hispanos had lost much of their numerical advantage in the cities, making up 33 percent of the population of Albuquerque and 60 percent of that of Santa Fe, they remained a substantial majority in northern New Mexico. In 1930, on the eve of the Great Depression, they still comprised 66 percent of the total, with Indians a bare 7 percent and Anglo Americans 27 percent.[16]

Through the years the Hispanos of New Mexico, like the rest of their brethren in the annexed territories, lost much of their land through litigation and fraud, government seizure, and tax delinquencies. They saw much of the rest destroyed through erosion and commercial overuse. Like other Spanish-speaking citizens of the United States, they became victims of racial and ethnic prejudice. But, because of their numerical superiority, especially in the Upper Rio Grande Valley, their leaders were able to play an astute political game at the state and local level.

Through their influence the 1910 Constitution, which went into effect in 1912 when New Mexico became a state, effectively laid the groundwork for the protection of both their legal rights and culture. It made New Mexico officially a bilingual state, putting English and Spanish on an equal basis for all state business. It provided for the training of bilingual teachers, prohibited separate schools for Anglo and Hispano children, and specifically, provided that the rights guaranteed by the Treaty of Guadalupe-Hidalgo would remain in force in the new state.[17]

During the second half of the nineteenth century New Mexico's Hispanos made the transition from a multiresource based, preindustrial economy to that of full, if second class, participation in the modern American economy. In the process of coping with the Anglo introduced forces of economic and technological change, they adopted new tactics for their economic and cultural survival. Migrant labor, in particular, became a means by which Hispanic men, and sometimes whole families, kept a secure foothold in the villages, while branching out in search of new sources of income to compensate for the loss of their grazing lands. The migrants brought much needed cash to the villages, while the villages preserved the migrant workers' ethnic roots and protected them and their families against the exigencies of seasonal flux. This measure of independence and mobility also permitted the villagers to protest unpalatable employer demands and working conditions. With little incentive to accumulate or increase their consumption of industrial goods, and without a fear of destitution, New Mexico's Hispanos sought and left work based as much on their own limited cash needs as on labor market demands. In this way they successfully resisted Anglo efforts to make them conform to individualistic competitive behavior, and they retained a remarkable degree of control over the development of their culture.[18]

The key element in this highly successful strategy of cultural and economic survival was the performance of Hispanic women in building and maintaining kin and cultural networks throughout an area that included all of northern New Mexico, much of Colorado, and parts of Utah, Montana, and Wyoming. The women kept village culture alive and well within this widespread "regional community," through patterns of visiting, ceremonial co-parenthood, and religious activities. At the same time they preserved the integrity and the economic stability of the villages by growing and processing food, and flexibly adopting whatever new gender roles were needed in their male depleted society.[19]

Despite these coping skills, by the 1930s the Hispanos of the Upper and Middle Rio Grande Valley were considered by national standards to be one of the poorest groups in the nation.[20] Statistics from the 1930 census and other surveys made later in the period emphasized the extent to which they fell outside the parameters of desired American norms. New Mexico had, by far, the highest birth and death rates in the nation, with infant mortality amounting to 136 deaths for every thousand births.[21] In the counties with 50 percent or more Hispanos, infants died at the rate of 144.4 per thousand, and in the county with the largest Indian population, they died at a record 212.4 deaths per thousand.[22]

By 1930 the average Hispanic farm family had only six acres under cultivation. It did well to net from this a little over $100 a year, not enough for subsistence living.[23] In the Upper Rio Grande Valley, where chile was the principal cash crop, the harvest was committed well in advance as credit at the village store.[24] Sheepherders who tended flocks on shares for large commercial wool merchants were caught in a similar escalating cycle of debt.[25] The Hispanic bean farmers of the Estancia Valley were no better off. Hard put to compete on their small plots with the large, commercial Anglo operators, they had so abused their land through overuse that dust storms and wind erosion were major problems.[26] In the Middle Rio Grande Valley, where the irrigable lands had been put into a Conservancy District, Hispanos were delinquent in their taxes on as much as 70 percent of all their agricultural lands.[27]

Without supplementary income from wage labor, few Hispanic families could pay their taxes. Ironically, because of the lack of commercial and industrial development, the large amounts of government lands taken off the tax rolls, and the indebtedness created by the numerous reclamation projects, the predominantly Hispanic counties of northern New Mexico had, proportionately, the highest property taxes in the state.[28] As a result ever increasing numbers of Hispanic families lost their lands through foreclosures and tax sales. Even more remained on the land unaware that, for lack of tax payments, they no longer owned it.[29]

As the tax collections declined, so did the benefits from tax supported public services. Public health facilities, institutions for the aged, handicapped, and mentally disabled were nonexistent. Welfare benefits were negligible.[30] Forced to cut back on expenses, the poorer Hispanic counties made school terms shorter. School buildings and instructional materials deteriorated for lack of money to repair or replace them. Because the predominantly Hispanic counties offered the lowest salaries and poorest working conditions, the teachers were generally the least prepared.[31] School attendance in rural areas was sporadic, especially in bad weather when the children encountered difficulties getting to school. More than one-fifth had to be bussed and the average length of a bus route in New Mexico was twenty-three miles one way. In addition, most children had to walk many miles to get to the bus.[32]

According to 1933 school statistics, 36 percent of all New Mexican first graders were eliminated before entering second grade. Only 44 percent of those eligible entered eighth grade, 39 percent entered high school, and a bare 13 percent graduated. Because of the increase in population from outside the state the figures hid the fact that the holding power of the schools was actually far worse than it seemed, especially in the counties with predominantly Hispanic populations.[33]

The results of this lack of schooling were hardly surprising. Illiteracy had fallen from 78.5 percent in 1870 to 13.3 percent in 1930, but New Mexico still ranked third from the bottom among the states in the Union.[34] More significantly, 72 percent of the illiterates were Hispanos and Indians, and four-fifths of the illiterates were aged twenty-one and older.[35]

Most of these grim statistics were compiled to justify massive efforts at cultural intervention designed to bring this blighted and "un-

American" ethnic population within the parameters of desired American norms. Other statistics compiled during the 1920s and early 1930s which attempted to demonstrate low Hispanic IQ were motivated by a desire to prove Hispanic racial inferiority. All were part of a concentrated effort to rid American society of the alien elements that many thought were eroding the nation's cultural values and diluting its racial purity. Americans, in general, during the 1920s and 1930s were bewildered and unsettled by the multitude of changes occurring within their rapidly urbanizing and industrializing society. They blamed these changes on the thousands of new immigrants that flooded yearly through the gates of Ellis Island, and concluded that, for the nation to prosper, all "alien" elements in the population must either be assimilated or eliminated as quickly as possible. Educators and social workers in the city slums de- voted themselves to turning the new immigrants into "100 percent Americans." Other Americans urged passage of the Immigration Acts of 1917 and 1924, which put severe quotas on immigrants from southern and eastern Europe.

In the Southwest, many people considered Mexicans to be even less desirable than the new European immigrants. Their fears derived from a number of factors. They objected to the fact that the majority of Mexicans entering the country were racially mixed and of dark skin color. They, and others, also objected to the fact that they were largely poor and uneducated, and that they came from a country troubled with po- litical unrest and revolutionary violence. Finally, many Americans har- bored deep suspicions concerning the Spanish character. They believed that people of Spanish ancestry were peculiarly untrustworthy, cruel, and lascivious—a set of negative stereotypes dating back to sixteenth- century England that historians call the "black legend."

Alarmed by the numbers of Mexican laborers that were entering the country, these Americans lobbied vigorously for their inclusion in the immigration legislation. But while they may have represented the ma- jority opinion, their efforts were defeated by an even stronger lobby of western businessmen, missionaries, politicians, and government ad- ministrators. United States officials, greatly concerned with the revo- lutionary turmoil in their southern neighbor, hoped to promote stability by providing Mexico with an escape valve and, in the form of returning workers, American dollars, and technological know-how. The mission- aries supported large-scale immigration from Mexico based on the con- viction that Protestantism could save both Mexico and its peoples from revolutionary and economic chaos. The strongest argument, however, was that presented by the business-agricultural lobby. It pronounced Mexicans to be "the preferred of all cheap labor available to the Southwest," uniquely capable of performing hard "stoop" labor under a blistering sun, and indispensable to the American economy. Though American workers resented Mexicans for their willingness to put up with low wages and miserable working conditions, and for their use by employers as strike breakers, the proponents of Mexican immigration prevailed and Mexicans were excluded from all immigration legislation.[36]

By the time of the Great Depression Americans had already had two decades of experience with the love-hate relationship that has characterized Mexican American labor relationships to the present day. Beginning in 1910 with the completion of the railroad from central Mexico to the United States border Mexicans were driven north by the chronic poverty and harsh working conditions of Mexican rural life, and the terrible upheaval of the Mexican revolution. At the same time they were pulled north by American employers seeking cheap, easily controlled, and dispensable labor. The primary impetus for both movements was the tremendous agricultural expansion in the American Southwest—in the Imperial and San Joaquin valleys of California, the Salt River Valley of Arizona, the lower Rio Grande Valley of Texas, and the sugar beet fields of Colorado and Wyoming.[37]

The common denominator in all agricultural employment, as well as that in many new southwestern industries, was its seasonal nature. Mexican laborers were regarded as ideal seasonal workers. They were plentiful, desperate for work, and when no longer needed, could be expected to return to their homes in Mexico, well satisfied with the money they had earned while in the United States.[38]

The labor market into which the Mexicans had flocked disappeared with the onset of the Great Depression. With it went the desire for Mexican workers. Always regarded as expendable, Mexicans were among the first to be dismissed as businesses closed down. Thousands of workers and their families were suddenly left without resources and dependent upon local charities or public relief. Almost paradoxically, Mexican workers who did not lose their jobs were accused of holding them at the expense of American citizens. As the depression deepened, so did nativistic pressures to find a scapegoat. Angry citizens throughout the country demanded that aliens be removed from the relief rolls. In the Southwest immigration officials searched for Mexican immigrants, and welfare agencies urged Mexican indigents to volunteer for repatriation. Some Mexicans, who had achieved a degree of financial success in the United States, decided on their own to return to Mexico, taking with them their automobiles and other material possessions. Others were lured home by Mexican government land reform programs designed specifically for *repatriados*. By far the majority, however, were repatriated under intense pressure from Anglo Americans. Included among the more than four hundred thousand individuals repatriated or deported to Mexico between 1929 and 1939 were numerous United States residents of such long standing that they believed themselves to be American citizens, many American born children, and some American born wives. For them Mexico was the foreign land.[39]

New Mexico's Hispanos endured the same kinds of hostility and job discrimination as other Mexican Americans during the 1930s, but they were spared much of their trauma and dislocation. They were, first and foremost, United States citizens of long standing. No matter how much the nativists of the 1920s might have argued about Hispanic racial inferiority, and attempted to prove it by way of statistics and IQ tests, New Mexico's Hispanos were indisputably a part of the American population. When jobs became scarce they had their home villages in northern New Mexico to return to, and even when village resources were exhausted in the early 1930s, they could not be deported or "repatriated," or denied access to local relief. On the contrary, as we shall see, they were given preferential treatment over their Mexican immigrant brethren. The otherwise narrow distinction between the native born and the foreign born drove an unfortunate wedge between linguistic and cultural brothers. With their economic survival dependent on their need to distinguish themselves from the more recent Mexican immigrants, New Mexico's Hispanos shunned the late arrivals and resented them for depressing their wages.[40]

Despite their favored position as United States citizens, the depression years were years of extreme crisis for New Mexico's Hispanos. The loss of wage labor, added to earlier losses, left both them and their regional community devoid of survival strategies. Lacking sufficient land to feed their enlarged population, and money to buy clothing and to pay taxes, the villagers could well have been forced off their lands to become rootless wanderers like the "Okies" and "Arkies." Instead, an unusual combination of forces channeled federal funds into a unique Hispanic New Deal.

Designed ostensibly to preserve Hispanic village life while "modern-izing" the villagers and teaching them Anglo, middle-class economic behavior and cultural values, the Hispanic New Deal resembled and, to a considerable extent, was modeled after John Collier's Indian New Deal. Like the Indian New Deal, its inspirational origins were deeply rooted in United States social and cultural history. Both programs were addi-tionally patterned after programs initiated a decade earlier in Mexico and, as such, were part of both the 1930's intellectual fascination with "primitivism," and with our southern neighbor's socialistic experiments in education and land reform. The more pragmatic economic origins of the Hispanic New Deal derived from a desire to preserve the native cultures as lucrative tourist attractions and prevent the villagers from becoming a rootless, landless population permanently dependent upon federal relief. The story of how this special New Deal program came into being, how it was implemented, and what it did, and did not, accom-plish, not only distinguishes the New Mexican Hispanic experience from that of other Mexican Americans during the Great Depression, but marks a unique chapter in Anglo–Mexican American relations.

# TWO

# The Roots of Dependence

There is a myth concerning the Great Depression in New Mexico. It holds that, because the state was not industrialized and was made up largely of self-sufficient small farmers, it suffered few of the pains felt elsewhere. In actual fact, the 1930s, which ushered in a decade of drought and depression throughout the American West, found the Hispanic villages of northern New Mexico in a state of near collapse. Long unable to sustain a self-sufficient agrarian life-style due to the loss of both farming and communal grazing lands, and the shift to a money economy, the native Hispanic population was inextricably tied to the national economy through its dependence on wage labor. When opportunities for outside income disappeared with the onset of the depression, great numbers of Hispanic laborers returned to their home villages. They were sustained by their extended families and by such mutual aid community groups as the Catholic auxiliaries and the Penitente lay brotherhood. When these resources were exhausted, the situation became critical.

If there is one single factor responsible for the transformation of a once proud, independent, and self-sufficient people to abject poverty and dependence, it is the inexorable seizure of wealth and power that accompanies the superimposition of a technologically and economically dominant culture upon a preindustrial civilization. What happened in New Mexico was, in microcosm, what happened throughout the Third World in the nineteenth and twentieth centuries.[1] The process began shortly after United States annexation in 1848 and accelerated rapidly after the arrival of the railroad in the 1870s.

From the beginning, the Anglo-American newcomers regarded the area as a great economic resource.[2] They made exaggerated claims as to the land's potential fruitfulness and, almost to a person, proclaimed the native inhabitants to be backward, lazy, and generally incapable of taking proper advantage of nature's bounty. In 1857, one wrote: "No branch of industry in New Mexico has been more neglected than that of agriculture. . . . It has been pursued merely as a means of living."[3] To a people preoccupied with material development and the goal of "progress" this apparent neglect was justification enough to move in and take over.

Despite these pronouncements, it was the Hispanos who first put the region's grass and farming lands to commercial use. The original expansion of the Hispanic frontier was, it is true, a folk movement along traditional lines, but trade had long been a part of a diversified regional economy.[4] Sheep were regularly driven to the mines of northern Mexico and, when the Americans introduced new markets and a money economy, the sheepmen simply expanded their activities, dramatically increasing their flocks and driving them to the California and Colorado gold fields, to Denver, and occasionally to Kansas and Nevada.[5] Those to whom large plots of land had been granted during the Mexican period grew in wealth and prestige and, under cover of the new security from nomadic Indians afforded by the American army, expanded their land holdings far out onto the plains.[6] Between 1876 and 1878 the 300,000 sheep shipped out of Raton each year belonged largely to Hispanos.[7]

Nor were the villagers as lacking in enterprise as proclaimed by the Anglo newcomers. The presence of the United States army and the growth of Anglo towns offered new outlets for trade and an opportunity to acquire the cash needed to buy the attractive manufactured goods increasingly available from Anglo merchants.[8] The villagers not only produced small surpluses of hay, wheat, onions, chile, cabbages, sheep, and wool for sale in such regional centers as Española and Santa Fe, but engaged in trading and freighting over long distances.[9] Such trade had been customary for many years. Now, with the rural village population rapidly outstripping the agricultural resources available to them, it became increasingly important.[10]

While the Hispano population was growing due to natural increase, it was nothing compared to the growth of the Anglo population. Between 1870 and 1910 Anglo numbers swelled from 2,760 (a bare 3 percent of the total population) to 119,406.[11] More important than the human growth, however, was the increase in pressure on natural resources from new forms of animal husbandry and commercial agriculture.

First came the Anglo cattlemen, led by Charles Goodnight and Oliver Loving, who blazed a trail in 1866 from Fort Worth to Fort Sumner to sell their beef to the Union army. Their success encouraged others and soon vast herds of cattle took their place on the range alongside the sheep. [12] What followed was a classic confrontation between cattlemen and sheepmen made more vicious by the introduction of racial and ethnic prejudices derived from a general Anglo American distaste for dark skin combined with the Texan's distrust of Mexicans.

On the heels of the cattlemen came the homesteaders, encouraged by companies that purchased large blocks of government and railroad lands. These homesteaders deemed it the inalienable right of American citizens to "take up" and "hold down" rights to any mines, farms, ranches, and water not actually occupied by inhabitants or covered with cultivated fields. [13] By so doing they violated the communal grazing rights presumed by both the Hispanic sheepmen and Anglo cattlemen. The homesteaders' efforts to fence the range prompted another rash of violence. However, dry farming even with the introduction of the windmill, was precarious except in unusually wet years. Many homesteaders gave up after a few years. Others shifted to livestock and picked up the lands abandoned by their former neighbors. By owning 160 acres about a spring a few men could control an immense range. [14]

In the meantime, the presence of so many hungry grass eaters upon the range depleted the luxuriant sacaton pasture grass which held down the soil in the wide, level valleys. The clumpy ring grass and smoke weed which grew up in its place left the top soil unprotected. At the same time, commercial timbering operations in the uplands, largely to provide ties for the rapidly advancing railroads, denuded the mountains of miles of ponderosa pine forests, leaving them bare and exposed to erosion for the first time in history. The runoff of snow and rain water cut deep gullies which served as drains, lowering the water table and further depleting the vegetation. [15]

As it became increasingly apparent that the days of the open range were limited, entrepreneurs scrambled to claim some sort of legitimacy, as well as exclusive use, of large sections of the range. They did this by acquiring title to portions of one or more of the old Spanish land grants.

The Treaty of Guadalupe-Hidalgo guaranteed all property rights existing at the time of annexation but great confusion existed concerning both exact boundaries and exact owners. Most of the grants had been awarded either to families or to villages on a communal basis, a factor difficult for Anglo-American law to comprehend, with its emphasis on individual rights and private property. The boundaries were recorded in relation to prominent landmarks such as rivers, mesas, and geologic outcroppings and the distances measured in metes and bounds. Transfers during the Colonial and Mexican periods were usually made only by verbal contract and those that were written down rarely found their way into provincial archives. In a sparsely populated land where sanctions to enforce agreements were provided through face-to-face community ties, nothing more exact was necessary. The result after annexation, however, was that few Hispanic communities or individuals possessed the kind of documentation of their land rights that would stand up in an Anglo court of law.[16]

Claims were at first investigated by the United States Surveyor General for New Mexico. This office, created in 1854, had the responsibility of ascertaining the origin, nature, character, and extent of all claims made by Mexicans under the terms of the Treaty of Guadalupe-Hidalgo and reporting to Congress which, in turn, confirmed or denied the titles. Unfortunately, the Surveyor General's office never possessed the expertise, manpower, or budget sufficient to carry out its charge satisfactorily and only a handful of claims were confirmed.[17] Political influence determined the outcome of many so-called "adjudications," which contained none of the procedures associated with due process.[18] Taking advantage of the general confusion, the "Santa Fe Ring," an "unholy alliance" of Anglo lawyers and power politicians, secured the political allegiance of powerful Hispanic leaders and their constituents in return for boosting their land grant claims.[19] Those communities and individuals who did try to establish their titles usually lacked the cash necessary to pay attorneys to represent them at court. They were even less able to secure a congressional lobbyist in Washington. Obligingly, lawyers often settled for a portion of the land, often as much as one-third or more.[20] Not surprisingly, most of the titles confirmed were those of large business interests that had acquired rights to a grant through purchase or by means of the age-old alliance, through marriage, of capital with land.

The failure on the part of the United States Territorial government to recognize the political and legal rights of the rural Hispanic communities permitted endless varieties of chicanery, fraud, and collusion to occur. Titles were bought and sold, often from and to several different individuals, all of whom claimed ownership.[21] Forgery and the fabrication of documents became a fine art and illiterate farmers and sheepmen were often tricked or coerced into signing deeds of sale.[22] Even when, in 1891, Congress created the Court of Private Land Claims to solve the region's land problems, no special notice was taken of the rights of the corporate land holding villages. Ninety-five percent of the land brought up for litigation was rejected and fewer than a dozen community grants were confirmed. Of these, several were lost shortly thereafter through the imposition of taxes based on the presumptive commercial use of the land. The general lack of cash in the Hispanic economy, combined with the necessity of collecting the unfamiliar and resented taxes from all members of the community, quickly led to tax indebtedness and fore-closures.[23] In spite of the unremitting pressures on the Hispanic lands, however, the process was often so subtle that the villagers were unaware of their losses for months and, occasionally, even for years.[24]

All unconfirmed communal lands reverted to the federal government to become part of the public lands and were open to settlement under various land laws. From them the government also made huge grants to the railroads which, in turn, leased the alternate sections of forty to fifty miles each side of the right of way to cattle and wool growers for revenue. Since their principal interest was the transport of these commodities to eastern markets, they favored large-scale commercial operators rather than the family-oriented sheepmen of the Hispanic villages.[25]

Portions of the public domain were also withdrawn by the Forest Reserve Act of 1891. The Santa Fe National Forest was the first created in 1892. Twelve years later in 1904 the Carson and Cibola National Forests were set aside and the Forest Service bestowed range privileges upon the principle of "prior use." These the Hispanic sheepmen had no trouble in claiming but, after the devastating winter of 1914–15, during which many lost as many as 30 percent of their ewes, they were hard put to rebuild their flocks. The large stock growers were only too glad to rent them sheep on a share-cropping basis, and gather up their rights to Forest range privileges as well.[26] Four million acres of public land were, additionally, given over to the New Mexico Territory for the support of public education.[27]

The loss of so much rangeland, along with the rapid expansion of the commercial livestock business, had the effect of imprisoning both the Hispanic and the Indian populations of New Mexico upon a land base entirely inadequate to their needs. At the same time it prohibited the colonization of new areas and the formation of new villages as a way of accommodating their growing populations.

The process called attention to the fact that Indian and Hispanic land titles were almost inextricably entangled. The confusion dated back to

Spanish Colonial times. The Spanish government had recognized the Indian's rights to land by awarding each of the Indian pueblos a large communal grant. Unfortunately for the pueblos, the exact dimensions of the grant were not clearly defined, since Spanish property laws were based on such flexible concepts as "need" and "use" rather than on measured geographic parameters. It was not until the mid-eighteenth century that New Mexico practice and custom recognized a four-square pueblo league, usually measured from the cross at the center of the Pueblo cemetery. By this time many Hispanos were already living on pueblo grants.[28]

Hispanic settlers made their homes on pueblo lands at various times and for a variety of reasons. In the early days many Hispanic families were invited to settle near the pueblos for purposes of common defense against raiding nomadic Indians. Other Indian and Hispanic families intermarried and the lands were passed down to offspring who might claim either Indian or Hispanic allegiance. The severe population decline that followed the first European-Indian contact had decimated many Indian communities. By the early nineteenth century many were still too sparsely populated to farm all of their grant lands. In order to make maximum use of the limited arable lands and produce enough food for the fragile colony, these so-called "surplus" lands were opened by law to landless Spanish settlers in 1813. After 1821 many Hispanos also bought land from individual Indians who, under the laws of Mexico, were citizens with the same rights as their Spanish-speaking neighbors. The greatest number of Hispanos, however, simply squatted in sizeable areas of unused, often uncleared, irrigable land within the sparsely populated pueblo grants during the late 1800s, in the same way that Anglo American settlers acquired Indian lands elsewhere in the country, but without the bloodshed. In point of fact, the rush to dispossess the Indians of their lands was considerably tempered in New Mexico by the reluctance of her officials to break radically with the long standing rights of the Pueblos.[29]

When the territory of New Mexico was acquired through annexation by the United States in 1848, both Indian and Hispanic land titles were guaranteed in the treaty of Guadalupe-Hidalgo. Under its terms the Indians, like the Hispanos, were presumed to be full citizens with the right to sell their lands. This right was brought into question in 1851 when the federal government extended to the Indians of New Mexico the provisions of the Indian Intercourse Act of 1834 which, among other things, prohibited the settlement of non-Indians within the boundaries of Indian reservations. The matter was brought to the New Mexico Territorial Supreme Court in the early 1870s by a Hispano from Taos named Antonio Joseph. When the Territorial Court ruled in Joseph's favor federal attorneys appealed the decision to the United States Supreme Court which, in 1876, upheld the *Joseph* decision on the grounds that the Pueblos were "civilized" farmers and being fully capable of handling their own affairs, had the right to sell land to whomever they pleased.[30]

In the years that followed, as more and more Hispanos lost title to their own land grants through fraud or litigation, they moved onto pueblo lands by buying property or by simply squatting. Historical research suggests that it was the availability of these Indian lands to accommodate the growing Hispanic population during the 1800s that explains today's presence of this ethnic core.[31] By the early twentieth century some of the largest Hispanic communities in northern New Mexico were located within the boundaries of the northern pueblo grants.

In 1913 the United States Supreme Court reversed the *Joseph* decision. In the *Sandoval* decision the area of contention involved the nature and extent of federal jurisdiction within the state of New Mexico. Although the United States had established its sole authority over the pueblos as a condition of statehood, and this authority was written, albeit begrudgingly, into the New Mexico State Constitution, this authority was called into question when a prohibition officer from the Indian Office apprehended a Hispano named Felipe Sandoval selling intoxicants to the Indians at Santa Clara Pueblo. Sandoval's attorney, a prominent Santa Fe resident named A. B. Renehan, argued that the federal government had usurped the police powers of the state and won him an acquittal. The matter was appealed to the United States Supreme Court which reversed the *Joseph* decision, making it retroactive to 1848. Ironically, the Supreme Court based its decision this time on the presumed incompetence of the Pueblo Indians. Declaring that the Pueblos were "Indians in race, customs, and domestic government . . . adhering to primitive modes of life, . . . [and] essentially a simple, uninformed, and inferior people," it ruled them entitled to the full protection of the federal government.[32]

The *Sandoval* decision immediately put into question some 3,000 Hispanic land titles. It not only had dire legal implications for the Hispanic villagers but paved the way for more problems and continued litigation in the years ahead—as we shall see in a later chapter. Given the interrelated nature of Hispanic and Indian society, the *Sandoval* decision was divisive at best. It also had the potential for grave injustice and interethnic violence.

In the meantime, with their land base so severely restricted, a common solution for many Hispanic sheepherders was to rent grazing land or enter into share-cropping, *partido,* contracts with the Anglo commercial enterprises that leased the railroad lands. The partido system, a pastoral institution of great antiquity in the Near East, had been transferred to the New World from Spain. By the time it reached New Mexico it had already become a means of lending capital at interest. Customarily, the *partidario* took responsibility for a certain number of ewes for which he was obliged to make annual payments to the lender of an agreed upon number of lambs and wool, about 20 percent of the original head count. At the end of the contract period of three to five years, he was to return the original number of ewes to the owner plus any increase not already delivered. In a land short of cash, the partido system offered poor sheepherders the opportunity to build up small flocks of their own, while providing meat for the family and generating cash from the sale of wool. The owner often assumed part of the risk, encouraged good management, and made advances if necessary. In return he received a healthy profit in addition to loyalty, deference, and prestige.[33]

With the introduction of commercial stock raising the partido relationship, under such Anglo Americans as the Bond brothers of Española, became more businesslike and less personal. The partidario rarely knew anything about his new patron but his name. Detailed contractual agreements called for the sheepherder to return the same number, age, and quality of animals that he had rented, plus a certain number, weight, and quality of lambs as a rental fee, regardless of any losses he might sustain due to unseasonable weather. As before, he was permitted to keep any remaining lambs and all of the wool, but he had no choice but to sell his wool back to the commercial operator who also owned the local store from which the sheepherder bought his supplies on credit. The generous extension of credit was part of the old patron relationship and the sheepherder, forced to sell low and buy high, was caught in a cycle of escalating indebtedness almost before he knew it.[34]

Although the extension of credit was essential in a region lacking a money economy, and was initially perceived by the Hispanos as an expression of the new patron's personal concern and generosity, it was clearly linked to the merchant's need to secure, by chattel mortgages, fall deliveries adequate to meet the competition. If the merchant let the sheepherders keep their sheep on a rental basis, and accumulate debts from one season to another, he was assured of future payments and a business monopoly. The sheepherders, even while eking out little more than a subsistence living, were thus incorporated into the capitalist national economy and made vulnerable to boom and busts as well as to the merchants' efforts to minimize costs and maximize profits. High interest rates and low wool prices kept the sheepherder's debts in excess of his profits, and the sheepherder himself, in a form of debt slavery.[35] Nevertheless, men like Frank Bond were held in great esteem by the rural Hispanos because they mediated between them and the puzzling and threatening Anglo world.[36]

Barriers to Hispanic trade also arose on all sides. Licenses were required to trade with the Indians, and agents tended to favor Anglos over Hispanos because they considered the latter a bad influence. The long established exchange of farm products between the residents of the Upper Rio Grande valley of New Mexico and the San Luis valley in Colorado came to an end when, by an Act of the Colorado legislature, all truckers were required to obtain commercial licenses in Colorado, carry public liability and property damage insurance, and pay three mills per mile on all tonnage hauled.[37] This was clearly an impossible burden on the small operators who had depended almost exclusively on barter. Other Hispanic freighters were hard put to compete with the railroads, and even the wealthiest lacked the capital necessary to gain access to the new means of long distance trade. Hispanic trade goods such as hand woven cloth and blankets were equally unable to compete with commercially woven cloth and sewing machines. Craft production, and the revenue it produced, all but disappeared from the villages. Hispanos still operated small stores and saloons in the villages, but the better education and equipment of the Anglos gave them a virtual monopoly of commercial activities in the cities.[38]

New Mexico's Hispanos resisted the continued oppressive encroachment of Anglo economic institutions and social controls throughout the territorial period. That much of the resistance was covert, rather than overt, explains why it has been relatively little reported or analyzed by historians. In its simplest form it consisted of simply ignoring the new laws. The resented taxes and grazing fees were not paid if it was possible to trespass. New owners were quietly defied. Because law enforcement was difficult and costly in the isolated rural areas it was often years before fences were erected, "squatters" and trespassers ejected, and foreclosure proceedings instigated.[39] However, when this happened incidents of violence occurred, especially in the areas of most recent Hispano expansion where the Anglo encroachments were most severe.

The struggle over the ownership and use of the land raged throughout the West, from Texas to Oregon, in the late nineteenth century. Hispanic resistance in New Mexico took on additional ethnic overtones when incidents of race prejudice separated Anglo and Hispanic participants. In Colfax County, protests originated early in the territorial period over the disputed and ever-expanding boundaries of the Maxwell Land Grant. When, over a period of years, the various owners of this grant pressed claims for as much as two million acres of land, threatening the homes and farms of hundreds of small Anglo and Hispanic farmer-ranchers, violence occurred in defense of squatter's rights. At first Hispanic and Anglo opposition followed separate but supportive, if not cooperative, tracks. Then, in the 1880s when Anglos refused to help Hispanos oust a hated company agent, the Hispanos vowed never to aid Anglos again. A Hispano suspected of wounding a deputy sheriff was shot while reportedly resisting arrest and the Hispano community was outraged. Violence escalated with Hispanos burning crops, cutting fences, destroying buildings, and stealing or killing cattle.[40]

Violence erupted in Lincoln County in the 1870s when the local Hispanic sheepherders came into conflict with Texan cattlemen. Described by the *Santa Fe New Mexican* as "an unfortunate war between Texans and Mexicans," the conflict actually involved a larger power struggle between the Republican and Democratic political parties. From it Juan Patron, clerk of the Lincoln County district court, emerged briefly as a hero.[41]

In the late 1880s violence occurred in San Miguel County when the Las Vegas Land and Cattle Company attempted to bar local Hispanos from the use of their communal grazing lands on the Las Vegas Grant. During the two years in which a civil suit was under consideration a group of masked, armed horsemen calling themselves *Las Gorras Blancas,* the "White Caps," cut fences, burned buildings, crops and farm machinery, destroyed railroad tracks and bridges, and intimidated Anglos. This secret organization claimed as many as 1,500 members and included respected officials of the villages, many of them also members of the local, largely Hispanic, Knights of Labor, which helped raise money for the defense of the Hispanic ranchers. The Knights' platform, published in the *Las Vegas Daily Optic* in March 1890, called for the protection of the rights and interests of poor people; condemned land grabbers, partisan bossism, and race agitation; and demanded a free ballot and a free court.[42]

In 1890 the "White Caps" joined the Populist *Partido del Pueblo* to seek redress from wrongs through the political process. Led by Felix Martinez, publisher of the Las Vegas *La Voz del Pueblo,* the party stressed such reforms as free public education and the creation of an office of county surveyor to clarify tangled land titles. With the victory of the People's Party at the polls in 1890 and the creation of the Court of Private Land Claims in 1891, the outbreaks of violence declined. But the victory was short lived. By retreating to the courts the Anglos effectively changed the rules of the game. The Hispanos lacked both the influence and the financial resources to carry the conflict onto the new terrain.[43] Although the Gorras Blancas never rode again, other groups, primarily the Manos Negras or "Black Hands" of Rio Arriba County, rode on sporadically into the 1920s.[44]

Hispanos expressed more traditional forms of resistance through their membership in mutual aid organizations, the oldest and most widespread of which was the so-called Penitente Brotherhood, more properly known as the Confraternity of the Brothers of Our Father Jesus of Nazareth.[45] Although the origins of the order are somewhat obscure, there is little doubt but that the lay brotherhood became a stronghold of traditional Hispanic Catholicism in the late nineteenth century. As such it was also a focus for Hispanic resistance to the increasingly Anglo dominated Roman Catholic Church.[46] Beyond the religious purpose, however, the "Penitentes" served as a benevolent society dedicated to the welfare of the entire community, particularly orphans and widows. Their meeting houses, called *moradas,* were kept well stocked with supplies for times of need. They also served as centers of cultural activity and community action. Preparations were made there for the annual *fiesta* in honor of the patron saint of the brotherhood and pageants were produced which reflected and preserved the musical and literary traditions of old Spain.[47] Members gathered there to discuss community problems while their wives, the *auxiliadoras de la morada,* attended to village matters of feminine concern.[48]

Inevitably politics came into these discussions because politics served as another form of resistance to Anglo control. So many rural Hispanos belonged to the brotherhood that the Penitentes represented a powerful political force. At one time it was alleged that no one could be elected to public office in northern New Mexico without the blessing of the society.[49] Nevertheless, the strength of the Penitente vote did not depend upon a "blind deference to their leaders," as often charged. According to historian Jack Holmes, studies of Hispanic voting records from this period reveal a deep and abiding interest in politics, a higher than average turnout at the polls, and a highly organized, stable, and competitive two-party system at the village, as well as at the precinct and county levels.[50]

Some villages had both Republican and Democratic moradas and, while the Republican vote was usually heavier than the Democratic in the predominantly Hispanic counties, there was definitely no monopoly of political power. The Penitente chapters did, however, become schools of politics and the Penitente vote, while neither deliverable nor inflexibly controlled, was large enough and variable enough, to make it a critical factor in the electoral strategies of both parties. Predictably, the Penitentes and other Hispanos were more influenced by ethnic concerns than political allegiances. In the late 1920s and early 1930s when the Progressive non-Hispanic political leader Bronson Cutting promoted issues important to New Mexico Hispanos, he carried his substantial following of Hispanic voters with him as he switched from the Republican, to the Democratic, and back to the Republican parties.[51]

In addition to influencing county and state elections, the Penitentes controlled the local administration of justice to the extent that in many counties it was almost certain that a member of the society would appear on a jury. In many cases the sheriff, local judge, and other leading officials were members as well, and reluctant to press a case against a brother. True culprits did not go unpunished. Though many escaped the jurisdiction of the "foreign" courts, the society exacted an even more effective punishment in the form of expulsion from the order and ostracism by the Hispanic community.[52]

At the local level the beleaguered Hispanic communities were concerned primarily with bread and butter issues. Jobs and contracts were essential to their survival and voters gave their support to the patron or *jefe politico* who could manipulate the political system so as to provide them. The politician, in return for "delivering" a group of voters, bargained for ethnic concessions, opportunities to further his own career, and jobs for his constituents.[53] His role was thus not much different from that of a city ward boss. Like him, he was known as much for his ruthlessness, graft, and corruption as he was for a personal, and usually sincere, commitment to his constituents. His role as broker to a largely poor, uneducated, and linguistically handicapped rural population was as essential to the Hispanos as it was frustrating to the Anglos.[54] As anthropologist Frances Swadesh has commented, Anglo Americans who gnash their teeth over the "crookedness" and "nepotism" of Hispanic political involvement should examine it in the context of the Anglo-American power bloc in the Southwest. The extension of patronage and the kin network into politics served as an effective countervailing force providing Hispanos with social and political leverage.[55]

For many Hispanos, the best resistance was a powerful offensive. Hoping to find an advantageous position in the new Anglo society they turned to education. Public schools in the poor Hispanic counties were few and far between, however, and most often inadequately equipped, staffed and open for only a few months of the year.[56] Hispanos with upwardly mobile ambitions sent their children to the Anglo-run and staffed nine-month Protestant mission schools, often braving miles of bad roads, fierce winter weather, and the dire warnings of the parish priests to do so.[57] From these schools emerged an elite corps of teachers, lawyers, politicians, and businessmen.[58] Despite their efforts, few positions opened for Hispanos in the Anglo economy. Nevertheless, they formed the nucleus of a new professional Hispanic middle class and paved the way for others to follow in their footsteps.[59]

Most rural Hispanos had more modest aspirations. They looked only for survival. That, for thousands, meant seasonal wage labor in the new Anglo enterprises that offered cash to be used for land taxes, grazing fees, and consumer goods. Villagers who did not want to become entrapped in the partido system of New Mexico sought work as sheepherders in Colorado, Utah, Wyoming, and Montana. Others found jobs closer by on the railroads, on cattle ranches, in mines and lumber mills, and as laborers in the growing cities. Still others migrated northward to tend and harvest sugar beets. In the latter case whole families were involved, wages being so low that it took many hands to make an adequate income. Hispanic village women found jobs in the new towns as cooks, servants, seamstresses, and washerwomen. Inevitably, some also found self-employment as prostitutes.[60]

But while wage labor permitted the Hispanic villagers to enter partially into the Anglo economy while holding fast to village roots and traditional culture, it exacted a price. The self-concept of laborer was considerably less desirable than that of *ranchero* so, to the extent that it was possible, village men endeavored to keep a toe hold in agricultural production. At best, wage labor required only a periodic absence from the community. If it demanded a longer tenure, wives and children were left behind to help older parents maintain the family lands. In spite of flexible gender roles that permitted village women with their children to take over much of the farming and irrigating, the absence of large numbers of adult males for varying periods of time each year disrupted communal patterns of planting and harvesting. Each family was left more and more dependent on its own resources. The procedure also increased the need for cash. Assistance in the fields, or with the care of livestock, which had been a communal responsibility, now had to be recompensed with wages. Since the productivity of the Hispanic village was predicated upon its corporate nature, the moment productivity became an individual rather than a group concern, it constituted the *coup de grace* to Hispanic economic independence.[61]

In the Hispanic villages land was generally divided equally among all the children, male and female. As the population increased the arable lands were split lengthwise into narrower and narrower plots, each one having access to the all important source of irrigation. Lands which had once barely sufficed for one family were cut into strips of only a few acres each to serve many families. The intensive use led to a rapid depletion of the soil and a further decline in the standard of living.[62] At the same time the end of cultural isolation brought new desires and influences that contributed to the breakdown of traditional social controls. A greater emphasis on the autonomy of the individual and his or her right to pursue private gain led to increasing acrimony in village social relations. To many older people it seemed that, with the separation of subsistence from tradition, God's blessing had been withdrawn from both the people and the land.[63] Most importantly, the dependence on wage labor made the villagers highly vulnerable to fluctuations in the national capitalist economy.

But the forces of change, once set in motion, were inexorable, and worse was yet to come. The next phase of land loss came about in most places without the perpetrators anticipating or even fully recognizing the results of their actions. The reason behind the loss was the continued destruction of the fragile ecological balance of the New Mexican landscape.

The early decades of the twentieth century were characterized by extensive efforts to extend or "reclaim" irrigable lands along the Rio Grande and its tributaries.[64] In the north, in the San Luis Valley of

Colorado, thousands of acres of land were put under irrigation for the first time in a vast agricultural enterprise. About the same time entrepreneurs in the southern part of New Mexico pushed for an even larger irrigation project to impound water for cotton production in the Mesilla Valley. Midway between the two, commercial farmers in the Española Valley urged the creation of a dam on the Rio Santa Cruz to bring more acres of land under production and assure a steady and predictable supply of water.[65]

The effect on the Rio Grande, squeezed from above and below, was disastrous. With so much water withdrawn from its headwaters in Colorado, thousands of acres of land in the Middle and Upper Rio Grande Valley had to be abandoned for lack of water. Elephant Butte Dam, completed in 1916 to bring water to the lower valley, only compounded the disaster. It backed up water all the way to Albuquerque leaving the soil water-logged and useless. Floods, which had always been a problem, became devastating. The heavy irrigation in the north reduced the flow of water that had scoured the channel of sediment. At the same time it increased the production of silt. The level of the river bed rose, sometimes higher than the adjacent valley land. The water table also rose dangerously near the surface and forced the swampy bottom lands out of use. Drains and ditches on the main channel needed constant repair and cleaning, an increasingly impossible burden in terms of manpower and money.[66]

By the late 1920s the Hispanic villages were besieged with problems, but they brought with them into the twentieth century a long tradition of tough, resilient, and resourceful adaptation and accommodation to changing circumstances. Deriving strength and identity from families and villages deeply rooted in the soil of New Mexico, they kept traditions alive, even when separated geographically from kinfolk, through work and visiting patterns which regularly sustained and restored these cultural roots. They may have harbored deep resentments of Anglo economic and social domination but reserved direct confrontation as an undesirable last resort, preferring instead to wage a deft political war that often as not left their erstwhile conquerors exasperated and frustrated. Theirs was not a winning position, but it offered no small amount of compensation in the retention of cherished values and ethnic identity.

# THREE

# The Mystique of the Village

Throughout the nineteenth century New Mexican Hispanos received treatment neither radically better nor worse than their counterparts in Texas and California, but early in the twentieth century a new wave of Anglo settlers established a special relationship with them that made their subsequent history differ greatly from that of their brethren. That they were chosen for this special relationship was no accident. It was directly attributable to the fact that the New Mexican Hispanos, protected by their poverty and the inaccessibility of their mountain lands, still lived within the context of a tightly knit and richly textured village culture. When, inevitably, their lands were invaded by Anglos the newcomers were of a far different stripe than the entrepreneurs who had earlier rushed into Texas and California, and onto the eastern and southern plains of New Mexico.

These Anglos wanted to escape from the driving forces of technological progress and economic gain. Rather than wishing to displace the villagers and their way of life, they wanted to merge with them, and learn from them, and preserve them from further change. They wanted to do this because they envisioned Hispanic village life as the ideal alternative to a mainstream society corrupted by a dehumanizing materialism. Within the village they hoped to preserve an earlier set of values long held dear by Americans—values by which most Americans still wanted to define themselves.[1] As part of an extended program of social engineering that emerged in the twentieth century on both the national and local levels, their efforts to preserve the Hispanic and Indian villages led directly to many of the New Deal programs of the 1930s.

The preservation of the primitive Indian and Hispanic villages of New Mexico was one of a series of attempts on the part of American intellectuals in the late nineteenth and early twentieth centuries to identify, glorify, and preserve intact for the future population groups within American society that appeared to embody the virtues and values of the preindustrial village. The effort was based on a number of popular nineteenth century myths. The first of these was the belief that human beings in the preindustrial village lived in ideal harmony with their neighbors and with their environment, sharing close personal relationships and a simple equality. Freed from the pressures of social and economic striving they were blessedly content. The second myth was a quasi-Jeffersonian idealization of rural values. People who lived close to the land were supposed to be honest, virtuous, industrious, frugal, pious, and incorruptible—in short, a sturdy mooring for the republican ship of state. A third myth held that people who lived close to nature were close to God, Who was embodied in nature. Since the natural state was always beyond the frontiers of civilization, those people who lived in the West, beyond the American frontier, held a promise of rejuvenation for civilized society, which had become evil and corrupt. Finally, Americans had begun to come to terms with their multicultural, immigrant society by developing the myth of the "melting pot." According to this myth, ethnic and national differences enriched the nation culturally as long as they were not allowed to impede it economically or politically.[2]

Americans would not have needed to make myths of these values had they truly wanted, or been able, to live by them. Since they found it increasingly difficult to do so, the myths provided a matrix for their expression and glorification. Beginning early in the nineteenth century merchant capitalism and a burgeoning national economy propelled Americans away from their colonial, subsistence farming origins and into an increasingly urbanized, industrial society. Survival in the new society required an entirely different set of values than those which had been extolled by the nation's founding fathers. Competition took the place of cooperation, resourcefulness and entrepreneurship worked better than honesty and virtue, expedience was more practical than incorruptibility, and efficiency produced more impressive results than piety.

But while these values were undeniably useful, Americans did not particularly like or admire them, or want to hold them up as a social charter for future generations. The solution to this national existential dilemma was to identify, and glorify through myth, groups outside the American economic mainstream which seemed to uphold the old preindustrial virtues. These groups, it was hoped, would serve as a moral anchor for American society and as role models for present and future generations. Paradoxically, while none of the groups so identified abided by all of the revered virtues, each upheld enough to make them appear as anachronistic aberrations. As such they were glorified in the abstract but devalued in everyday practice. As Americans sought to save each group by bringing its people within the pale of modern industrialized civilization and up to some standardized American "norm," they destroyed the very values for which the group had been glorified.

The first group to be so identified and glorified was that of women in their separate sphere within the home. Home was the place where the original integration of labor with life was preserved. It was where the young were nurtured and instructed in the old virtues and where men could find a secure haven from the frantic pace and irreverent complexities of the marketplace. Home and "women's sphere" became, not only an antidote for the perceived desecration of the human spirit, but its justification. By establishing the preservation of the home and the family as the ultimate reason for the accumulation of wealth, both men and women avoided the necessity of challenging the new pecuniary standards. As a symbol of the preindustrial village, the home, and women's role, both glorified and devalued, become the source for the regeneration of society.[3]

This effort on the part of American society to salve its conscience and relieve its anxieties by finding an "other," less powerful group, tangential to the economic mainstream to carry the treasured and endangered virtues was followed quickly by two more "others." Both of them idealized visions of the American West, they reflected competing value complexes associated with different stages in the settling of the frontier.

To the fiction writers of the early nineteenth century, as well as to the Transcendentalists, the untamed West was a symbol of republican virtue. In the wilderness beyond the confines of civilization man, God, Nature and intuitive wisdom were at one. In the popular imagination, frontiersmen, such as the semilegendary Daniel Boone, the fictional Leatherstocking and his companion, the noble savage Uncas, played out an allegorical conflict between nature and civilization.[4] While "nature" was all that was noble and divine, civilization was clearly fated to win; just as "progress" and "Manifest Destiny" were to carry American society and government to the far shores of the continent by destroying the wilderness frontier. Nevertheless, there seemed to be important consolation in the belief that the West contained within its primeval bosom some mystical antidote to the social ills generated in the process.

The other vision of the West was that of an agrarian utopia of simple agricultural communities just within the cutting edge of the frontier. There, in the collective imagination, sturdy, self-reliant yeomen farmers transformed the wilderness into a peaceful and fruitful garden and lived in a happy state of harmony with nature and with their fellow men.[5]

In the years before the Civil War a number of communitarian colonies were deliberately founded by men desirous of separating themselves from an increasingly complex and, to many, sinful world. The Mormon farm villages were a large-scale departure. Their rich social life, which combined handicrafts with farm work, offered an appealing alternative to the isolated farm life characteristic of most American rural development. In 1870 Horace Greeley promoted a successful agricultural colony at Greeley, Colorado, and Archbishop John Ireland of St. Paul, Minnesota, established five more in Minnesota and Nebraska.[6]

Upon these visions of the frontiersman and the agrarian community there grew up a body of social theory related to free land. It seemed to follow that, if nature were a source of spiritual renewal and the highest social values were to be found in the relatively primitive agrarian communities on the edge of the frontier, then the preservation of democratic values depended upon the continuing availability of free land. So long as there were lands to be explored and settled they would serve as a safety valve, drawing excess population away from the industrial areas of the East, thereby keeping wages high and preventing the evils of poverty and urban slums. At the same time, the continued infusion of strong egalitarian, democratic values from the West would mitigate the worst effects of industrialism and rejuvenate American society.[7] As with the idealization of the home and "women's sphere," the theory made it possible for Americans to look backward to preserving the values of morality and community while justifying rapid geographic expansion and a full-scale development of technology. This Janus-faced model for the future of American society, enacted into law in 1861 as the Homestead Act, became an article of faith as well as Republican national policy. It received its classic expression in 1893 in a paper entitled "The Significance of the Frontier in American History" by the University of Wisconsin historian, Frederick Jackson Turner.

The occasion for Turner's thesis was the 1890 report of the United States Census Bureau that an unbroken moving line of settlement no longer existed and that the frontier must be considered officially "closed." Turner, speaking before a meeting of the American Historical Association in 1893, masterfully summarized American history in its relation to the frontier, repeating all the elements of the agrarian myth and arguing forcefully that the frontier was the ever-renewing source of American democracy. By implication he warned that the end of the frontier could bring an end to American uniqueness, individualism, democracy, and economic growth.[8]

In 1893 it did indeed appear that could be so. The year ushered in the worst depression the country had yet experienced throwing hundreds of thousands of people out of work without savings or relief. In the West and South, in the rural heartland, Populist farmers rose up against the dominance and exploitation by Eastern industrialists, financiers, and railroad tycoons. Young people left the countryside in droves, fleeing the hardships, loneliness, and deepening poverty of the farm. Disillusioned with the old slogans about the primacy of agriculture and the superiority of yeomen, they determined that, even with their appalling slums, the cities offered greater opportunity.[9]

The closing of the land frontier left the farmer as the next logical "other" to be held responsible for maintaining the endangered democratic, communitarian values, but the farmer was clearly in the process of discarding them. Americans reasoned that unless he could be restored promptly to his proper place, as contented husbandman of the nation's natural and philosophical resources, the country would be in deep trouble. With the material forces that had given vitality to Western democracy passing away, Turner believed Americans had to look to the domain of ideals and legislation for the preservation of democratic institutions. In particular he suggested that the rejuvenating effect of the frontier might be replaced by the salutary efforts of the Midwestern state universities, science, and education.[10] Others agreed, and out of this consensus grew the Country Life Movement of the early twentieth century. It established an agenda of goals and methods for the preservation of rural life that led directly to the New Deal programs of the 1930s.

Except for the fact that all proponents of the movement agreed that the countryside was in need of immediate social renovation, the Country Life Movement was remarkable for the diversity of its membership. Among the first to diagnose problems and offer solutions were, as Turner suggested, the academicians in the land grant colleges. Together with bureaucrats in the United States Bureau of Agriculture, leaders of the new twentieth century farm organizations, and editors and publishers of prominent farm journals, they called for a revolutionary modification of rural America. They were joined by all manner of businessmen who hoped to benefit by a revitalized, more prosperous rural clientele; and by teachers, ministers, and social workers, many of them inspired by the "Social Gospel." While the first group urged technological progress and efficiency, however, the latter emphasized social regeneration and moral uplift. [11]

Dean Liberty Hyde Bailey of Cornell's Agricultural School and Kenyon L. Butterfield, president of Massachusetts State College and a rural sociologist, became the principal spokesmen for the Country Life Movement. Both men were deeply concerned with the social, economic and technical problems confronting agriculture and hoped through the application of new methods and scientific technology to improve both the quality of country life and the efficiency of food production. This, they believed, had to start with the inclusion of agricultural economics, rural sociology, and home economics in the curriculum of the agriculture colleges. Next, it meant the reeducation of the farm family to be more efficient and more responsible stewards of the nation's agricultural resources. Farmers should be taught conservation, crop rotation and methods for preventing soil erosion; and they should be given advice in how to market their produce. Their wives were to learn new methods of food preparation and preservation, better nutrition, health, and sanitation, modern methods of child care, and home beautification. The spirit and social environment of the community was to be strengthened through neighborhood pageants, organized recreation, country theater, and traveling libraries. [12]

The social institution most in need of reconstruction, all Country Lifers agreed, was the rural school. The courses traditionally taught in the primary grades, they believed, had little relevance to farm life and fitted children only for white collar occupations. This emphasis not only caused the children to disdain physical labor but encouraged them to flee the countryside. [13]

To accomplish their goals, Country Lifers called for practical courses in industrial arts and domestic science to teach children "to do in a perfect way the things their fathers and mothers are doing in an imperfect way." Such courses would not only elevate farming and housework, making them interesting to intelligent rural youth and encouraging them to stay in the country, but would influence the children's parents to adopt better methods. By working together on projects children would also be led to more cooperative attitudes and away from the individualistic orientation so deplored by Country Lifers.[14]

Bailey, the principal philosopher of the Country Life Movement, advocated a more humanistic, if no less manipulative, direction for rural education. A prolific writer, his works were widely read in both city and country. Bailey believed the earth was holy and to be close to it was to set one's life in order and to return to the simplicities that were the moral bulwarks of civilization. Agriculture was not only the rock foundation of democracy, but the very basis of humanity, morality, and justice. Cities could and would grow, but to prosper they had to have the support of a morally strong and economically productive countryside. If the rural population was at present out of harmony with the earth and with nature, given to wasteful, inefficient, and speculative use of the land, and too ready to desert the countryside for the spurious pleasures of city living, it could be restored to its proper role through a new system of education. Based on real life problems, Bailey's curriculum called for a program of active learning in the shop, the field, and the garden. His pedagogical ideas, which bore a striking resemblance to those that John Dewey was developing independently at the same time, were based around the study of nature as a way of remedying the alienation of man from the land and from his neighbor. Like other Country Life educators, Bailey's "school of the future" was to be of, by, and for the country, oriented to rural needs and concerned with rural problems.[15]

In 1908 Bailey's ideas gained national recognition when President Theodore Roosevelt appointed a Commission on Country Life and formally charged it with gathering information and formulating recommendations for alleviating rural distress. In its report the Commission, following Bailey's lead, recommended a nationwide system of rural education taught in ways that were visual, direct, and applicable to the immediate needs of the farm, the home, and the community. It also recommended that the schooling be supplemented by a vast, national extension program embracing farm demonstrations, boy's and girl's clubs, reading circles, traveling teachers, farmer's institutes, and publications. Although no immediate legislation was forthcoming, the efforts of Bailey and his colleagues resulted eventually in the passage of the 1914 Smith-Lever Act. This Act established a national system of extension work in agriculture and home economics and initiated a massive effort to coordinate agricultural colleges, experiment stations, federal and state agencies, and local organizations in the uplift and regeneration of the rural community. [16]

Ironically, by the time the Country Life Movement was institution-alized at the national level, it had fallen into considerable disarray at the local level. The reasons were not hard to discern. For the most part Country Lifers were quite uninformed about the true nature of rural problems. The group that viewed farming as a business enterprise which should be operated efficiently and profitably put heavy emphasis on increasing production—an emphasis that ran counter to the farmer's lifelong experience with the laws of supply and demand. Most farmers lacked the financial means to avail themselves of the new technology, and resented the patronizing manner in which it was presented to them. They were even more suspicious of the efforts of the agrarian romantics to uplift them socially and morally. Farm wives resented the implied criticism of their homes and husbands and blamed the continual lectur-ing of the reformers for the farmers' lack of social esteem and the mi-gration of farm boys to the city. They especially took issue with the argument that the country was not a healthy and sanitary place in which to live. [17]

Both parents feared the efforts to change their schools would result in a loss of local control and tended to view them as part of a massive take-over by a centralizing and consolidating bureaucracy. Women, espe-cially, objected to school consolidation because of the long trips in the wagon, the waiting at crossroads in cold weather, the possibility of improper conversations and immoral acts, and the influence of bus driv-ers who might corrupt their children with their smoking and profanity. Some farmers, of course, welcomed the new practical education. Others feared the introduction of ideas and concepts contrary to their own no-tions of morality. Still others saw in it a way of undemocratically denying their children access to the same channels of upward mobility available to urban children. [18]

The Country Lifers were mystified and disillusioned by the steadfast resistance to their enthusiastic and well-intentioned efforts. They com-pletely failed to see the central paradox: that the rural values that they were trying to retain were in large measure the product of isolation and that they were, by their very presence, pulling the rural communities into the orbit of city life, and exposing their inhabitants to a world of conflict, change, and insecurity, rather than to harmony, stability, and protection. The reason that the Country Lifers had, in fact, perceived the need for reform was that the urbanization of the countryside was already well underway. The population of the rural communities had fallen below the point necessary for efficient economic and social cooperation. In the vacuum, farm parents were unable to teach their children the familial and societal values they needed for the life ahead because no one really knew what they were or would be.[19]

Like other reform groups, before and after, the Country Lifers also failed to perceive the fact that they were trying to face two directions at once—backward to a largely mythical arcadia, and forward to an industrialized world increasingly concerned with efficient business practices and monetary gain. They were telling the farmers that they wanted them to adopt all the attitudes and methods of modern capitalistic production except for one—the desire to become wealthy.

While the goal of restoring an arcadian world which had never existed was patently absurd, the goal of rationalizing agricultural production to fit the needs of an industrial nation was neither sufficiently informed nor sufficiently radical to meet the magnitude of the problems involved. Clearly, while the debate concerned what one historian has called the "industrialization of American agriculture," it was less about the nature of farmers than about the image of American values that farmers seemed to embody. The American farmer, for his part, was more than ready to join the mainstream and become in fact, what he had been in potential from the very beginning, an aspiring capitalist.

Sharing the Country Lifer's belief that the evils of industrialism could be mitigated by an infusion of preindustrial agrarian values, settlement workers in the cities tried to restore the integrity of the European peasant community to the immigrant slum. Like the Country Lifers they used education as their medium and, like them, they established an agenda of goals and methods that also led to the federal programs of the 1930s in New Mexico. However, instead of depending upon nature study to restore a holistic community of life, spirit, and work, the settlement workers used art, and in particular the native handicrafts of their immigrant clients. Drawing heavily for inspiration upon the writings of the English art critic and social reformer, John Ruskin, they endeavored to bring hope and meaning to drab lives by introducing them to things of beauty and good design.[20]

Settlement workers, and their successor social workers, lived and worked directly with the immigrants in the city slums on a sustained, face to face basis. In the process they acquired a sympathetic understanding of cultural differences. They also came to realize that working people needed to learn things that were useful, concrete, and closely related to their daily lives. "Americanization" came to mean more than just classes in English and citizenship. It meant classes in child care, hygiene, home making, cooking, sewing, and shopping. It also meant ethnic pageants, festivals, and music to dramatize the heritage of each immigrant group, together with art exhibitions, lectures and classes in fine arts and handicrafts. Most of all, the experiences of the settlement workers convinced them that poverty was not the result of individual inadequacy but was related to economic and social opportunity. Education was not only a means of enlarging that opportunity but was a way of directly influencing social reform.[21]

Like most progressives, the Country Lifers, viewing the problems of rural America, and the settlement workers, those of the cities, blamed them on the individualistic tradition of nineteenth century liberalism. The promise of American life could only be restored, they reasoned, if men rejected individual goals and worked for the good of the community. On the national level, Theodore Roosevelt's "New Nationalism" symbolized the beginning of a new political tradition based on a modern, collective reaction against individualism.[22]

John Dewey brought all these disparate elements together. Just as Liberty Hyde Bailey had been led to his educational ideas through his analysis of the problems of country life, so Dewey was influenced by his first hand observations at Hull House in Chicago, and his enduring friendship with its founder, Jane Addams. But Dewey did more than learn from observation. He drew upon the entire philosophical, social, and psychological climate of his time to develop both a program and a rationale for the reform of American society.[23] His classic statement, presented in 1899 in *The School and Society*, postulated that in the older agrarian society youngsters shared in meaningful work and in the process learned discipline and developed character. Now that society had been transformed, he argued, the school had to assume all of the educative aspects of traditional agrarian life. It could do this if each school became an embryonic community reflecting the life of the larger society, permeated throughout with the spirit of art, history, and science. In this way, he concluded, the larger society would be made more "worthy, lovely, and harmonious."[24]

Dewey's new philosophy, radical empiricism, was idealistic in its view of man, had a high moral content, was extremely practical, and made a religion of democracy.[25] It not only provided a framework for the development of the social sciences, including economics, sociology, political science, and anthropology but placed education in the role formerly served by the frontier as the fountainhead of democracy. "The New Education," Dewey wrote in 1899, is "part and parcel of the whole social evolution and, in its most general features, at least as inevitable."[26] Twenty years later he had expanded his vision to bring in the notion of class. "The schools," he argued, "have now to make up to the disinherited masses by conscious instruction . . . for the loss of external opportunities consequent on the passing of our pioneer days."[27] While it may have seemed to some a radical philosophy, Dewey presumed no revolutionary class conflict. Instead, he was the first philosopher who dared to read democracy into the ultimate nature of things and social reform into the meaning of knowledge.[28] Little did he realize how, when vulgarized and widely disseminated, it could provide the basis for undermining some of the most cherished ideas in American life.[29]

The progressive years before World War I were heady with purpose, excitement, and unbridled optimism. Settlement houses, as well as schools and universities, were centers of intellectual ferment and experimentation. In them a generation of American men and women were fired with an idealistic, humanitarian drive to make the nation a better place. Given the right institutions, they were convinced that they could do it.

Between 1916 and 1918 they carried their idealism onto an even broader stage. Their soaring faith that they could preserve and regenerate the old republican verities, not only in American society, but in a worldwide community of nations, and thus make the entire world safe for democracy, was, however, dashed against the bitter realities of World War I and its political aftermath. The experience shaped the future directions of progressivism.

One of the new directions, which came directly from the successful mobilization of business and government in the War Industries Board, was a more somber, frankly manipulative direction to social reform. If people and governments would not, or could not, reform themselves, then social planners using the power and the science of government, could bring it about. In 1919 the New School for Social Research, founded in New York City, set the course for such efforts by using Dewey's instrumentalist approach to build the philosophic bridge between the scientific method and social control. A number of its students in due time helped to shape the course and direction of the New Deal. In particular, Rexford Guy Tugwell, a member of Roosevelt's "brain trust," steered the President toward a full commitment on national economic planning in the summer of 1932.[30]

Other social workers turned "social engineers," as they called themselves, who would later play key roles in the New Deal were Harry Hopkins, Frances Perkins, Felix Frankfurter, Harold Ickes, and John Collier. Putting their new sense of professionalism to work as paid employees of voluntary associations in the major cities they emphasized the prevention of social ills rather than their amelioration or cure. They not only put full responsibility upon society for having created the conditions that trapped certain groups in a state of economic dependency, but argued that society had an obligation to provide subsistence to them during times of unemployment, help them to find other jobs, and otherwise fill the vacuum in their lives. Behind all their efforts lay a burning desire to overcome the divisive forces of class, race, and religion; to democratize industry; and to build a finer, more responsive community.[31]

The desire to build a better community surfaced in the rural south through the Southern regionalist movement. Looking to the indigenous culture of the southern Appalachian mountains, an influential group of southern agrarians praised the supposed self-sufficiency and simplicity of southern rural life and sought to enrich it by encouraging the adoption of trades that involved the spirit and mind as well as the pocketbook. They urged the government to "restore people to the land, and land to the people" by replenishing the worn out soils, and by making scientific agriculture the equal of industry, finance, and commerce. To prevent the use of land for speculation or for profit they urged the government to establish a modified feudal tenure in which the state would exact services and duties, institute reforms, and sustain a political economy fitted to the region.[32]

In the west, Elwood Mead, a civil engineer and irrigation authority, advocated an Australian idea for an organized rural society that involved an equally revolutionary increase in the role of government. He believed that the place to start was in the area of reclamation where rural planning would create a new community around a recreational and social center. Mead outlined his ideas in a speech before the prestigious Commonwealth Club of California in May 1914. His ideas spread quickly to Washington, D.C. where they were endorsed by Theodore Roosevelt and President Woodrow Wilson. Two southern congressmen, Senator

John Bankhead and Representative William B. Bankhead, were particularly impressed and later proposed similar settlements during the New Deal. Very much a Country Lifer, Mead considered such settlements necessary to prevent social chaos from erupting in the United States over land hunger as it had erupted in Russia.[33]

Finally, a number of progressives, disillusioned with the failure of pre—World War I reform in the countryside and the cities, and embittered by the crass materialism of the postwar world, gave up hope of reforming America entirely. Many traveled to Europe, hoping to find a more congenial society. Others, a small and very diverse group, thought that they had found an Eden, unexpectedly, in the remote and starkly beautiful state of New Mexico with its two large agrarian populations— Indian and Hispanic—just emerging into the industrialized world of the twentieth century. Among them they were sure they had found the simple communitarian values and the respect for land and nature that had been lost elsewhere in America. Yet these societies were already under attack by a number of programs designed to Americanize and assimilate them. To people like D. H. Lawrence, Mabel Dodge Luhan, Mary Austin, Edgar Lee Hewett, and John Collier it became imperative to preserve these cultures to serve as an example for the rest of America. Moreover, they represented an almost untouched human laboratory for progressive reform and experimentation. With these two new "others" in the very bosom of the old Western frontier they hoped that the community values, the respect for land and nature, and the unity of life, spirit, art, and work, might yet be preserved, and the American mainstream even yet be saved from itself.

FOUR

# Assault on Arcadia

In 1893, the same year that Frederick Jackson Turner announced the closing of the American frontier, a slim book of rather dreamy prose appeared on the nation's bookshelves. Entitled *The Land of Poco Tiempo,* it described the charms of New Mexico as the perfect antidote to the frantically competitive world of the industrialized East.

> Sun, Silence and adobe—that is New Mexico in three words. If a fourth were to be added, it need be only to clinch the three. It is the Great American Mystery—the National Rip Van Winkle—the United States which is *not* the United States. Here is the land of *poco tiempo*—the home of "Pretty Soon." Why hurry with the hurrying world? The "Pretty Soon" of New Spain is better than the "Now, Now!" of the haggard States . . . Let us not hasten—mañana will do. Better still, pasado mañana.[1]

The book's author, Californian Charles Lummis, was the first of a number of writers to describe his fascination with the land and the native cultures, the Hispanic folksongs, and the ancient ruins of New Mexico.[2] Given the temper of the times and the yearning for arcadia, it is not surprising that word of New Mexico spread quickly. By the turn of the century a number of artists and writers had established a small colony in the Hispanic village of Taos. Prophetically, many of them had been introduced to the state by the Atchison, Topeka and Santa Fe Railroad and its aggressive advertising manager, William Simpson.[3] While Arcadia beckoned, American business enterprise was already at work changing a centuries-old way of life. The first wave of artist-intellectuals was followed by another, and another—many of them, especially after World War I, reform-minded progressives eager to put their own distinctive stamp upon the state. Their combined efforts to develop the area economically while preserving the "quaint and picturesque" nature of its native inhabitants amounted to a cultural invasion far more pervasive than anything yet experienced. The process reopened the complicated issue of Pueblo/Hispanic land titles, roused enmity between erstwhile friends, and threatened Hispanos with a further loss of land. It also led to further invasions by tourists and to probings by innumerable investigators bent on analyzing the workings of Hispanic village culture.

Interest in the life and culture of so-called New Spain did not originate in New Mexico. It started in California as a literary movement romanticizing California's past. With the Indian no longer a threat and the actual influence of Mexican culture all but eliminated, Californians turned to these now harmless native cultures for a bit of exotic local color. But while Indians had appealed to American romantics from the beginning, there was a problem with Mexicans who had been almost universally despised as dirty, backward, ignorant, and lazy. To romanticize Mexican culture it had to be "cleaned up" and relabeled as Spanish. The result was a marvelous rewriting of Southwestern history. California writers such as Helen Hunt Jackson and Bret Harte invented a romantic Spanish heritage for the state, and Mexican culture was split into opposing categories of "good" and "bad." That which was considered "good" became Spanish or Spanish Colonial. That which was considered "bad" continued to be called, derogatorily, Mexican.[4]

The Santa Fe Railroad and its affiliate, the Fred Harvey Company, picked up the Spanish Revival theme with the completion of its line to California and the opening of other transcontinental railroad routes in the 1880s and 1890s. Plunging feverishly into the tourist business the Santa Fe built hotels throughout the Southwest in the familiar pseudo-mission style characterized by red tile roofs and stuccoed arches. The Fred Harvey Company began selling Indian "curios" and, to stimulate business, bought up Hispanic and Indian folk art for exhibition. It encouraged both groups to produce for the tourist market. The Fred Harvey agents became authorities in the field and were even responsible for introducing many so-called Indian designs into Navajo blankets and jewelry as well as into Hispanic blanket weaving. The latter, though frequently marketed and sold as Indian products, benefited from the receptive frame of mind already associated with the Indian and helped transfer interest to other Hispanic elements of the Southwest.[5]

To further publicize its route the Santa Fe Railroad brought artists to the West to paint its grandeur and its exotic inhabitants. The railroads provided transportation in exchange for paintings, which were hung in midwestern and eastern ticket offices, while the Fred Harvey Company provided food and lodging, and also purchased paintings. Western trips for artists became annual affairs after 1900 and in 1907 Simpson initiated the famous Santa Fe Railway calendar. Distributed to over three hundred thousand homes, schools, and offices, it provided unprecedented exposure to the artist whose work was selected.[6]

A number of artists introduced to New Mexico by the railroad decided to make it their home. They found the village of Taos, with its brilliant light, dramatic landscapes, and colorful native peoples especially appealing. By 1912 they had established the Taos Society of Artists to promote the sale of their work, most of which was devoted to Indians, Hispanos, and the landscape, with the Indian the dominant theme. Hailed by critics as an American Renaissance, the artists sent out annual exhibitions throughout the United States after 1915. A few years later a similar society was formed in Santa Fe which became known as *Los Cinco Pintores*. Both communities attracted artists and writers, with more of the former settling in Taos, and the latter taking up residence in Santa Fe.[7] Living expenses were low in the territory and the newcomers, most of whom lived comfortably on the income from sales and commissions of their works, as well as from private family endowments, were able to devote themselves wholeheartedly to the pleasures of creation.

It was, of course, this freedom from the daily pressures of earning a living that also enabled them to "renounce" civilization. And renounce it, as they knew it in the bustling, work pressured East, they did. Captivated with the grandeur of the scenery and the romance of the indigenous cultures, the artists sought both to record a dying way of life and emulate its simplicity. Some, like European aristocrats who, at an earlier time, had played at being shepherds and shepherdesses, also played at being villagers. They bought old adobe houses, usually enlarging them and fitting them with such amenities as indoor plumbing. To add to their charm, they carved and painted lintels, doorways and window frames, or incorporated architectural elements from other old houses and even from churches. Fascinated with both Indian and Hispanic folk art, they bought up as much of it as they could find, reasoning, like Lord Elgin with the Parthenon marbles, that it was a form of cultural preservation. And while the Hispanic and Indian villagers often parted reluctantly with their family icons and heirlooms out of economic necessity, the Anglo newcomers waxed romantic about the superiority of their simple, nonmaterialistic neighbors who wanted, and needed, nothing more than what the earth provided. They considered themselves privileged to be accepted by the native people, attended and even at times participated in Indian and Hispanic festivals and religious rites, and adopted a modification of native dress.[8] The Indians and Hispanos, for their part, accepted the newcomers with great dignity. They appreciated their sympathetic interest in their culture and accorded them the same respect they gave to artists in their own societies.

At the same time that the railroad began promoting the special wonders of New Mexico, the New Mexico Bureau of Immigration began a vigorous campaign to promote the territory. With its boosterish publication, *The Land of Sunshine*, it promised immigrants a garden paradise of unexploited agricultural land and drew nearly twenty thousand of them to New Mexico in its first seven years.[9] In 1906, concerned that the territory's large population of native peoples might deter some of the more squeamish Easterners, it confidently predicted that a few more decades would witness their complete amalgamation in both language and culture.[10]

While many New Mexicans were still eager to rid the territory of its economically "backward" native populations, others seized upon their presence as a distinct cultural asset that could yield economic dividends. Among them were Dr. Edgar Lee Hewett and his long time friend and associate, Paul A. F. Walter. Walter, first as editor and later as owner of the *Santa Fe New Mexican*, carried on a vigorous advertising campaign promoting the distinctiveness of New Mexico's native cultures. Hewett promoted their study and preservation.

Hewett, a teacher and amateur archaeologist, began by directing the activities of the Santa Fe Archaeological and Historical Society. By 1909 he had persuaded the Archaeological Institute of America to locate its School of American Research in Santa Fe and had become its first director. He had also persuaded the New Mexico legislature to give the old Palace of the Governors to the Institute to house both its permanent headquarters and the new Museum of New Mexico, of which Hewitt was to be director.[11]

Hewett next turned his abundant energies toward cultural and historic preservation. He began by stripping the old Palace of its victorian facade and repairing it, in accordance with the terms that he had set forth in the Act creating the Museum. These terms required that the building be restored to an external appearance in harmony with the Spanish architecture of the period of its construction. They also required that it be preserved "as a monument to the Spanish founders of the civilization of the Southwest."[12] But Hewett did not stop with the old Palace. He wanted all of Santa Fe to be restored to a prescribed "Spanish-Pueblo" style of architecture. Archaeologist Sylvanus Griswold Morley and School of American Research associates Kenneth Chapman and Carlos Vierra assisted Hewett by drawing up complete plans and constructing a model of the Santa Fe of the future. Morley, in an editorial in the *New Mexican,* declared that "the relics of a romantic history" are an asset beyond "climate, healthfulness, prehistoric ruins and scenery," and recommended that architectural conformity be assured before building permits were issued. The Santa Fe Planning Board recommended a remission or rebate on taxes "for any structure built in the hundred variations of the Santa Fe style," while the Chamber of Commerce awarded prizes for the best designs and structures.[13] The high point in the architectural revival was the design and construction of the New Mexico State Building at the Panama-California Exposition in San Diego in 1915. The target of an intense publicity campaign by the legislature, New Mexico's participation in the fair was a sort of "coming out" party celebrating its admission to statehood three years earlier. The beautiful and tremendously popular Spanish Pueblo structure built especially for the event became known as the "Cathedral of the Desert." It later served as a model for Santa Fe's new Museum of Fine Arts, dedicated in November 1917.[14]

Builders in Taos and Albuquerque followed Santa Fe's lead and soon virtually every public building in New Mexico, and most private homes, were built of adobe with beam construction. The results were not uniformly lovely and some were criticized as anachronistic enormities. Even gasoline stations often absurdly sported bell towers and false beams. But the fusion of Indian, Spanish, and Anglo American architectural elements, especially as expressed in the designs of architect John Gaw Meem, gave a distinctive elegance to New Mexico city planning.[15]

In 1918 the School of American Research initiated the Santa Fe Fiesta. Under directors Hewett and historian Ralph E. Twitchell, who was also president of the Santa Fe Chamber of Commerce, it became a historical pageant celebrating the history and civilization of the state. Field expeditions were sent to the Pueblos to solicit their participation and in 1924 prizes were offered for the first time for Indian art works of superior quality. That same year, in response to what some artists and writers considered an over emphasis on Indians, poet Witter Bynner led a movement to introduce a Spanish carnival atmosphere into the Fiesta with

Hispanic folk dances, songs, and games, as well as an exhibition of Hispanic arts and crafts.[16]

The Fiesta was enormously popular. In 1921 the *Santa Fe New Mexican* smugly lauded it as a patriotic service for America "in an age which has tended toward commercial commonplaceness and absorption in the material things of the present."[17] Three years later the journal's new editor, E. Dana Johnson, summed up local sentiment as follows:

> We are keeping alive all the beauty and grace of the Spanish culture, because it is beautiful and graceful, and because a country that becomes too much steeped in the commonplace and the ugly needs to preserve all the picturesqueness and artistry and all the beauty to which it is heir from the civilizations that have contributed to it.[18]

The response in Santa Fe to the tourist souvenir trade was an interest in the revival of both Indian and Hispanic crafts. Once again Hewett was involved, but while he was largely responsible for the development of Indian painting and pottery-making, credit for the Hispanic crafts revival must go to Mary Austin and Frank Applegate. Austin's contribution, in particular, hit New Mexico with what art historian, Roland Dickey, has aptly described as "the fire of an old fashioned Methodist revival."[19]

Austin first came to New Mexico in the winter of 1918 to make a study of Hispanic folk literature and music among the villages of the Rio Abajo south of Albuquerque. According to her autobiography she stayed to conduct a survey of the Spanish-speaking population of Santa Fe and Taos counties for an Americanization Study sponsored by the Carnegie Foundation. Confident that these experiences qualified her as an authority on the state's native resources, she returned to Santa Fe to live and to orchestrate its cultural revival.[20]

Austin began her adult life as a rather unsuccessful school teacher in California. A newcomer to the state, having only recently moved there from Illinois, she was fascinated with the Indian and Hispanic inhabitants and quickly formed a romantic and strongly mystical attachment to their cultures. Her burning desire was to be a writer and to make an impact on the world. In 1903 she published her first book, *The Land of Little Rain*. It was a success and with this momentum she moved to Carmel, to join a writer's colony, and from there to Los Angeles where she became part of another literary circle surrounding the charismatic Charles Lummis. Eventually her curiosity and her ambition took her to

Florence, Paris, London, and, finally, to New York. There, among other activities, she lectured at the People's Institute, an educational institution devoted to restoring a sense of brotherhood to urban neighborhoods through a union of intellectuals and working class people.

Austin had the soul of a social worker. Just as in California, where she had taken to the defense of the Indians because "they were the most conspicuously defeated and offended against group at hand," in New York she rented rooms in the poorer sections and took odd jobs in order to understand the lives of the immigrants. She also continued her association with the celebrities of her time and, through her close friendship with the writer, Lincoln Steffens, she gained entry into the circle of radical intellectuals that frequented the glittering Greenwich Village salons of Mabel Dodge, a socialite known for her Bohemian life-style. [21]

In Santa Fe, Austin called on Hewett who gave her an office and an unpaid position with the School of American Research. She immediately launched a campaign to expand the city's cultural activities. Holding court in her home on Santa Fe's famed Camino del Monte Sol, she demanded and commanded homage from whomever she met. In failing health, she determined to devote the remaining years of her life "to rebuilding the shattered cultures of the Southwest as a legacy to the world." [22]

Austin's commitment was twofold. She intended to preserve the native traditions as a means of restoring integrity and self-esteem to their cultural practitioners, and she intended to use them as a profound object lesson for her fellow Americans. In an article written for the *Survey* in 1931, she declared:

> What we have to deal with in the mixed populations of both Old and New Mexico, is an item that the American people cannot face too soon and too completely, the *socio-political inheritance of communistic living*. . . . We must rid ourselves of the fetishistic idea that group mindedness is inferior to individualism. . . . The most affronting trait to the 100%er is the capacity of the Mexican to find satisfaction in communal rather than individual expression of economic conquest. [23]

Austin's first efforts were among the Pueblo Indians and in 1925 she helped to organize the Indian Arts Fund. [24] She then turned her attentions to the Hispanic New Mexicans and began to collect folk literature, plays, legends, and songs. With her neighbor, Frank Applegate, she founded the Spanish-Colonial Arts Society and added a Spanish Colonial Arts and Crafts Exhibition to the Spanish Market at the Santa Fe Fiesta. This led

to the beginning of a permanent collection of native arts and the establishment of a Spanish Arts Shop in Santa Fe's Sena Plaza. When the
famed pilgrimage shrine known as the Santuario de Chimayo was put
up for sale by its owners, Austin found a Catholic benefactor to purchase
the building and hold its contents in trust for the Church, as a place of
worship and as a religious museum.[25] In 1931 she organized the New
Mexico Folklore Society.[26]

Austin's friendship with Applegate and his interest in collecting Hispanic religious images inspired the two of them to consider reviving the
native folk arts which Austin labeled "Spanish-Colonial." By holding
prize competitions at the Santa Fe Fiesta, she and Applegate succeeded
in calling attention to the work of local craftsmen and in providing both
an incentive and a market for their products, even though at first they
"actually knew of but one person who could be counted on for contributions." This was Celso Gallegos, a woodcarver. Fortunately for everyone, Gallegos's carvings sold so well at that first fair that he earned over
sixty dollars. Some years later Austin reminisced, "the old man was so
overcome that he wept and tried to kiss Frank, which, in view of Frank's
great length of limb, was not easily managed."[27]

In what anthropologist Charles Briggs considers a particularly ser-
endipitous association, Applegate "discovered" José Dolores López, a
creative genius steeped in the traditional Hispanic cultural system. By
1921 Lopez had evolved a highly individual interpretation of the religious images of his society. With Applegate's friendly advice, Lopez
subtly molded his artistic creations to meet the tastes of the Anglo art
market. By so doing he provided himself with a satisfying new source
of cash income and the Anglo Americans with a new product for their
art collections.[28]

Austin and Applegate did more than simply expand the market for
the works of Lopez and others. They also defined "traditional" Hispanic
art and determined which works conformed to this definition on the
basis of their own historical assessment and aesthetic judgment.[29] That
this smacked heavily of paternalism did not go unnoticed. Austin's
contemporaries found her to be generous and sympathetic but with "an
arrogant assumption that the Southwestern field was primarily hers."
According to some she insisted "upon her position as the oracle and
interpreter of Indian and Spanish culture," and rarely acknowledged the
source of her ideas.[30] But, as author Carey McWilliams, a friend and
contemporary, noted she believed devoutly that the West was destined

to be the center of the "next great and fructifying world culture," and furnished it with faith, program, tradition, and ideas.[31]

Austin's prolific writings and her espousal of regionalism in literature created and sustained a distinctly New Mexican ethos and directed national attention to the state's indigenous peoples.[32] The missionary zeal of another dedicated egotist made them a national progressive *cause célèbre*. Of all the events of the 1920s and 1930s in New Mexico, the one that most threatened New Mexican Indian and Hispanic village life was the enormously complicated Indian Pueblo Lands Controversy. The fact that it reached national proportions was almost exclusively the work of a young social worker from the East named John Collier.

Collier, like many of his fellow progressives, believed that the supremacy of the machine over man had alienated men from their work, destroyed neighborhoods, and starved the soul. Like Dewey, he also believed that man could regain a social consciousness and control over his future through social planning. To put theory to practice he worked as an administrator for the People's Institute in New York where he urged immigrants to keep their national dress, their customs, diets, religion, and all of their folkways in an effort to stem the tide of Americanization. With Mary Austin, whom he met at the People's Institute, he was drawn into the intellectual circle that frequented Mabel Dodge's salon. It was through this association with Dodge and Austin that he was drawn eventually to New Mexico and to the cause of preserving American Indian culture—a preoccupation which, as it turned out, had an equally profound influence on New Mexican Hispanos.[33]

The People's Institute experiment collapsed in 1918 shattering his hopes for a better world and Collier retreated to the countryside. His dispair was short lived for in 1920 he received an invitation from Mabel Dodge to visit her in her new home in Taos. Intrigued by Dodge's description of a "magical habitation" of Pueblo Indians, Collier accepted the invitation.[34]

In Taos Dodge introduced Collier to Antonio Luhan, the Taos Indian whom she later married. Together they visited Indian homes, participated in the Pueblo's Christmas festivities, and witnessed its powerful religious dances. Collier was transported. There, among the Indians, he believed he had found a "Red Atlantis" where a deep sense of community still existed. With hope born anew he concluded that Pueblo culture offered a model for the redemption of American society and that this model of beauty, joy, comradeship, and the connection of man with God must never be destroyed.[35]

America's Indian cultures had, of course, long been under attack. With the Americanization of all foreign elements a top priority of the late nineteenth and early twentieth centuries, government policy had made a point of destroying tribal communities, breaking up communal land holdings, and absorbing the Indians as individuals into mainstream American society. The Indians, completely unprepared for such measures, had already lost much of their land along with their heritage and cultural pride.[36] Collier determined to dedicate his life to reversing this trend and immediately found a ready-made issue in the so-called Bursum Bill of 1922.

Introduced into Congress by New Mexico's Senator Holm Bursum at the request of his fellow New Mexican, Secretary of the Interior Albert B. Fall, the Bursum Bill was intended to settle the decades long dispute arising from the Supreme Court's *Joseph* and *Sandoval* decisions concerning Hispanic land titles within the Pueblo Grants. According to Fall such a settlement was desperately needed. So many Hispanic families were being threatened with the loss of lands that they had occupied for generations that he feared violence and armed conflict would ensue. Incidents had already occurred in Nambé.[37] The problem, as far as Collier and numerous other concerned citizens were concerned, was that the Bursum Bill would have validated virtually all non-Indian land titles on Indian lands provided the owners could prove continuous possession from June 1900.

Fall's argument in favor of Hispanic rights might have carried more weight had he not also had a reputation for favoring the break-up of communal Indian lands so that they could be purchased for private exploitation by local interests.[38] Those who opposed the bill argued that it would deprive the Indians of at least sixty thousand acres and destroy their unique self-government by placing them, and their land disputes, under the jurisdiction of the district courts. These courts, it was maintained, were "unfriendly" to the Indian cause, because so many were under the control of Hispanos.

Collier determined to stop passage of the bill at all costs. He hired on as a research agent for the Board of Indian Welfare of the Federated Women's Clubs, and waged all out war against Fall, Indian Commissioner Burke, and anyone else whom he perceived as an enemy of the Indians.[39]

Mary Austin, one of his earliest allies, joined him and the two orga-nized the American Indian Defense Association.[40] In addition to raising funds they enlisted the intellectuals of the Taos and Santa Fe art colonies in a great letter- and article-writing campaign under the slogan of "Let's Save the Pueblos." The flood of publicity that appeared in the national press denounced the Bursum Bill as a "blot on the [Harding] adminis-tration" and suggested that the Pueblos had been betrayed because most of the claimants were Hispanic Republicans.[41]

There was some truth to the suggestion that party politics in New Mexico was behind the Indian's plight, but the matter was far more complicated. Both Fall and Bursum, "Old Guard" Republicans from the Rio Abajo south of Albuquerque, did indeed owe much of their political strength to the support of the local Hispanic *patrones,* but they also had to take into consideration their large Hispanic constituency, especially with matters that concerned land and water rights. They felt consider-ably less obligated to New Mexico's Indians who had the Indian Service to take care of them and were neither voters nor taxpayers.[42] There were also the many legal complexities explained earlier.

Collier cared nothing for the legal complexities or for the fact that some three thousand claims by twelve thousand non-Indians, most of them poor, rural Hispanos, had been thrown into doubt. Caught up in the Collier charisma, many of his New Mexican followers also ignored them at first. They cheered as Collier and Tony Luhan orchestrated a growing chorus of Indian protest. There was almost as much pleasure when Albert Fall, who had instigated the affair, resigned in disgrace from the Harding administration in March 1923.[43]

Once efforts were made to draft a suitable compromise bill, however, cracks began to appear in the Collier team. Most New Mexicans, whether Anglo or Hispanic, who attempted to understand the historic roots of the problem, wanted Hispanic land claims to be considered along with Indian claims.[44] The very idea infuriated Collier. He angrily attempted to purge the Defense Association of all who opposed his one-sided and single-minded approach, suggesting that they lacked honesty and fair play. In spite of his objections, a revised bill known as the Pueblo Lands Act passed Congress and was signed into law by President Coolidge in June 1924. According to its terms a statute of limitations allowed non-Indians to claim lands on which they had lived continuously without title for thirty years and with title for twenty years. The relatively recent recognition periods adopted by the act, when combined with the long presence of Hispanos in the federally recognized pueblo grants, guaranteed that the Pueblo Lands Board had to confirm in non-Indians many small tracts of the Pueblos' best irrigable land. Both Indians and Hispanos who lost lands were to be compensated monetarily at fair market value so that they could, presumably, purchase new lands to make up the loss.[45]

The result of the adjudication of private land claims by the Pueblo Lands Board was that Hispanos acquired legal title to approximately 18,200 acres of land, most of them irrigable, on eight northern Pueblo grants, along with their appropriate water rights. The northern Pueblos reclaimed by purchase and relinquishment nearly nine hundred acres of mostly non-irrigable land along with additional non-irrigable grazing lands added by the government prior to 1924. The paradoxical result was that the Hispanos lost their self-assumed grazing privileges on the pueblo grants and thereby the means to pursue their traditional pastoral activities; while the Indians, traditionally horticulturists, were left without farming land and water rights. Neither group possessed the desirable ecological components within their domain to develop economic units sufficient to engage in large scale and profitable agriculture. The Hispanos had no alternative but to increase their dependence on wage labor. The Indians turned to tourism.[46]

Both Pueblos and Hispanos were compensated monetarily for their lost lands but, because of apparent budgetary restraints from the Hoover administration, the awards were scaled down more than 50 percent below the figures determined by the board of appraisers as just compensation.[47] Rather than compensate the Pueblos for their lost water, the Board determined that the Pueblos had, in fact, lost none of their water because the Indians retained a prior water right to all lands within the pueblo grants. This theory, which represented a radical departure from existing practice, served neither the Pueblos nor the Hispanos and set the stage for more legal battles that would continue throughout much of the remainder of the century.[48] Even had the awards been adequate, there were no comparable agricultural lands, with or without water, available at any price.

There was no satisfactory resolution possible for the Pueblo Lands controversy in the 1920s but the fault lay with neither the Indian nor the Hispanic litigants. It lay with the loss both populations had suffered of their original land base. Most significantly for the 1930s, however, Collier's crusade for Indian rights had mobilized national sympathy and concern for the Indians. In New Mexico it forced many influential civic and state leaders to take a hard and realistic look at the plights of both rural populations. Finally, reaction to Collier's domineering and inflexible ways may well have been the catalyst that awakened Anglo interest and concern for the preservation of Hispanic village culture.

Collier was harshly criticized in editorials in the *Santa Fe New Mexican* and the *Albuquerque Journal* for his methods and intentions and for his unwillingness to compromise and consider the rights of the Hispanic villagers.[49] New Mexico's three man Congressional delegation also opposed him. Senators Bronson Cutting and Sam Bratton, in testimony before the Senate Indian Investigating subcommittee, agreed that the Indians, in some instances, had been "treated disgracefully," but they insisted that, on the whole, they had come nearer to receiving fair treatment in New Mexico than anywhere else. Bratton took Collier to task, specifically, for insinuating that the United States District Judge for New Mexico was unfair to Indians.[50] Cutting put the blame for the whole "Pueblo Land mess" squarely on the government for its confusing reversal of Indian land policy between the *Joseph* decision of 1876 and the *Sandoval* decision of 1913. Insisting that the non-Indian settlers, most of whom were poor Hispanos, had been dealt with "just as unjustly as have the Indians," he declared that the government should straighten out the controversy with "equal consideration and fairness to both."[51]

The Bratton-Cutting bill, drawn up with the help of New Mexico's Representative, Dennis Chavez, added compensation for both Indians and Hispanos to make up for the niggardly actions of the Pueblo Lands Board. Hoover threatened to veto the bill and the House killed it, but it was one of the first pieces of legislation enacted during the ensuing Roosevelt administration.[52]

Collier eventually alienated almost all of his New Mexican supporters. Mary Austin supported him initially and, in an interview published in the *Santa Fe New Mexican* in September 1923, defended him against accusations and actions taken by the New Mexican Association of Indian Affairs.[53] It is apparent, however, that even at this time her allegiance was wavering. When Collier denounced the compromise bill that attempted to deal fairly with both Indians and Hispanos she and another of Collier's supporters, Harold Ickes, found his objections incomprehensible.[54] Edgar Lee Hewett feared that Collier was "inciting the Pueblos to an alarming extent to distrust the government."[55]

The last straw for many New Mexicans was Collier's aggressive badg-

ering of Herbert Hagerman, a respected former territorial governor, for
his actions as special commissioner to the Navajos. Amelia Elizabeth
White and Oliver La Farge, both prominent members of the Eastern
Association of Indian Affairs, rushed to Hagerman's defense. When Hagerman returned to New Mexico following Senate Hearings, during which
he had been harried into exhaustion by the Collier forces, he was met at
the train by a delegation of writers and artists led by poet Witter Bynner.
In a gleeful procession they wound their way to the Santa Fe plaza where
they burned Collier in effigy.[56] Bynner accused Collier of deliberately
alienating the Pueblos from their Hispanic neighbors and forcing the
Hispanos to spend their meager savings on attorneys in order to defend
their titles.[57]

Collier admitted in his autobiography that he eventually had only
four friends left in Santa Fe. One of them, by his account, was Mary
Austin, but Austin was incensed with the way he had presumed to take
over the Indian Arts revival.[58] Collier continued to experience opposition
from the New Mexico press and Congressional delegation throughout
the 1930s and 1940s. In spite of this outpouring of sentiment, however,
it is doubtful if he ever realized how deeply he had offended New Mexicans with his assaults on Hispanic village lands.

The widespread publicity surrounding the Hispanic and Indian arts
revivals and the Pueblo Lands controversy, not surprisingly, brought
large numbers of curious tourists to the Southwest. Expanding the promotion begun earlier in the century, in which transcontinental passengers were given the option of a side trip to the capital city and the choice
of several different tours to prehistoric and historic sites, the Santa Fe
Railroad in 1925 announced its "Santa Fe Indian Detours."[59] In the
colorful brochure the passengers were offered a three day trip through
the Indian Pueblos between Las Vegas, New Mexico, and Albuquerque.
The Indian Detours were greeted enthusiastically by both the Santa Fe
and Albuquerque Chambers of Commerce. Local businessmen were de-
lighted at the prospect of thousands of monied people visiting the state
and touted the tours as comparable to a visit to India, Egypt, Europe,
or Asia.[60] Attractive women guides, called "couriers" added to the appeal.
They were trained as carefully as their predecessors, the famed Harvey
Girls, and were given crash courses in the history, politics, sociology,
anthropology, geology, and native arts of the area by such experts as
Hewett, Alfred V. Kidder, and Sylvanus G. Morley. They were also
expected to know enough Spanish to carry on a basic conversation.[61] By

1927 the "Roads to Yesterday" brochure offered a tour to Taos and the Hispanic villages of Truchas, Cordova, and Chimayo. In the latter, visitors were treated to a demonstration of native weaving and a visit to the famed Santuario, described as the "Lourdes of New Mexico." The brochure suggested that on Sundays, tourists might see pilgrims inching their way to the shrine on their knees.[62] Although changes in the American life-style and the onset of the Great Depression put an end to the railroad's Santa Fe Detours after 1931, tourism by private motorcar continued unabated.

New Mexican villagers had by now been invaded by artists, writers, Senate investigating committees, and tourists. But there was more to come. From the late 1920s onward, they were studied and analyzed by rural sociologists, psychologists, anthropologists, medical health and nutrition specialists, agricultural scientists, and educators. These experts moved into the villages singly or in small groups, some for just an hour, others to live for weeks or months as "participant observers." They carried with them survey sheets, questionnaires, diaries, and cameras and recorded myriads of details concerning virtually every aspect of village life. Stimulated by the crisis of the depression the experts gathered enough statistics to destroy for all time the idyllic vision of the village nurtured by the cultural preservationists and promoted by the business interests. These statistics pointed to grave problems in arcadia.

The statistics would have been alarming under the best of circumstances, but in the 1930s, New Mexico, along with the rest of the United States, was entering into one of the worst of times. No individuals or industries within the state served to benefit by the creation of a displaced, landless, and illiterate rural proletariat. The agricultural and extractive industries had a more than sufficient labor pool to keep wages low and costs down. With tourism the state's most important industry many served to lose if the state lost the special exotic quality provided by the Indian and Hispanic villages. Even the health industry, which closely approached tourism in its economic importance and brought in many prominent men and women, depended in considerable measure on the preservation of New Mexico's tranquil beauties. No one, Anglo or Hispanic, rich or poor, urban or rural, wanted to see the Hispanic villages destroyed through poverty, ignorance, or land loss.

On the other hand, everyone served to benefit if the villages remained economically self-sustaining and did not further strain the state's limited tax base. For the businessman they were a source of tourist revenue. For the politician they held a still sizeable constituency, one that could wield the balance of power in an election.[63] For the general Anglo public they harbored an industrious, nonthreatening population that gave the state a unique regional flavor. For Hispanos at all levels they were home, a source of physical and emotional security, and a continuing fount of ethnic solidarity and identity.

The intellectuals, as they saw mainstream American society breaking apart, apparently rotten to the core, were more convinced than ever that the New Mexican villages held the key to America's future. Some, like Austin, even dreamed of a new world culture evolving in the Southwest in the region soon to be watered by a great reclamation project on the Colorado River. Elaborating on the writings of Elwood Mead, she explained that life in the new land would express itself in groups, not individuals, and would be organized around the principle of the irrigation system. Seven states and the federal government would create it, and three bloodstreams, "the Indian, the Spanish, and the so-called Nordic American," would inhabit it. As a concept, she explained, it would be God in a group relation.[64]

While most New Mexicans did not share Austin's euphoric vision, they did feel a sense of crisis with the beginnings of drought and depression. Action had to be taken, they decided, and quickly, to restore the economic stability of the villages and the integrity of village life. A beginning had been made in the Hispanic arts revival but much more was necessary. Setting in motion a new cycle of social engineering, they renewed their assault on arcadia, intent on rationalizing its economy, while preserving its antiquarian values. That reform and preservation were opposing concepts disturbed them not one whit. Through their efforts they were convinced that they could turn the worst of times into the best of times.

# FIVE

# The New Mexico, Mexico, New Deal Connection

A variety of action programs were initiated in New Mexico during the 1920s and early 1930s. They established an agenda of methods and personnel that needed only additional funds to accomplish what were expected to be millennial results. When these funds became available through federal agencies instituted to combat the worst problems of the national depression, they were funneled into a uniquely New Mexican Hispanic New Deal. Several of these programs had their immediate origins in the social revolutionary climate of Mexico—a country which held great fascination for the intellectuals of New Mexico, as well as for many of their colleagues throughout the United States. Through the New Mexico connection these programs became part of both a Hispanic and Indian New Deal and affected even the thinking of national New Deal leaders.

In New Mexico, as elsewhere, federal relief programs for Indians were funded separately through the United States Bureau of Indian Affairs. The state-run federal programs were designated for the relief of all needy New Mexicans, from the drought-stricken Anglo farmers of the eastern and southern plains to the urban destitute, whatever their racial and ethnic origins. Nevertheless, a significant proportion of federal funds was channeled into programs designed to assist Hispanic villagers to regain economic independence by augmenting their small-scale agricultural activities with native arts and crafts cottage industries, by modernizing Hispanic village agriculture, and by restoring the fertility of the land. These programs also sought to educate the villagers in a more efficient and productive use of natural resources; to make them healthier, more literate, more culturally aware, and better able to function in the economic mainstream; and to document, preserve, and revive native

Hispanic culture as a source of ethnic pride and identity for Hispanos. Not completely coincidentally, they were also intended to preserve Hispanic village life and culture as a source of nationalistic pride and tourist dollars for New Mexico. Since the village was the focus of Hispanic economic and cultural life, it was the village that had to be preserved.

Prior to the 1930s the federal government had done virtually nothing to assist its recently acquired Hispanic citizens to learn either English or the customs of their adoptive country. Since the United States Congress did not consider it important to appropriate money for free public education, and the New Mexico Territorial legislature consistently refused to allocate funds for this purpose, money for the public schools had come from a variety of territory-wide taxes and fines. At least three of them, the fines for the burial law, the strict Sunday law and the new marriage law, were intended to eliminate traditional Hispanic customs which the Anglo community considered to be unhealthy or immoral. The fourth, a poll tax of one dollar per voter established in 1872, was meant to eliminate all voters too poor to pay it, most of them poor Hispanos. The burial law forbade the traditional practice of interring the parish dead beneath the floors of churches or within the church yard whenever the church was within the limits of the town. The strict Sunday law forbade any games, sports, dancing, fairs, markets, or paid labor on Sundays, the traditional day for Hispanic *fiestas* and markets, which always took place after the weekly church service. Finally, the marriage law forbade any marriage between close relatives, including first cousins—a long established practice in the small, closely interrelated Hispanic villages. It also forbade marriage for women under age eighteen and for men under twenty-one.[1] When these laws were later abolished or modified, school funds were allocated almost entirely from county property taxes. The predominantly Hispanic counties had the lowest property valuations and the highest percentage of tax delinquencies so their rural schools languished in something less than benign neglect, inadequate and poorly attended. For most villagers the lack of educational opportunity was no misfortune. They, along with their Catholic clergy, viewed the new Anglo, protestant-oriented education with suspicion, concerned that it was an effort to train their children away from their traditional values. At best, it seemed to bear little relevance to their daily lives. Those villagers with upwardly mobile ambitions took advantage of the numerous protestant mission schools.[2]

The first substantial infusion of federal funds into New Mexico for educational purposes came in 1914 with the passage of the Smith-Lever Act establishing a national system of agricultural extension services in cooperation with the United States Department of Agriculture, the land grant colleges, and the county governments. The act's purpose was, as described in the enabling legislation, "to aid in diffusing among the people of the United States useful and practical information on agriculture and home economics and to encourage the application of the same through field demonstrations, publications, and otherwise. . . ." In addition to increasing farm crops it was to be "a system of rural education for boys and adults by which a readjustment of country life can be effected and placed upon a higher plane of profit, comfort, culture, influence, and power."[3] Under its auspices, the New Mexico Agricultural Extension Service was instituted at the New Mexico State College of Agricultural and Mechanical Arts at Las Cruces. The county agents, who were hailed as "trained social engineers," urged a variety of methods to lighten the toil of rural women by simplifying their work and making their lives happier by beautifying their homes and grounds. The teaching of canning, in particular, became an aspect of government policy.[4]

Despite the fact that in tax-poor New Mexico not every county could afford an agricultural agent, programs in farm and home education were instituted widely throughout the state along with health and nutrition programs. They failed to reach most Hispanic youngsters and adults, however, because they were offered only to seventh graders and above, and only in the larger towns.[5]

Success among the Hispanic rural population of New Mexico also necessitated new methods and bilingual Hispanic agents, neither of which were immediately forthcoming. Hispanos, as a rule, did not trust Anglos and employees of Anglo government agencies. They also lacked the money to invest in new tools. Hispanic women did not feel comfortable in school houses or other public buildings in the presence of Anglo women who did not belong to the community. Anglo women were just as reluctant to meet with a group of Hispanic women. In spite of the many areas of need, therefore, Hispanos did not respond as quickly or as positively as Anglo farm families.

For a brief period during World War I the need for increased food production, combined with a concern for Hispanic assimilation, led the Extension Service to employ several Hispanic county agricultural agents and at least one Hispanic home demonstration agent. The latter translated federal circulars on cooking, serving, and the preparation of poultry into Spanish, gave over 162 demonstrations in seven counties, and visited over three hundred homes in the course of her work.[6] In addition to mobilizing Hispanos to produce more food, government workers instructed them in patriotic citizenship. With attention focused on their cultural needs and differences, the Hispanos responded enthusiastically. Hispanic women planted larger gardens and many switched from the traditional method of preserving foods by drying, to canning. Both women and children joined Red Cross clubs and took over work on the farms as over ten thousand of their men, making up 60 percent of New Mexico's contingent, entered the armed services.[7] Wartime experience in the army provided many Hispanic men with a new sense of identity as Americans, a new understanding and closeness with Anglo peers, and experience with outright discrimination on the part of officers at stateside training camps.[8]

Ironically, just as large numbers of Hispanic veterans returned to their home villages, eager to take advantage of modern facilities and services, the availability of these services evaporated. Despite efforts by the Extension Service, only a few Hispanic county agricultural agents were retained after the war, and there were no Hispanic home demonstration agents until Fabiola Cabeza de Baca joined the staff in 1929. Reflecting the lack of contact, as well as the cost of pressure cookers, canning supplies, and the scarcity of water, Hispanic women continued to preserve their food by drying until well into the 1930s when the New Deal took over and again promoted the canning program.[9]

While this neglect on the part of the Extension Service may have been rooted in an unwillingness and inability to deal with the severe problems of Hispanic rural poverty, it was not unique to New Mexico. Throughout the country surveys demonstrated that agricultural extension programs were more effective in reaching families in the upper social and economic classes. Participation in county agent meetings, as well as contacts made between agents and farmers, were all found to correlate closely with class structure. Even so, the failure to reach the lower rural classes was not a concern. Agents argued that diffusion of information from the upper classes to the lower classes was more rapid than diffusion in the opposite direction.[10] In the case of New Mexico, as in some other areas of the South, however, communication between the classes was so poor that the diffusion was almost nonexistent. Nevertheless, the brief wartime exposure of many Anglos and some upper class Hispanos to conditions in the Hispanic villages aroused in them an awareness and interest in their problems. Combined with new research into rural problems by rural sociologists, it paved the way for the social action programs of the next decade.

The passage of the Smith-Hughes Act in 1917 provided federal aid for vocational education in both agriculture and trades and industries. It also provided for the training of vocational education teachers. Like the Smith-Lever Act, it was an important infusion of money into the New Mexico school system, but like its predecessor, it was slow in reaching the Hispanic villagers. Courses were given in the public schools only to youths over the age of fourteen and to those who intended to enter a trade or an industrial pursuit.[11] Since most Hispanic village children had dropped out of school by the age of fourteen, few were able to take advantage of the courses. Fewer still met the prerequisite of planning to enter a skilled trade or industry, there being little demand for either in rural New Mexico. Finally, because of the need to match federal funds dollar for dollar, the schools in the poorest Hispanic counties were least able to afford the programs.[12] Nevertheless, many educators agreed on the need for vocational education and in 1919 and 1920 some part-time and evening domestic science and agricultural courses were offered in a few northern New Mexico Hispanic communities.[13]

More significantly, in March, 1919, A. B. Anderson, State Supervisor of Trade and Industrial Education, organized a vocational education conference at the new Museum of Fine Arts in Santa Fe. At this conference he proposed the establishment of a "school for New Mexico architecture and handcrafts" to be located in the capital city. Anderson, like many of his peers, was caught up in the enthusiasm of the Spanish architectural revival. Calling attention to the fact that great numbers of Hispanic villagers had been forced to work as wage laborers in extractive or agricultural industries outside the state, he noted that their earnings, rather than benefiting the New Mexico economy, were spent on goods from "mail-order houses in Chicago or New York for furniture and furnishings that should be made right here at home in accordance with New Mexico traditions and designs." Echoing the sentiments of many in his audience, he added that, "New Mexico has a noble history, it has beautiful traditions, it has its own architecture, its own design, its own arts, all of them far finer and more fitting than anything that can be purchased or imported from other states." Anderson resigned his position in 1921 so he never realized his dream for a school in traditional crafts.[14] No further action was taken on this idea by his successor and, except for minor programs, vocational education for Hispanos had to wait until 1932 when, with the onset of the depression, new federal funds became available.

If New Mexico was slow in developing formal programs in vocational education, Mexico, its neighbor to the south, was not. The Mexican Revolution had inspired a wave of buoyant nationalism and, in a search for their origins, Mexican intellectuals had turned to their indigenous cultures and made them the focus of a national artistic renaissance beginning in 1922. Contemporary Mexican painting was born. The popular arts were revived, the old songs sung again in schools and in concert halls, and regional dances performed for national audiences. [15]

Some of the greatest accomplishments made during this period were under the direction of José Vasconcelos, minister of education under President Alvaro Obregón. A philosopher who united classical learning with the love of his native Mexican culture, Vasconcelos created a school system designed to serve both the practical and aesthetic needs of the Mexican people. Education, formerly the privilege of the few, was used as a means of integrating the indigenous populations into the national fold. Inspired by the precepts of Deweyan progressive education, Mexican leaders adopted the slogan *Educar es Redimir,* "to educate is to redeem." "Cultural missions" were established throughout the countryside for the purpose of training prospective rural school teachers and to improve the quality and availability of rural education. In them instruction was given in academic subjects along with intensive preparation for teaching agricultural and vocational subjects. [16]

The 1920s also brought a rush of American intellectuals to Mexico, eager to judge for themselves the results of this social experimentation. Among them were such writers as D. H. Lawrence, Katherine Anne Porter, Waldo Frank, and Stuart Chase. Almost all were fascinated by Mexican politics during the eight year period in which the Mexican presidents, Alvaro Obregón and Plutarco Elías Calles, began to implement the goals of the Mexican Revolution. They were powerfully stimulated as well by Mexico's artistic renaissance and by its indigenous cultures. Desperately eager to discover some new value system to fill the void left by their disillusionment and loss of faith in the American Dream, they traveled like pilgrims to Mexican villages in search of some mystical experience unavailable in the United States. Societies outside the pale of capitalist society were particularly attractive since the intellectuals' central purpose was not so much to study life in preindustrial arcadias as it was to launch a serious cultural critique of conditions back home.[17]

John Dewey visited Mexico in 1926 to advise the government on its educational program after Vasconcelos resigned. When he returned he wrote a series of articles for the *New Republic* that were later collected in a book entitled *Impressions of Soviet Russia and the Revolutionary World.* In them Dewey applauded the directions taken by the Mexican Revolution. He particularly praised the work of Vasconcelos, commenting that, "there is no education movement in the world which exhibits more of the spirit of the intimate union of school activities with those of the community." He also noted the importance and freshness of the concept of incorporating Indians into the national life of the country.[18]

Katherine Anne Porter also praised the Mexican school system and the work of Vasconcelos. In a monograph entitled *Outline of Mexican Popular Arts and Crafts* she lauded the native arts revival and the fact that the cultured Mexican artist had returned to his native roots. "The artists are," she declared, "one with a people simple as nature is simple: that is to say, direct and savage, beautiful and terrible, full of harshness and love, divinely gentle, appallingly honest."[19]

Waldo Frank and Stuart Chase shared her enthusiasm. Frank, like Dewey and Porter, gave specific praise to Vasconcelos, writing in *America Hispana:*

> He organizes his Teachers' Missions to spread the revival of dignity through the remotest villages. From town to town goes the group: physician, nurse, craftsmen, agriculturist, painter, teacher of letters and numbers, and draws to it potential local teachers, and inspires them to work among the Indians, in order to recreate their sense of creativity with the past and with the land. . . . Everywhere the crafts awaken. . . . In the Capital, the young artists climb on scaffolds, cover the walls of schools and official buildings with plastic splendor whose equal America has not seen since the Incas. . . . Two Essential wills have moved the Mexican Revolution: the will to economic independence and the will to cultural rebirth.[20]

In *Mexico, A Study of Two Americas,* Chase contrasted life in the Mexican village of Tepoztlan, as studied and described by anthropologist Robert Redfield, with life in Middletown (Muncie, Indiana), as described by sociologist Robert S. Lynd. Impressed with the Mexican village's handicraft economy, its "natural integration of work and play," and the people's sense of partnership in a common enterprise, Chase concluded that Mexicans had a happiness and peace of mind entirely unknown to frenzied America. He ended his book with the dream of one Mexican for his people. It was a dream, Chase declared, which must never die.

> With their own communal lands, with good roads, with schools in every hamlet, with a self-sustaining diversity of farm products, with a social organization in each village that will serve spiritual and social needs, with the cultivation of more than one export crop, with cooperative consumer's and producer's organizations, with a cultivation of the handicrafts, the native music and dance, with a deliberate introduction of every scientific improvement, we will, in a single generation . . . preserve all that is rich, beautiful and useful in the traditions . . . and at the same time . . . have absorbed all that can be used of the new and modern in science. We will cherish our soil, harbour our group life, grow and develop into a free and strong people, an example to Mexico and even to the world.[21]

Author D. H. Lawrence, was among the earliest and the most influential of these enthusiasts. Perhaps in response to a 1920 essay in the *New Republic,* in which Lawrence urged Americans to look to the culture of the Indians for their future, Mable Dodge invited him to join her at Taos. In 1922 he accepted her invitation. A year later he, and a poet friend from Santa Fe, Witter Bynner, toured Mexico and returned to New Mexico to praise its innovations in education and art.[22] Among those listening with more than casual interest must have been Mary Austin and John Collier.

In response to the example from Mexico and the general alarm over the implications of the Bursum bill a number of influential New Mexicans determined to effect a similar cultural renaissance for the state's Indians and Hispanos. As previously noted, Hewett, Austin and others established the Indian Arts Fund in 1925 along with an Indian Fair to promote and market Indian handicrafts. In 1923 Austin and Applegate initiated the revival of Hispanic handicrafts and in 1925 they formed the Spanish-Colonial Arts society. By 1928 the Santa Fe Fiesta had a Spanish Market. Even the agricultural extension agents for Santa Fe and Rio Arriba counties were involved. Under their direction, students prepared exhibits of agricultural products and brought them into the Fiesta in old fashioned covered wagons.[23]

Austin and Applegate were motivated from the beginning by a desire to improve the economic conditions of Hispanic New Mexicans, convinced that by so doing they were also making a statement concerning American values and helping to turn them in more humanistic directions.[24] But the preservation of the preindustrial village was often justified by Anglo Americans through a variety of pseudoscientific racist arguments. An editorial in the *Santa Fe New Mexican* written in April, 1921, asked "Is there such a wide difference between cutting up a giant redwood into flooring and making an imitation 'civilized man' out of a Pueblo Indian?"[25] Austin was no less explicit about the proper future of Hispanos. In an article entitled "Mexicans and New Mexico," she argued that Hispanic "group mindedness" did not fit them to survive in large industrial cities, but that they were quite able to take care of themselves in an economic environment they understood [i.e., the village]. The worst thing that could happen to Hispanos, she declared, was to be taught to want things. If taught "to keep up with the Jones's," they would no longer be "cheap labor," satisfied to express themselves in making and being.

Austin believed that Hispanic children learned quickly only to age fifteen, at which time "the racial inheritance rises to bind them to patterns of an older habit of thinking," and so was convinced that the educational system failed them by trying to train them for a university education. "Why ask them to become average installment plan Americans, socially and intellectually inferior to standardized Anglo labor, when they can be highly individualized artist-craftsmen?" she asked. Her conclusion, so blatantly but unconsciously exploitative, was that "It is for us to make the most sympathetic, happiest, and so effective, use of them."[26]

In a later article Austin expanded her educational theories to include a curious accommodation between assimilation and cultural pluralism. She argued that the reluctance of Indians and Hispanos to part with their native language derived from a revulsion at being forced to join a society divorced from artistic expression and believed that they would take a greater interest in learning and adapt more quickly to American ways if permitted to be creative in their own ways. The "New Mexican Experiment," she wrote, was to apply a different scheme of education to each "racial genius." It was possible because New Mexicans had discovered "how peoples of profoundly differing levels of culture and stages of experience can set up among themselves a thoroughly rewarding state of society."[27]

While Austin and others took Mexico's experiments in education in directions neither Dewey nor Mexico intended, they were not alone in advocating a new educational system based on differing cultural needs.

The concern for ethnic issues raised by the vocational arts and crafts revivals also found expression in efforts by a group of progressive New Mexican educators to refute notions of Hispanic racial and intellectual inferiority.

During the 1920s a series of standardized tests administered to urban and rural children in Texas, Colorado and New Mexico had indicated that Hispanic children were retarded by rates ranging from 89 percent in the fourth grade, to 63 percent in the eighth grade.[28] By the end of the decade, a number of young southwestern educators had begun to challenge these figures.[29] When the beginnings of the national depression brought even graver problems to New Mexico's rural schools and focused attention on the economic future of the Hispanic villagers, they called for a special research program. It materialized in January 1930, when Atanasio Montoya, the state superintendent of schools, succeeded in interesting representatives of the Rockefeller Foundation in the problem. By May the Foundation had appropriated twelve thousand dollars for a five year experimental program to be run through the College of Education of the University of New Mexico and the state Board of Education. New Mexico's Senator Bronson Cutting, with his usual concern for Hispanic welfare, provided the money to match the Rockefeller donation.[30]

With the Rockefeller Foundation Grant the University established the San Jose Experimental school program in the southern Albuquerque suburb of San Jose in the fall of 1930. Directed by Dr. Lloyd S. Tireman, associate professor of elementary education at the University of New Mexico, its twofold purpose was to study the educational potential of Spanish-speaking school children under controlled conditions, and to train teachers for the rural elementary schools of the state.[31]

The program Tireman established in San Jose evolved directly from his experiences in Mexico. He had observed, and been enormously impressed with, a training school for rural teachers at Oaxtepec, Morelos, where Deweyan progressive education was used to incorporate Indians and poor Mexican peasants into the national culture.[32] The school of Oaxtepec was one of Vasconcelos's "cultural missions." Like other such missions its personnel consisted of a director/coordinator, an agricultural social worker, a home demonstration agent, a nurse, a music teacher, an arts and crafts teacher, and a mechanic. Located in an old convent, students and teachers lived together as a family, working together on the repair and renovation of the building as one of the school projects.

The curriculum, outlined by the federal government, combined practical work on the school farm with housework and academic subjects, most of which were also based on the students' interests and practical usage. Native crafts were taught along with hygiene, health, and recreation. The emphasis on practical education was justified by the argument that unless basic needs for food and shelter were satisfied intellectual pursuits would have little meaning.[33]

Tireman also emphasized practical, vocational education in native crafts, beginning with the construction of the school building and its furnishings—a project in which both the children and their parents were involved. Determined "to overcome the now prevalent feeling that unless a building has a tin roof and mail order house furniture, it is something of which to be ashamed," Tireman introduced woodworking, weaving, tanning, and tin work into the curriculum. As in Mexico, the teaching of crafts was accompanied by a revival of Hispanic songs and folk tales. The school also taught Spanish along with English in the lower grades.[34]

Austin, a member of the school's board of directors, and its chief publicist, summarized the goals of the project as well as its larger vision for New Mexico. Rural New Mexican villages, she wrote, had suffered a total loss of community identity after a half century of indifference and contempt on the part of the dominant Anglo population. All that was dramatic, entertaining, poetic, and generally cultural had dwindled to the vanishing point and village education was completely severed from the community. What was needed was a renewed sense of the school as a focus of community interest—something that could be best achieved if the village contributed equally with the state in the building of the school as a social institution.

What rural New Mexicans most needed, she believed, was training in the normal activities of rural community life. The skills of adobe-making, carpentry, weaving, fruit-canning, and bread-making should be taught by selected individuals from the region who would travel from village to village. Campaigns for health, sanitation, and pest-fighting should be correlated between the farm agent and the school. School gardens should be planted. Finally, these practical skills should be the basis for teaching the children habits of observation and deductive reasoning.[35]

Although the San Jose training school program was discontinued after five years for lack of funds, it accomplished many of the goals set out in the original proposal. It also inspired a number of other projects. Due

to the financial support of millionaire Cyrus McCormick and the cooperation of several New Deal agencies, another program, which even more
closely resembled the Mexican cultural mission concept, was established
in the village of Nambé in 1937 with Tireman as director.[36] In 1936
following the gift of a house and endowment from the Harwood family,
a similar educational mission was established at Taos under the direction
of Professor J. T. Reid of the extension department of the University of
New Mexico. George I. Sanchez, who had worked with Tireman throughout
the life of the San Jose training school program as Director of Research
for the New Mexico State Department of Education (a position funded
through the same Rockefeller Foundation grant), was asked to prepare
a thorough study of Taos County. Before accepting this new assignment,
however, he received a commission from the Julius Rosenwald Foundation to make a nationwide educational survey of Mexico. Sanchez
published the results of this survey in 1936 under the title *Mexico: A
Revolution by Education* and it served as the basis for much of his later
thinking, including the landmark book written as a result of the Taos
survey, *Forgotten People: A Study of New Mexicans*. Published in 1940,
*Forgotten People* received nationwide attention and marked a new chapter
in the history of the Spanish-speaking people of the Southwest.[37]

Finally, the San Jose training school program forged the link uniting
the arts and crafts revival with the New Mexico State Department of
Vocational Education, the New Mexico State Agricultural Extension
Service, and later, with the New Deal agencies. In 1931 the School's
director of vocational work, professor Brice H. Sewell, an industrial
sculptor who was also director of Spanish handicrafts at the University
of New Mexico, prepared a paper for New Mexico's Governor Arthur
Seligman on the prospects for vocational education in New Mexico.
Sewell's recommendations, which followed closely the philosophy of the
San Jose training school, were well received. They formed the basis for
a statewide program when, the following year, the Governor appointed
Sewell Supervisor of Trade and Industrial Education for the State Department of Vocational Education.[38] Using Smith-Hughes federal funds,
Sewell hired a number of gifted individuals who combined the skills of
craftsmen and educators, some of them people he had worked with at
the San Jose training school. Their threefold challenge was to establish
vocational schools for the teaching of New Mexican crafts in the rural
Hispanic communities, to develop a means of successfully marketing

the crafts produced in the schools, and finally to encourage the village vocational schools to develop self-sustaining local industries.[39]

It would be interesting to know what the Hispanic villagers might have thought of these programs, but the voices of virtually all Hispanic New Mexicans were muted by a decades long tradition of accommodation to the dominant Anglo culture and by the state's popular myth of tricultural harmony. While far from passive in matters concerning their cultural and economic future, with the exception of Sanchez, Hispanos rarely expressed ethnic concerns publicly, and almost never in English. Until the Hispanic crafts revival neither Anglos nor Hispanos had found it productive to dwell upon ethnic and cultural differences. A conspiracy of silence maintained the peace and forbade any overt expression of discrimination, while a polite separatism kept hostilities from rising to the surface. With as little implication as possible of inferior or superior status, each group kept to its own neighborhoods, churches or church services, schools, clubs and social events.[40] Upper class Hispanos, while not entirely exempt from prejudicial treatment by Anglo Americans, maintained such a strong feeling of class status that they did not identify with the lower class villagers. Instead, acting and thinking like the *patrons* of an earlier day, they, like Nina Otero-Warren, saw themselves as culture and power brokers, mediating between the villagers and the Anglo reformers, whose romantic aims and goals they accepted as their own.

So with the possible exception of those whose lives would be most directly affected, there was by the early 1930s a virtual consensus in New Mexico concerning the values of progressive education, bilingual education, and the revival of New Mexican arts and crafts. Though some groups still tended to view this education in Hispanic folkways as a means of keeping the rural Hispanic population contented with a quaint and exploitable peasant life-style; others, chief among them Sanchez, Tireman, and Sewell, saw the new educational methods as a first step in restoring Hispanic economic and cultural independence. While unconsciously limiting the options offered to the villagers, they encouraged the growth of ethnic awareness as a springboard for a new beginning based on pride of heritage and language. In so doing they hoped that it would be a bridge to complete equality.

By the early 1930s there was also a consensus concerning the need to preserve New Mexico's village agriculture and to supplement it with local cottage industry—though few, if any, people in the state understood the magnitude of the problems involved. Priorities were set and programs planned that needed only money to be carried from theory to practice. When the New Deal supplied the necessary funds along with a variety of programs designed to revive and preserve a rural life-style, New Mexico's business and cultural elites greeted them like manna from heaven.

It was hardly a coincidence that the New Deal programs came along just at this time. In 1933 Franklin Delano Roosevelt drew into his new administration a number of social workers, educators, and economists of the same progressive stamp as those who had worked so hard to preserve agrarian values and promote cultural pluralism in New Mexico.[41] Little more was needed in the way of a direct link with the New Deal. There was a further link, however, that connected the New Mexican experience to Washington. That link existed in the person of John Collier.

Collier's involvement with the Pueblo Indians and the Bursum bill put him in the vanguard of those espousing cultural pluralism and the rights of American minorities. He had long urged the preservation of ethnic customs and the revival of ethnic arts and crafts. Once in New Mexico he competed with Mary Austin and others to control the nature and direction of the revival insofar as it concerned American Indians. The crafts revival led him, in turn, to an interest in Mexican vocational education and land reform. In 1929, and again in 1931, he visited Mexico and came away convinced that it had revolutionary and epoch-making lessons to teach the United States in the matter of land redistribution and management as well as rural education. To Mexico's innovations he recommended only a greater respect for the preservation of America's indigenous languages and cultures. With them, he predicted the emergence of a new Western civilization.[42] When Collier was appointed Commissioner of Indian Affairs in 1933, he introduced these ideas into the Roosevelt New Deal.[42]

The cause of Indian rights brought Collier into direct contact with a number of people who became influential members of the Roosevelt administration. A. A. Berle, Jr., a member of Roosevelt's "brain trust," was principal author of the brief condemning the Lenroot compromise in the Pueblo Lands controversy and was an active supporter of Collier and the policies advocated by the American Indian Defense Association.[44] Harold L. Ickes, the man who, as Secretary of the Interior under Roosevelt would become Collier's boss, was a social worker in Chicago when, in the early 1920s, he and his wife joined Collier's crusade for Indian rights.[45] Collier and Ickes locked horns on several occasions and Ickes disliked and distrusted Collier's unwillingness to compromise, but he respected his dedication to the cause of Indian rights. Since they shared many of the same assumptions the two, working together, were able to institute, with federal funds and Roosevelt's support and encouragement, many of the reforms they and others had been agitating for since 1920.

Once based in the New Deal Collier went on to interest many others in the "cooperative community action" he had admired in the indigenist revival in Mexico and which he and others hoped to institute in New Mexico.[46] He found in Secretary of Agriculture Henry A. Wallace a receptive spirit who shared his appreciation of Indian spiritual life and agreed with him that the American Indians were America's "true subsistence farmers." Wallace, Rexford Tugwell, Harry Hopkins, and Robert Fechner all supported Collier's efforts to have matters of concern to New Mexico's Indians included in his Indian New Deal.[47] In turn, they served as channels through which some elements of the Mexican experience may have flowed back into the broader program.

In *From Every Zenith,* Collier's biography, he describes how he was directly responsible for interesting Harold Ickes and Hugh Bennett in the catastrophic soil conservation problems of northern New Mexico and in influencing the direction of later soil conservation policy. To acquaint the administration with the severity of the problem, Collier's son, Charles, a BIA field representative, "borrowed" Bennett from his post in the Department of Agriculture to direct a survey of conditions on the Navajo, Acoma, and Laguna reservations. Bennett, who was later named head of the Soil Conservation Service, was appalled at conditions on the western range. Even more significantly, Bennett observed the way the Pueblo Indians discussed their range problems and reached a community consensus to reduce their herds. According to Collier, Bennett found the success of the Pueblo consensus such a striking contrast to the failure of the authoritarian program imposed by the Navajo Tribal Council that he concluded that local participation was essential at the grass roots. From this insight came the idea of the Soil Conservation District, one of the most successful and influential programs of the Roosevelt New Deal.[48]

Unquestionably elements of Collier's Indian New Deal served as a prototype for New Mexico's Hispanic New Deal. Apparently Mexico's Indian New Deal served as an example and inspiration for both programs. Through Collier, they may have influenced the direction of America's "Community New Deal," as well.

# SIX

# Federal Relief Comes
# to New Mexico

The Great Depression crept into New Mexico so quietly that at first no one knew it was there. Even when officials became aware that the state had a severe unemployment problem they thought exclusively of the many transients who rode the freight trains or trailed across the state in old jalopies looking for work. Few expected anything to affect the stability of the Hispanic villages.

But the villages were affected, drastically, by the declining opportunities for wage labor both in New Mexico and throughout the Western states. Although no statistics existed as yet to document the fact, as many as seven to ten thousand villagers from the Middle and Upper Rio Grande valleys had migrated annually to labor in the beet and potato fields, the mines and smelters, the railroad and sheep camps, of Colorado, Utah, Wyoming, and Montana. As these jobs disappeared the erstwhile migrant workers retreated to overcrowded home villages with inadequate and worn out lands. Families made room for homeless relatives and mutual aid societies shared community resources as long as their reserves held out. By early 1932 the reserves were gone, and with all credit resources exhausted, the villagers were destitute.[1]

State and local officials were totally unprepared for such a scenario. Completely unaware of the multiresource nature of the Hispanic economy, they were at first disbelieving, then puzzled. Finally they embarked on a period of fact finding in order to discover why a population they had thought so self-sufficient on the land should be suffering such misery. In the meantime they offered what they could in the way of relief. But just as poverty at the grassroots led to the exhaustion of community resources, so the loss of tax revenues at the local level led inexorably to bankruptcy at the county and state level. When state reserves were exhausted state officials turned in desperation to the federal government for relief. The relief came in time to prevent outright starvation but exacted a heavy price in village pride and independence. The first efforts were experimental and fraught with conflicts. While local officials were deeply concerned about the welfare of the Hispanic villagers, federal representatives questioned whether they were eligible for emergency relief, given the fact that their distress stemmed largely from such long term factors as soil exhaustion, insufficient farm land, and long term unemployment. They even questioned whether a population so "backward" and alien could be brought into the American fold. New Mexican leaders, determined to maintain the paternalistic relationship with these villagers that they had long enjoyed, ignored and circumvented federal efforts to impose strict guidelines. They also brought what influence they had to bear on redesigning the federal programs to meet specific state needs.

Some of their concerns derived from the cultural agenda that had been developing over the past two decades. Others arose suddenly and dramatically as the result of John Collier's efforts to improve and expand Navajo and Pueblo Indian land holdings. Collier's rise to power as the Commissioner of Indian Affairs in the Roosevelt administration gave him an unprecedented opportunity to attempt to alter the balance of Indian/Hispanic/Anglo land relationships. His equally unprecedented access to federal funds gave him the means to do so. Collier's use of federal wealth and power threatened state officials as well as representatives of other competing federal agencies. It thus stimulated them to take quick action to thwart his plans and direct the federal bonanza to their own purposes. With New Mexico's Indians under the care of the Bureau of Indian Affairs, Hispanos made up the bulk of New Mexico's relief load—fully 80 percent of it.[2] No more justification or incentive was needed for state officials to direct the majority of federal programs toward a special New Mexican Hispanic New Deal. New Mexico's Hispanos, stripped of their multiresource based coping strategies by the rigors of depression and poverty were, for the first time in their history, unable to direct their own destinies. Stunned and demoralized, like many other groups in the United States in the dark days of the early 1930s, they could do little but accept with some degree of gratitude the new federal invasion of their lives.

Because of their pride, and their tradition of self-help, their plight was not immediately obvious. In November 1929, New Mexico's governor, Richard C. Dillon, reported confidently to the United States Employment Service that New Mexico had no unemployment problem because most of its people lived pastoral lives. "This does not bring them into sharp competition in the matter of earning a livelihood," he explained. Nevertheless, at the request of President Herbert Hoover's Organization for Unemployment Relief (POUR), Dillon inquired about prospective municipal public works projects and urged business interests to "fall into line" with the President's program to stimulate employment. In early December he announced that over one and a half million dollars of local money had been budgeted for public construction in New Mexico for the year 1930.[3]

Local business leaders were equally optimistic concerning the local economy. Reflecting the state's earlier boosterism, the executive committee of the New Mexico Banker's Association reassured its members that New Mexico's financial basis was sounder than in many years. Agricultural statisticians at New Mexico State College in Las Cruces reported that crops for the year were 120 percent above average, and an economist confidently predicted a labor shortage. A columnist in the *Albuquerque Journal* even speculated that the Southwest might become the chief beneficiary of the business depression since it offered a "wonderland of new chances where a worker could find any climate, industry or vocation."[4] The ill-placed optimism was short-lived. In 1930, with ever increasing numbers of jobless migrants entering the state from Oklahoma, Arkansas, and Texas, both Republican and Democratic politicians ran on platforms which advocated limiting state employment to state residents. In 1931 the New Mexico Legislature passed an act limiting employment of nonresidents on public works projects to fifteen percent.[5]

Arthur Seligman, who took office as governor in January 1931, dedicated much of his first two years in office to gathering information about the seriousness of the problem. Like his predecessor Dillon, he labored under the early impression that New Mexico's rural population was exempt from want, a conviction that seemed to be confirmed when a federal unemployment agent visited "nearly every town in New Mexico" and reported "no real need or suffering." Still, Seligman's inquiries revealed that most of the larger towns had had to establish relief organizations funded through charitable contributions. In the meantime, local tax collections had fallen off to such an extent that the public works projects reported earlier could not be implemented. Public officials doubted whether future bond issues for civic improvements would be approved. They were certain that they could not be counted on as a means of providing work for the unemployed.[6]

Early in 1931 Seligman launched the state's first active unemployment relief program. With three and a half million in federal aid funds and one and a half million dollars in federal building and forest program funds he initiated a five million dollar highway construction program. The funds, which were simply advanced to the state, were to be repaid at a later date from future federal appropriations. The effort came none too soon. With the state's unemployed now numbering between twenty and twenty-five thousand the crush for jobs was so great that the New Mexico Federation of Labor proposed limiting employment on government construction projects to one wage earner per family.[7]

Herbert J. Hagerman, now president of the New Mexico State Taxpayers' Association, was among the first to grasp the situation realistically. In an article in the *New Mexico Tax Bulletin* he warned that the state was in serious trouble. Mines had shut down and agricultural prices had fallen because New Mexico could not compete with its neighboring states. The farmers were "broke" and, because they could not pay their taxes, education, the main source of public expense, was endangered. Efforts to relieve unemployment through federal highway construction programs did little but line the pockets of contractors. Because of the extensive use of machinery, they provided relatively few jobs. Worse, they pulled the state deeper into debt because of the required state share of construction and maintenance costs. Soil conservation programs were essential to the restoration of the state's agricultural economy but, Hagerman wrote, funding them would put such an intolerable burden on farmers and ranchers that it might drive many out of business. He urged a drastic reduction in state spending and the imposition of a sales tax to reduce the tax burden on property owners.[8]

New Mexico's depression problems were compounded in 1931 by the desperate condition of its vital midsection, the densely populated Middle Rio Grande Valley. Problems had been building there for years but in August and September 1929 the Rio Grande south of Albuquerque raged out of control and flooded hundreds of Hispanic farms. Several Hispanic villages were completely destroyed, the most prominent of which was San Marcial. The Red Cross provided emergency relief, feeding up to 1,200 people a day, but there was no money to reclaim land and rebuild homes. Even though cotton growers in Arizona and in New Mexico's

Mesilla Valley offered jobs, wages, and housing, the refugees refused to give up either their lands or their desire to rebuild their villages. With no industries in the valley to provide jobs their future was bleak. Moreover, experience suggested that the flooding would reoccur yearly unless work were continued on the vast reclamation project known as the Middle Rio Grande Conservancy District.[9]

The conservancy district, as it happened, was both the cause and the solution for the region's distress. Organized in 1923 as a political subdivision of the State of New Mexico, it was designed to correct problems caused by the enormous agricultural development in the San Luis Valley of Colorado during the 1880s and 1890s, as well as to prevent silting up of the newly constructed Elephant Butte reservoir. The old Hispanic irrigation system, unable to cope with the heavy new demands, had given way repeatedly, drowning some crop lands and leaving others without a source of water. The district had applied to the Bureau of Reclamation for funds to construct a new system of dikes, levees, and reservoirs, but was told that the project would have to wait ten to twenty years before federal funds would be available. Unwilling to wait that long, district officials persuaded the federal government to contribute one and a half million dollars on behalf of the Pueblo Indian lands. It then issued two million dollars in district bonds to cover the remaining construction costs.[10]

Launched with high hopes that it would bring thousands of new acres into cultivation and scores of industrious new settlers to the state, the project was ill-fated from the outset. The bonds, issued in 1929 under the most unfavorable market conditions in a decade, were sold to a syndicate of bankers at a prohibitive $5^{1}/_{2}$ percent interest rate. District officials and many Anglo farmers blamed the high interest rates on delays caused by the Hispanic farmers who, because they opposed the project on the basis of cost, demanded to be excluded from its boundaries. The Hispanos called attention to the fact that they were already contributing a great deal of free labor each year in the maintenance and repair of ditches and levees. Even so, an editorial in the *Magdalena News* blamed them for the disaster that had left them homeless. "It does not pay to oppose or try to stop the wheels of progress," it claimed self-righteously.[11]

Construction finally got underway in the spring of 1930 but armed conflicts broke out between conservancy officials and Hispanic farmers when the latter resisted the destruction of their irrigation ditches at the start of the planting season. Several tumultuous meetings were held between district officials and an organized body of small farmers, both Hispanic and Anglo, who protested that they could not pay even the interest on the heavy assessments imposed on their lands. Eventually state officials responded and the legislature passed a law exempting many agricultural tracts in the conservancy district from payments on both interest and principal for five years. By that time, it was claimed, construction would be completed and the lands reclaimed to the point that they could begin producing a profit. In the meantime construction costs rose. In 1932 with only thirty percent of the work completed, the district ran out of funds. Unable to sell more bonds because of the business depression, it faced bankruptcy.[12]

North of Santa Fe, in the Santa Cruz Valley, another conservancy district was in similar trouble. Organized by commercial farmers in the Española area, the district had as its purpose the building of a storage reservoir on the Santa Cruz River. As in the case of the Middle Rio Grande Conservancy District, it was opposed by local Hispanos, this time by seventy-five residents of the Hispanic village of Chimayó. Ignoring their protests the district was organized in 1925 without them. Members passed a bond issue for $250,000 with only a few dissenting votes. A bond company in Los Angeles, California, bought the bonds and work began in September 1926.[13]

It soon became apparent that the district had greatly overestimated the amount of irrigable land that could be developed. It had also underestimated the costs of construction. A second bond issue was floated in 1928 after the first three contracting firms were forced into bankruptcy. The bonds were sold at 6 percent interest and construction of the dam was completed in November 1931. In the meantime the yearly water tax, calculated in 1926 at sixty-nine cents per acre, had shot up to $8.36 per acre. By 1929 it was an impossible burden for land given over primarily to wheat and corn raised for home consumption. When tax delinquency grew to over 60 percent, the bond holders formed a protective association and reduced the taxes to $6.00 an acre. Delinquencies continued to rise, however, and by 1932 the Santa Cruz Irrigation District was once again on the verge of bankruptcy.[14]

Thanks to the efforts of New Mexico's congressional delegation, Senators Bronson Cutting and Sam Bratton, and Representative Dennis Chavez, the first federal monies paid out under Title II (Self-Liquidating Projects) of the newly established Reconstruction Finance Corporation (RFC) went to finance the beleaguered Middle Rio Grande Conservancy

District. Although Title II projects were, by statute, to be paid off by means other than taxation, the legal staff of the RFC determined that the assessments levied on the lands were not the same as taxes. The RFC bought up the bonds from the original bond holders at a reduced rate and spread out the repayment period to forty years. The RFC also rescued the Santa Cruz Irrigation District, but only after the bond holders had been forced into receivership. When the receiver, acting for the bond holders, agreed to accept twenty-five cents on the dollar on all back taxes, the RFC took over the district.[15]

Additional relief came to New Mexico through Title I of the Reconstruction Finance Corporation (the Relief of Destitution). This clause empowered the RFC to make loans to the various states for both direct relief (commodity distribution) and work relief (payment for services rendered on public works projects). Repayment at 3 percent interest was to begin in 1935. Margaret Reeves, director of New Mexico's Bureau of Child Welfare, administered the program sharing fiscal responsibility with the State board of Finance.[16]

In response to Seligman's request to survey relief needs in the state, Reeves found them to be far greater than anyone had imagined. In one rural county the bureau's field representative found women and children with nothing to wear but one flour sack apiece. Hundreds of children were badly undernourished and some were emaciated. Despite their plight, Reeves reported, the Hispanic villagers were technically ineligible for relief since they were not the victims of recent crop failures but had been made destitute through long term unemployment.[17]

Storekeepers throughout the state complained that they had extended credit as far as possible. Louis Ilfeld, a prominent Las Vegas attorney and merchant, had loaned villagers seeds and insect poisons. Other merchants by choice or necessity had been less generous. In at least one village the storekeeper had closed credit and gave assistance only to those willing to sign affidavits that they were starving. Reeves urged a statewide promotion of subsistence gardens as a stopgap measure and asked local agencies to help in financing the purchase of seeds.[18]

By July 1932 only one out of three individuals offered relief were transients. It was late summer, however, and in some rural counties a bare $4.50 to $5.00 a month was sufficient to supplement food raised by the family, particularly since the government also distributed flour supplied by the Red Cross. Food and clothing were top priorities with some limited funds available for the purchase of medicine. Nothing was allotted for fuel and shelter. Counties most urgently in need of relief were, in order: Bernalillo, Colfax, Rio Arriba, McKinley, Doña Ana, Valencia, Eddy, Curry, San Miguel, and Socorro. In providing relief Reeves worried about its effect on the villagers' sense of independence. The custom of mutual aid, she noted with pride in her report to the RFC, was developed to a further degree in New Mexico (among the Hispanic villagers) than in any other state. Aid would have to be provided strictly on the basis of need lest it encourage lack of initiative and dependency.[19]

Governor Seligman stressed the state's impoverished condition in his request for $240,000 in emergency aid from the RFC. County indigent funds were exhausted, he explained, and the only way New Mexico could provide state monies for direct relief would be for the people of the state to vote a bond issue for this purpose. He very much doubted that such a measure would pass, considering the impoverished condition of so many of the state's voters. Moreover, a special election would be time consuming and expensive. There was clear desperation in his plea for "all possible haste." When the state received the first installment of its RFC loan it was permitted to use some of the funds for state relief administration—the only state in the Union to be so permitted.[20]

The rules for federal relief were translated into Spanish by Louis Ilfeld and printed at the expense of the San Miguel County Emergency Relief Committee. True need had to be demonstrated, and the local relief agency was required to determine if an emergency existed. Authorities estimated relief needs based on individual or family income including wages, produce from the farm or garden, and other resources. To keep expenses at a minimum and discourage dependency, only enough was given to cover the minimum necessities. Even compensation for work relief was in the form of groceries, medicines, clothing, or fuel, figured at the rate paid locally for the same kind of work. To be eligible, projects had to be of a public nature and of benefit to the community or locality as a whole. For the most part they consisted of street repairs, clean-up, beautification of school grounds, and road work.[21]

Up to this point federal relief had, as intended, rescued some financial institutions and some property owners from immediate bankruptcy, but at the cost of borrowing with interest against the future. Starvation had been staved off in the more destitute villages, but at the cost of village pride—the need to admit, and give evidence of, abject need. Worse, the aid was purely temporary in nature. As Herbert Hagerman had pointed out, prosperity would not return to the state unless old industries were revived, new industries introduced, and greater efforts were made to repair the ravaged ranges and watersheds.

Franklin Delano Roosevelt, as a candidate for the Democratic presidential nomination, spoke directly to many of these concerns. As governor of New York state he had stressed the responsibilities of government to protect the rights of the "underdog" and to assure the equitable distribution of wealth and production. He had backed up such objectives with programs to regulate utilities, reform prisons, and extend old age pensions—programs which struck a responsive chord in the hearts of the state's many Progressives. Moreover, he was known to share his cousin Theodore's passionate love of the land. Always partial to the farmer, he had asked for tax relief and inaugurated studies on land use. His Temporary Emergency Relief Administration, set up in 1931 under his disciple, Harry Hopkins, not only provided work relief for 10 percent of the families in the state, but tried to get people back to the land. Roosevelt also urged the conservation of natural resources. Following guidelines established by Teddy's Chief Forester, Gifford Pinchot, Franklin had restored the exhausted land and planted trees on his Hyde Park estate in 1910. As governor of New York, he had sponsored an amendment to the state constitution giving the state government authority to purchase marginal land and reforest it. When, in 1932, he developed this plan as part of New York's unemployment relief program, his reputation was assured nationwide among conservationists.[22]

Much to the dismay of New Mexico's Old Guard Republicans, Roosevelt won the support of the powerful Seligman-Cutting coalition. This alliance, which united Seligman Democrats with Cutting Republican Progressives, even more significantly included substantial numbers of Hispanic voters attracted to the Cutting banner by his steadfast support for Hispanic ethnic concerns. In November 1932 Roosevelt won New Mexico handily, as he did every other Western state.[23]

Because of the many important posts throughout the government that Roosevelt filled with Westerners, many of them imbued with the progressive, social worker ethic, his New Deal quickly took on a western, progressive focus. Given more to optimistic generalization than to specifics, he encouraged and permitted his appointees to set much of the agenda for the turbulent activities that followed. New Mexico, as we have seen, was not only well represented in Washington, but the President's policies received strong support from Santa Fe. Through the active involvement of the intellectual and business communities, a rapid, two-way exchange of ideas and information developed between Santa Fe and Washington.

Key participants in this pipeline were, as would be expected, New Mexico's congressional delegation, now consisting of Senators Cutting (until his death in an airplane accident in 1935) and Carl Hatch, and Representative Chavez. Others contributed in important ways to keeping attention focused on New Mexico's people and its special agenda. Until her death in 1934 the flamboyant Mary Austin lectured throughout the country and her books and articles were widely read, along with those of other New Mexican poets and authors. Their efforts were augmented by those of such civic leaders as Paul A. F. Walter and E. Dana Johnson.[24]

Walter succeeded to the position of president of Santa Fe's First National Bank in 1933 following the death of its former head, Governor Arthur Seligman. The confidante and adviser of many of the state's politicians, scientists, and bankers, Walter was also a long time member of both the historical and archaeological societies, and the editor of both the *New Mexico Historical Review* and *El Palacio,* the magazine of the Museum of New Mexico. Like so many of his contemporaries he was deeply interested in, and concerned about, the future of New Mexico's Hispanos. As one of the state's leading businessmen, he was frequently consulted and so was in an ideal situation to influence public policy.[25]

E. Dana Johnson, the editor of the *Santa Fe New Mexican* from 1913 to 1937, may have been equally influential. Handpicked by the paper's owner, Senator Cutting, Johnson shared his employer's concerns, not only for progressive government, but for New Mexico's history, cultures, folklore, and environment. He supported every cause and movement that tended to keep New Mexico and Santa Fe, its capital, a symbol of the peoples who made it. Recognized as a good fighter, he was a master of witty, satiric invective, a weapon he used most effectively in promoting and defending special causes.[26]

While national and state leaders such as Cutting, Chavez, Austin, Walter, and Johnson influenced and directed public policy, others at the county and municipal level supported and shared their goals. In fact, there appears to have been a remarkable unanimity of opinion concerning New Mexico's needs and how to meet them that cut across party and ethnic lines. These needs were—not in priority order but so intertwined that one could not be accomplished without the other—the opening up of northern New Mexico with a system of roads linking Santa Fe to the Colorado border and isolated villages to the capital; the stabilization of the agricultural population on the land through more efficient farming and marketing, and the revitalization of village life; the introduction of home based industries to supplement farming and bring in additional revenue; the restoration and revitalization of the land, itself; and, finally, the preservation of such tangible elements of New Mexico's historic cultures as its architectural monuments, folklore, music, and art.

The road system was necessary to improve the flow of goods, produce, and tourists to and from the capital. It was also necessary to bring the villages into the state's market economy, and to make them accessible to both the control and the services of the state's educational establishment and the county agricultural extension services. With no prospects of industrial employment in sight, the only future for the state's rural Hispanos seemed to be a better, more efficient life on the land. But since neither the present amount or condition of arable land was adequate to support the rural population, steps had to be taken toward more efficient and less costly methods of farming, better methods of preserving and marketing farm produce, and better care and use of the land.

Village life had to be revitalized because this, it was assumed, would make for happier, more stable rural citizens. Supplementary income had to be introduced and, what better than with the production and sale of historic crafts? The revitalization of village life included the repair and restoration of decrepit irrigation systems, the building of new schools and community meeting and recreation centers, the digging of new, more sanitary wells and privies, and the construction of farm-to-market roads. It meant the improvement of community livestock and better use and access to public grazing lands. It included, as well, the introduction of educational opportunities for young people and adults, the encouragement of recreational programs based about traditional Hispanic culture, and instruction in the art of self-government. Finally, the restoration and preservation of the state's historic monuments, its Hispanic villages, Indian pueblos, and colorful folklore would add to its exotic appeal and introduce more tourist dollars into the local economy. And it would preserve some unique bits of Americana to enrich the nation's cultural heritage and provide for the pleasure and edification of future generations.[27]

In their efforts to direct and control the destiny of the state and its native populations New Mexico's ruling elites were aided by the localized nature of the New Deal programs. Harry Hopkins, who headed the new

Federal Emergency Relief Administration (FERA), signed into law on May 12, 1933, believed that its programs should be decentralized and local in character. The bulk of the FERA projects were state and locally sponsored, as were those of the Civil Works Administration (CWA), which ran concurrently in the winter of 1933–34, and the Works Progress Administration (WPA), which succeeded the FERA in 1935.[28] These federal funds gave local officials both the money and the power to carry out long desired programs and develop new ones. Although the drought-stricken farmers of the eastern and southern plains, the transients, and the urban dwellers of whatever ethnic composition received their just due, programs directed toward New Mexico's rural Hispanos and the preservation of their village life and agriculture constituted the bulk of the state's federal expenditures during the 1930s.

As had happened during the Pueblo Indian Lands Controversy of the 1920s, John Collier's efforts to promote Indian rights at the expense of the state's rural Anglos and Hispanos inspired concern and resentment. As before, this concern tended to be couched largely in terms of its denial of traditional Hispanic rights.

Collier's success as New Deal Indian Commissioner in acquiring federal funds to carry out his plans inspired cupidity as well. Upon the announcement that Collier had obtained one million dollars of National Industrial Relief Administration (NIRA) money for the improvement of land and facilities on the Navajo Indian reservation, the *Santa Fe New Mexican* demanded to know, in an editorial, why similar government lavishness had not been extended toward New Mexico's "suffering native peoples"—"native" being the euphemism for Hispano. The editorial declared,

> Uncle Sam has had nothing to give the northern New Mexico farmers who needed $50,000 to $75,000 to remedy unemployment, save the waste of their water, and the toil of fighting floods and drought. . . . A modest sum for their relief in the building of third class roads is now asked which is a small fraction of the golden flood poured into the Indian country.

Resentment ran so high that former Governor Miguel Otero, now chairman of New Mexico's Public Works board, felt constrained to announce that NRA did not stand for "Navajo Relief Act" and that not a single National Recovery Administration project in New Mexico was for Indians. In December 1935 the *New Mexican* again expressed concern that "the right of native valley farmers to the waters of the Rio Grande and its tributaries was being shoved into the background" in an interstate conference. "With scores of millions being spent on Indians," it declared, "someone needs to take up the cudgel for those whose fathers first watered the lands in the valley."[29]

Though the state was indeed impoverished, the realization that federal funds for Indian relief were outright grants to the BIA may have played a role in hardening state resistance toward providing its matching share of relief money. In accordance with the federal statute, FERA money was initially awarded on the basis of one dollar for every three dollars of local, state, and federal funds expended on relief by the state. Since New Mexico had neither the legal basis nor the inclination to raise such relief monies, FERA field representative Pierce Williams recommended confidentially to Harry Hopkins in July 1933, that the federal government agree to carry New Mexico's relief load in full.[30] Even after Congress abandoned the "matching" provision in November, state officials were reluctant to hold the special legislative session required for the state to receive FERA funds. They feared that federal officials might try to pressure them, as they had Colorado some months earlier. The governor did eventually call the special session, but only after being assured in writing that the federal government would not interfere. The legislature, when it finally convened in April 1934, went only so far as to enact a 2 percent sales tax and a liquor stamp tax to provide three million dollars in additional school revenue. State administrators hoped that these school funds would reduce New Mexico's need for federal educational grants and so partially satisfy federal requirements. FERA officials welcomed even this limited gesture of self-help and excused New Mexico from its matching obligations. Only in later years, with the depression easing, did the legislature set aside a franchise tax, a use tax, liquor and tobacco taxes, and part of the severance tax for matching federal welfare grants.[31]

New Mexico's governing elites and state officials may have thought they knew exactly what New Mexico needed and how its relief moneys should be spent, but representatives sent out from Washington often disagreed with their priorities. The outsiders, who failed to understand the nature of the Anglo-Hispanic relationship in New Mexico had a different set of prejudices and virtually no historical perspective concerning the state's native cultures. They were frequently at odds, frustrated and puzzled by the actions and arguments of state officials.

FERA had been in effect only a few months when a field examiner reported that the whole state relief organization was incensed about the census schedule which listed "Mexican" as a separate and nonwhite category for the first time. Refusing to use the schedule in its original form, state relief officials were mollified only when the federal representative agreed to let them block out the category "Mexican" and allow the census taker to insert that information later without the subject knowing it. Nevertheless, state officials must have continued to classify many Hispanos, native born and otherwise, as "white." A year later, in April 1934 a federal representative telegraphed the Bureau of Child Welfare with instructions that "native born Mexicans" were not to be called "white" if one or both parents had been born in Mexico and was a Mexican.[32]

Federal field representatives repeatedly described state relief activities as chaotic, in part, it would seem, because state workers insisted on following their own priorities. Marie Dresden, a regional social worker, reported that state relief director Reeves and her staff of state and county social workers were highly trained. They had done an excellent job of creating and using local committees and getting the cooperation of the strongest groups within each county. But, she complained, they were dismally unable to cope with government regulations. They continually dealt with their enormous case loads on an individual basis instead of setting up standardized budgets and procedures. They also insisted on caring for all needy persons, in particular women and children, instead of properly distinguishing between "eligible" relief recipients—those only recently impoverished due to drought and depression—and the "chronically indigent." Dresden was outraged when Reeves reported that one-third of the population of the state might soon be on relief. "Considering their type of population," she declared, "I think that is ridiculous." She was equally unhappy with state workers who set the budgetary needs of Mexicans at "too high a level" in order to qualify them for work relief as well as for direct relief.[33]

Other supervisors also found case loads too high. Alice Clements, an acting FERA field representative, demanded that they be "whipped down" from three to four hundred to nearer one hundred. Field representative Maude Van Kemp thought that this might be accomplished by employing more aides and teaching them how to conduct thorough investigations. She did see a problem, however, in the bare eighteen dollars a month salary that made it virtually impossible for an aide to work outside her home district.[34]

Early in 1935 Reeves was forced to resign by the administration of incoming governor Clyde Tingley. Tingley, a Democrat, wanted Republican Reeves out because she had steadfastly refused to permit the usual kinds of patronage within the relief organization. When he complained to FERA officials in Washington about the alleged inefficiency of her department they welcomed the opportunity to encourage her to leave and looked forward to working with a bureaucrat more amenable to following government regulations. At the end of April Alice Clements noted that matters had definitely improved under the new administration. Not only were workers relieved of the pressures formerly placed on them by local, small town politicians, she declared, but "another noticeable change is the few relief clients at the various offices. In January, hordes of people could be found at almost any time around any relief office. This situation has cleared up noticeably." Clements, apparently, was quite unaware of the realities of seasonal labor![35]

Another of the government regulations Reeves and her staff ignored concerned the use of FERA funds for medical relief. With New Mexico one of the most disease-ridden areas in the nation her concern was understandable.[36] FERA regulations restricted medical and surgical treatment to emergency conditions "causing acute suffering and interfering with earning capacity, endangering life, or threatening some permanent new handicap that is preventable when medical care is sought." This did not include hospitalization which, federal authorities insisted, should be furnished by tax supported charity hospitals. Reeves overrode this regulation in a supplementary statement to the "Rules and Regulations in Respect to the Administration of Federal Relief in the State of New Mexico" issued in October 1932. In her statement she declared that federal relief funds were inadequate to take over the treatment of indigent medical care, but a sick patient in an isolated locality in need of the services of a doctor was to be attended and the doctor paid at a rate previously determined between him and the certified relief agency. Reeves asked physicians to give charity rates, just as merchants were asked to give special prices. Hospital bills were to be paid only in exceptional cases and then only at charity rates.[37]

When local authorities tightened the rules after Reeves's departure it caused considerable discontent among members of the medical profession. As one state physician explained in a letter to the New Mexico FERA, there were no tax supported charity hospitals in New Mexico. Another physician cared enough to write a personal letter to Harry Hopkins telling him of cases refused by the local relief authorities. "Yesterday I tried to get help for . . . a sixteen year old Mexican boy," he wrote. "He is suffering from tuberculosis, motherless, without food, medicine, or care of any kind." The day before another Hispanic family had called on him for help. The mother and father both had active tuberculosis and five children to care for. With only four dollars' worth of groceries from relief for the entire month, they were on the verge of starvation. In another case an Anglo mother of five children, who worked in the relief sewing room for twenty dollars a month, had been refused treatment for her little girl who had broken her wrist. "Our indigent fund has been drawn on heavily and they are almost without funds . . ." the physician explained. "I have personally given funds, clothes, and lots of medicine and have helped in every way possible the Democratic cause and have not been reimbursed with just bills that the Government owes me."[38]

Beyond the sense of personal injustice, the state's doctors were vitally concerned with the high incidence of syphilis, tuberculosis, malaria, and typhoid among New Mexico's rural poor. Reporting on the Medical Relief Program in New Mexico, another doctor suggested that it was very important to get a ruling whereby indigents suffering from illnesses requiring emergency treatment could be attended whether or not they were actually on the relief rolls. The problem was acute because the annual incidence rate for syphilis in the non-Indian population in New Mexico, as reported in a bulletin published in 1934, was more than twice that of the general United States population. About three-fourths of the cases were within the rural Hispanic population. With only one-twentieth of the existing cases in the state under medical supervision due to the isolation of the population, the problem of control was formidable. Malaria was rampant in the Middle Rio Grande valley because the destruction of the old Hispanic irrigation system had created many marshy stagnant areas which were perfect breeding spots for mosquitoes.[39]

The fact is that the hardships of the depression had destroyed for all time the idyllic myth of the contented, self-sufficient, "wantless" Hispanic villager. Anglo newcomers to the state were more inclined to view Hispanos with the more common set of stereotypes applied to other Mexican Americans—as chronically indigent, dependent, and disease-ridden, and beyond the scope of federal relief. These views were expressed bluntly and candidly by Lorena Hickok, a newspaper woman sent out by Harry Hopkins to gather first-hand information on the extent of the national suffering and advise him on each region's specific needs and problems. Although Hickok was sympathetic to a degree with the problems of the nation's minorities, and recognized the effect of wage and job discrimination in perpetuating their poverty, her report reflected dominant Anglo attitudes. It must be presumed that many of her impressions were gained from conversations and interviews with leading New Mexicans. These impressions, in turn, influenced Hopkins and other FERA officials in determining the relief needs of New Mexico's Hispanos.[40]

According to Hickok New Mexico's Hispanos were an economically helpless people. They were easygoing and pleasure-loving but didn't seem to know how to take care of their stock or what to do with good land when they had it. Nevertheless, because of their low standard of living they were not a particularly serious relief problem. They could, she said, survive on as little as eight to ten dollars a month and their adobe houses were cheap and comfortable. Unless rehabilitated, however, Hickok feared they would become permanently dependent. They needed education, she declared, in what to raise and how to raise it. That would not be easy. "They're perfectly docile, but not particularly energetic."[41]

Hickok worried about the effect of uniform federal wage scales, particularly as they affected white males. From Tucson she wrote,

> It's the same old story wherever I go. Two classes of people. Whites, including white collar people, with white standards of living, for whom relief, as it is now, is anything but adequate . . . Mexicans—or, East of the Mississippi, Negroes—with low standards of living, to whom relief is adequate and attractive.

Many were able to get work but at wages so low that they were better off on relief. However, with so many Mexicans and Negroes on relief, "we are compelled to force the white man's standard of living down to that of the Mexicans and Negroes."[42]

Hickok thought one way to solve the problem would be to force anyone who could get work at whatever wages to take it and get off the relief rolls. She admitted, however, that there were people in the relief organizations who believed that such a policy would force people into peonage. They argued that employers, particularly farmers and housewives, would take advantage of the situation. Some housewives, they said, thought Negroes, Mexicans or "even" white girls ought to be glad to work for their room and board, and in New Mexico sheep growers wanted herders to work for a bare seven dollars a month. If farmers could not get herders to work for that amount because they got eight or ten dollars on relief, Hickok thought they ought to raise their wages a little.[43]

On the other hand, Hickok continued, doctors had shown that the Mexican or Spanish American diet of "chile beans, red beans, flour, and cornmeal" was highly nutritious.

> If these people can live on ten or twelve dollars a month and be reasonably healthy and so contented that they won't even take work when it is offered them, let alone go out and look for it, why, in the name of common sense, raise them above that? . . . I doubt if the Relief Administration is financially in a position to battle low wages all over the South and Southwest. Dammit, man, our job is to feed people and clothe them and shelter them, with as little damage to their morale as possible. . . . I've never been able to see that it was the job of the Federal Emergency Relief Administration to fight the battle of the American Federation of Labor![44]

The wage problem in New Mexico attracted official notice in January 1934 when the Civil Works Administration work projects began paying the federally mandated wage of fifty cents an hour. With the tremendous need for jobs and money, and the limited funds, Margaret Reeves decided to hire twice as many workers for two weeks each, at a monthly wage of thirty dollars, rather than create dissatisfaction by paying half as many workers the full monthly wage of sixty dollars. Other New Mexicans were quick to agree. Both Louis Ilfeld of Las Vegas and the Vice-Chairman of the Bernalillo County CWA expressed this argument in letters to Senator Carl Hatch, and a similar argument was expressed in an editorial in the *Tucumcari Daily News*. The most telling argument, however, was the petition signed by 700 unemployed farmers from Taos requesting that they be allowed to work staggered shifts in order to increase the number of employed from 250 to a total of 600.[45]

The problem was whether or not this was discriminatory. In January 1934 Jacob Baker, the assistant administrator for the CWA in Washington, notified Hatch that the federal government could not make exceptions to the hours of labor permitted without letting all states do the same. Hopkins contradicted him one week later when he informed Hatch that staggering would be permitted in rural New Mexico counties so long as workers were paid the prevailing wage for that kind of work and received a minimum of fifteen hours of work per week. Hopkins modified the plan the following month by once again prohibiting the rotation or staggering of employees but reducing the minimum wage from fifty cents to thirty cents an hour. He also directed that hours be limited so that the maximum weekly earning not exceed the amount necessary to meet the budgeted requirements of the family. When the directive was printed in the *New Mexico Relief Bulletin* a month later it informed workers that county wage committees would be appointed by the local relief chairman to determine the prevailing rates for each locality. The committees were to be made up of one representative each from organized labor, business, and the local relief committee.[46]

The problem of "staggering" work hours came up again in 1936 when Democratic Committeewoman Mrs. W. F. Kirby reported receiving complaints of wage and work discrimination from a great number of Hispanic women working on government projects. They objected to the fact that they were permitted to work only part time and to the fact that they averaged $25.26 a month while men, working the same number of hours, averaged $37.05 a month. Mildred Andrew, director of the New Mexico Women's Projects, justified the discrimination on familiar grounds. Most of the women had never been previously employed, she argued. The security wage for men was far in excess of the prevailing wage of fifteen cents an hour for unskilled women workers. Moreover, she continued, contradicting her earlier statement, many women were leaving private employment where they received three dollars to five dollars a week to participate in the program. Since there were already far too many eligible women to be absorbed into the work relief programs Andrew believed that they were better off with some work than with none at all. The arrangement gave them more time to be at home with their families and created an incentive for them to return to private employment.[47]

Ellen S. Woodward, national director of Women's Programs, disagreed with Andrew on the basis that the WPA had not lowered its standards in the case of Negro women in the Southern states. Rather than take a stand on the issue, however, she referred the matter to the regional director of Women's Programs in Salt Lake City, Mary H. Isham, who turned it over to her superior, Assistant Administrator, Robert H. Hinckley. Hinckley discussed the matter with Assistant Administrator Thad Holt in Washington. In the end, the men agreed to instruct New Mexico State Administrator Lea Rowland to continue the employment of women in New Mexico on the same basis as before.[48]

With all the jockeying of wages and hours on New Deal work projects it would be surprising if there had been no attempts by Hispanic laborers to control or protest the process. There were, in fact, many. Besides the fact that villagers frequently complained and held "mass meetings" to protest discrimination and politics in the distribution of relief, there were numerous incidents of organized protest. Many workers dependent upon wage work in the Middle and Upper Rio Grande valleys joined the *Liga Obrera de Habla Español,* or Spanish Speaking Workers Union, a leftist Hispanic labor union organized in Colorado with the help of the International Workers of the World in 1928 and brought to New Mexico by returning beet workers. They used it as a medium for exerting mass pressure on the relief agencies and other employers. In August 1934 FERA workers in Gallup called a strike to protest the wage cut from fifty cents to forty cents an hour recommended by the FERA wage committee. The reason given for the cut, according to the committee, was to put Gallup FERA wages in line with those paid elsewhere in the state. The following year the *Liga Obrera* protested FERA relief policies on at least two occasions. In February it demanded that a uniform family budget be set by the county welfare agencies based on the number of members in a family and the individual needs and limitations of those members. In May it protested what it deemed the improper use of a man to pull a sod plow on a construction project. In August a notice appeared that the Solomon Esquibel branch of the International Labor Defense had cited cases of discrimination in relief at Gallup.[49]

These efforts notwithstanding, Hispanic labor in New Mexico had never seen a harder time. It had always been difficult to organize because of the isolated nature of the population, the predominance of farm labor, the lack of industries large enough to bring together large groups of workers, and the conflict of economic interests between various groups. During the two decades preceding the depression native New Mexicans had had to compete with great numbers of their impoverished brethren from below the border. Mexican migrant workers lured north by the railroads, sugar beet growers, and other western employers, provided cheap labor and were used to discourage or break strikes. When the onset of the depression put jobs at a premium these Mexican laborers were forcibly repatriated on a scale previously unmatched in United States history. In this climate it was easy for employers to accuse workers who made problems of being communists and threaten them with deportation. Most New Mexican Hispanos could prove their American citizenship but that did not protect them from harassment or, at the very least, being removed from relief rolls. Not surprisingly, most attempts at organized protest occurred in the centers of greatest Hispanic population. For most rural Hispanos, any job at any wage was better than begging or letting one's family starve.[50]

For many of New Mexico's Hispanos it must have seemed as if the world had closed in on them. Free for generations to range widely throughout the West in search of wage labor, they now found their options greatly narrowed. As the depression deepened, employers cut back on their labor forces. Mines, smelters, and railroads reduced their activities. Many Western growers, faced with drought and other natural disasters as well as plunging prices, went bankrupt. Others cut back drastically on both labor and wages. Even those workers who found employment were unable to live on their meager incomes and were forced to apply for relief to make it through the lean winter months. Worse, many beet growers who had previously allowed their Hispanic laborers to winter on their farms now denied them even this refuge. With no place else to go, they flooded into the cities or returned to their home villages in New Mexico.[51]

Throughout the West employers gave preference to in-state workers even in the livestock industry, which had long depended upon highly skilled Hispanic cowpunchers and sheepherders. New Mexican workers, who had to be provided with transportation to and from their homes, became of marginal value to ranchers in Montana, Wyoming, Colorado and Utah, and were the last hired and first fired.[52]

Other employers, given the opportunity, discriminated against Hispanic labor in favor of Anglos who previously would not have deigned to take menial labor. As the numbers of unemployed and on relief spiraled upward, state relief agencies began to refuse help to out-of-state residents. Numerous New Mexican workers, unable to find work and denied relief in the states where they had formerly been employed, came home only to be told that, by virtue of their absence, they were no longer eligible for relief in New Mexico. Since most had had to borrow money to go in search of work they were also deeply in debt and devoid of credit.[53]

In May 1939 New Mexican Hispanos even found the Colorado border closed against them. In an effort to keep unwanted Mexicans from flooding the relief rolls in Colorado, Governor Edwin Johnson ordered all "alien" beet workers turned back at the New Mexico state line. The following year he called out the National Guard and declared martial law along the entire Colorado–New Mexico border.[54]

United States citizenship provided no protection to New Mexico born

Hispanos. In one incident twelve sheepherders from Abiquiu and Peñasco on their way to jobs in Wyoming and Utah were taken from a train by the Colorado militia, loaded into trucks, and dumped out on the New Mexico border. All were traveling on passes issued by sheep companies. Hoping to avoid another such incident, Juan Vigil, the New Mexico State Comptroller, addressed a letter to Governor Johnson on behalf of a group of Taos sheepherders who for years had been employed by Colorado sheepmen during the lambing season. Arguing that "to prevent these citizens from going into your state means that they will be deprived of their only means of livelihood," he assured Johnson that they were skilled "professionals" who could be counted on not to become public charges. In like protest, New Mexico Governor Clyde Tingley threatened to boycott goods from Colorado. In the meantime, Anglo employers in Colorado decried the loss of dependable seasonal labor, and several Hispanic groups in Colorado protested the completely unwarranted harassment of native born Americans. Johnson eventually lifted the blockade but only after it had been an effective "last straw" in breaking the generations-old migration pattern between New Mexico and its neighboring states.[55]

In one way or another the onset of the Depression stripped New Mexico's Hispanos of virtually every aspect of their multisource survival strategy. Those Hispanic farmers who had previously eked out a living close to home were no better off than those who had migrated in search of work. The dry-land pinto bean farmers of the Estancia Valley found that they could not compete in scale with Anglo farmers because of the relatively small size of their acreage and the lack of money to mechanize their operations. They tried to raise larger and larger crops only to be defeated by crop failures due to weather, insects, and the loss of topsoil through wind erosion. When the lumber mill that had provided dependable employment closed in 1932, they also lost their source of supplementary income.[56]

Farmers in the Middle Rio Grande Valley were, if anything, in worse shape. With water tax delinquency on all tracts of agricultural land at 70 percent, they had to adjust to the loss of much of their accustomed wage labor in Albuquerque. The process was unremitting. As tax delinquency increased, so did the tax rate. Throughout the Middle Rio Grande Conservancy District farmers were threatened once again with foreclosure, a fate they shared with farmers in the Santa Cruz Irrigation District. As their lands became available, land hungry newcomers from

Texas, Oklahoma, and elsewhere bought them up.[57] By late 1934, 60 percent of the villagers in northern New Mexico were receiving government aid and in some villages every family appeared on the relief roll.[58] Unable to sustain themselves independently, the villagers could no longer retain control over their interactions with the larger, Anglo dominated economy.

By late 1934 the experimental phases of the Hispanic New Deal were over. Geared up and ready to go in early 1935 the newly instituted Works Progress Administration (WPA) provided funding and personnel for a multitude of programs directed toward the preservation and improvement of Hispanic village life. The institution of the Soil Conservation Service (SCS) and the Resettlement Administration (RA) provided the funding and personnel for programs designed to improve village agriculture and restore village lands. The Hispanic villagers, no longer able to direct their own destinies, were targets and an ideal living laboratory for the massive but short lived experiments in social engineering that followed.

(Top) The revival of so-called Spanish Colonial architecture is illustrated by the graceful proportions of the Fine Arts Museum in Santa Fe as photographed in 1917. Courtesy Museum of New Mexico, Neg. No. 12986.

(Bottom) The revival could also appear ridiculous, as manifested in this curio shop in Albuquerque. Note the beams that project at right angles. Photo by John Collier. Courtesy Library of Congress.

(Opposite top) New Mexico's fascination with its Hispanic heritage peaked in the late 1920s. Fiesta costumes, ca. 1928. Courtesy Museum of New Mexico, Neg. No. 117680.

(Opposite bottom) Skilled artisans like Francisco Delgado had a thriving business thanks to the "Spanish Colonial" Crafts Revival. Santa Fe, ca. 1935. Courtesy Museum of New Mexico, Neg. No. 71180.

(Above) Harvey "Indian Detour" Car with tourists and tour guide in the Hispanic village of Truchas, New Mexico, 1930s. Photo by Edward A. Kemp. Courtesy Museum of New Mexico, Neg. No. 46949.

(Opposite top) View of Valdez, New Mexico, in late 1930s. Photo by Irving Rusinow. Courtesy National Archives.

(Opposite bottom) WPA road workers. Photo by Irving Rusinow. Courtesy National Archives.

(Above) New Mexico women were happy to be paid WPA wages for the traditional woman's job of house plastering, July 1940. Photo by Russell Lee. Courtesy Library of Congress.

(Above)  Numerous New Deal agricultural programs emphasized the importance of home canning. Photo by Russell Lee. Courtesy Library of Congress.

(Opposite top)  WPA craft projects encouraged the revival of traditional crafts for additional household revenue and to preserve the cultural heritage. Photo by John Collier. Courtesy Library of Congress.

(Opposite bottom)  WPA weaving projects encouraged women to try their hand at this traditionally male craft. Costilla, New Mexico, September 1939. Photo by Russell Lee. Courtesy Library of Congress.

(Opposite top)  Both the WPA and the NYA taught classes in the traditional Hispanic craft of woodworking. Photo by Irving Rusinow. Courtesy Library of Congress.

(Opposite bottom)  The WPA brought schools and teachers to many communities that had never had them before. Photo by John Collier. Courtesy Library of Congress.

(Above)  WPA hot lunch programs were among the most popular of all New Deal programs. Photo by Irving Rusinow. Peñasco, New Mexico. Courtesy National Archives.

(Above)  United States Agricultural Administration representative explaining a farm plan to Hispanic ranchers, Taos County, January 1943. Photo by John Collier. Courtesy Library of Congress.

(Opposite top)  Hispanic family bringing a sick child to the Taos County Cooperative Health Association clinic in Peñasco, New Mexico, January 1943. Photo by John Collier. Courtesy Library of Congress.

(Opposite bottom)  Nurse Mary Lennard, Red Cross nurse from Taos County Cooperative Health Association making a house call. Questa, New Mexico, January 1943. Photo by John Collier. Courtesy Library of Congress.

(Opposite top) The major thrust of many of New Mexico's New Deal agricultural programs was to restore communal grazing lands and return them to the exclusive use of village sheep herders. Photo by John Collier. Courtesy Library of Congress.

(Opposite bottom) WPA literacy and trade classes prepared New Mexican Hispanos for their heroic performance in World War II. Photo by John Collier. Courtesy Library of Congress.

(Above) Village of El Cerrito, New Mexico, today. Photo by James T. Forrest.

Water is still the lifeline. Acequia (irrigation ditch), El Cerrito, New Mexico.
Photo by James T. Forrest.

(Above) Street in village of Cordoba, New Mexico. Photo by James T. Forrest.

(Below) The largest and best kept building in every village is still the Catholic Church. Cordoba, New Mexico. Photo by James T. Forrest.

Calvario Cross near village of Nambe, New Mexico. Photo by James T. Forrest.

# Implementing the Cultural Agenda

The programs instituted by the New Deal agencies were in great part a continuation of the progressive policies of the 1920s directed toward the modernization of Hispanic village life. Herein lay one of the major tensions, and the source of multiple contradictions in the New Deal ethic. While the reformers yearned to preserve the cooperative, communitarian values of a preindustrial life-style, they abhorred its inefficiency and wastefulness. Hoping to bring to it new methods and techniques of scientific agriculture, homemaking, and child care, they found themselves battling on a practical level the very forces they hoped, on an intellectual level, to preserve. In like fashion they unconsciously distinguished between "good" and "bad" aspects of Hispanic ethnicity. Purporting to value cultural pluralism they extolled the virtues of Hispanic arts, crafts, music, and folklore but worked mightily to eradicate such other aspects of Hispanic ethnicity as the "superstition" and "irresponsibility" that brought Hispanos to put devotion to church, family, and culture over secular and monetary values. Other aspects of Hispanic ethnicity were variously, and pejoratively, labeled as docility, lack of ambition, and just plain ignorance.

With so much emphasis on behavior modification it is not surprising that progressive education—learning by doing—was pervasive throughout all New Deal community programs. Every agency had its educational goals and either had its own corps of teachers or worked cooperatively with another which did. Selected villages were invaded by Anglo arts and crafts experts, English teachers, health and nutrition specialists, recreational leaders, and county farm and home agents with demonstration projects in everything from soil conservation and home canning to the construction of sanitary privies. In time these efforts were variously and sporadically augmented with craft workshops and cooperatives, community or mobile libraries, adult literacy classes, health clinics, nursery schools and hot lunch programs, school demonstration gardens, community laundries and cooperative canneries, food dehydrators, livestock associations, and machinery cooperatives. Many villages were also invaded by urban intellectuals, both Anglo and Hispanic, eager to record and transcribe old Hispanic myths and legends, songs and musical rhythms, dances and ceremonies, folk customs, and folk medicine.

In exchange for this invasion of their lives, the villagers received wages for their labor, much of it directed toward the improvement of their roads, school buildings and grounds, and irrigation systems. Typically, they provided simple equipment and such native raw materials as wood, rocks, and earth, while the government agency paid their wages and provided mechanical equipment and any manufactured items that were needed. So far as was possible, construction methods and materials were kept simple enough that the villagers could maintain them in the future with the resources at hand. In exchange for their cooperation with these programs many villagers also learned to read and write in English, to figure, to articulate their needs in the form of letters and petitions to government agencies and representatives, and to make the most of an often bewildering and conflicting array of government services and regulations. While their most immediate needs of cash for food and clothing were met, and their village life brightened with new amenities, they were often bitterly disappointed at the short-lived nature of the improvements and their own continuing inability to provide for themselves. Anticipating these results, they were reluctant to trade old ways that were tried and proven, for new ways that were both problematical and beyond their capacity to maintain. The government agents who directed and participated in these programs were alternately transported in a euphoria of perceived accomplishment or as bitterly depressed as the villagers with the transiency of their efforts.

Predating both the New Deal and the depression, federal, state, and county highway programs provided a highly popular means of bringing the isolated and economically backward areas of the state into the urban business and governmental orbit. Local politicians promoted road programs because of the possibilities for patronage, and because they provided much needed jobs for local laborers. Road programs were popular with businessmen because of the lucrative contracts for construction companies and local suppliers, because they encouraged trade with the hinterland, and because they opened up vast new areas of scenic beauty to tourists and sportsmen. State and local authorities were equally enthusiastic. They knew that roads were essential to their programs of educational and agricultural modernization.

When John DeHuff, Secretary of the Santa Fe Chamber of Commerce, asked Paul A. F. Walter in June of 1933 to suggest public works projects that would be of benefit to the region, Walter's first thought was the construction of highways to the San Luis Valley of Colorado, across the Jemez Mountains to the Gallup-Farmington road, and across the Sangre de Cristos to Las Vegas.[1] The Chamber needed little prodding. Most annual reports from 1933 to 1938 noted efforts made by the staff to promote highway construction and, in particular, the program of secondary roads into and throughout the northern counties.[2] Not surprisingly, therefore, a major proportion of FERA and CWA funds were devoted to secondary road work. Although ostensibly for the purposes of relieving conditions in the drought-stricken counties of the state's eastern border, most federal highway funds were put at the disposition of a general road construction program designed to meet the requirements of the state as a whole.[3] The great majority of workers on these projects were Hispanos from rural communities.[4]

Although citizens frequently requested politicians to bring road projects to their areas, much of the impetus behind the road building program remained with the Santa Fe Chamber of Commerce.[5] In April 1935 the chamber gathered together a delegation of representatives from Santa Fe, Taos, and Rio Arriba counties to meet with the State Highway Commission to request the completion of first class highways from Española to Taos; to Ojo Caliente, Tres Piedras, and Antonito; and to Chama and Lumberton. An article in the *Santa Fe New Mexican* noted that this program would cut the distance to Denver via the Alamosa route by fifty miles and open much of northern New Mexico to visitors.[6]

By October 1935 New Mexico's road program consisted of improvements to 180 miles of federal roads, 736 miles of state roads, and 1707 miles of county or farm-to-market roads. Several of the latter in Taos and Catron counties were justified on the basis that they served smaller communities financially unable to improve or maintain their roads and would provide continuous work during the winter months for their large relief load.[7]

Once again, New Mexico found its particular set of priorities sharply criticized. The *New York Sun,* looking for ways to expose inefficiencies in the New Deal, singled out the road program in Catron County as "Today's Boondoggle" and asked why New Dealers wanted to pour out Federal funds "building roads that lead from forgotten towns to nowhere at all." The *Santa Fe New Mexican* charged to the defense and editorialized that "if the forgotten men in the sticks are getting scraps of the millions in overbuilt main racetracks in less sparsely inhabited localities, we experience no agony at the thought." That may have settled the matter in New Mexico but the *Sun* did not relent. In February it criticized the construction of roads in Catron and Valencia counties and in March, the road building program in Taos County. Replying to the criticism, Lea Rowland and Fred Healy, administrator and assistant administrator of the State WPA program, argued that there were 148 men on relief within a twenty-five mile radius of Quemado. Seventy-five of them were employed on a road which would provide a direct connection north to Gallup. Without this connection, residents of the area had to take a three hundred mile roundabout route by way of Socorro and Los Lunas.[8]

In February 1937 the Santa Fe Chamber organized another even more impressive highway promotion, this time bringing together some two hundred representatives of communities in northern and eastern New Mexico to meet with Governor Clyde Tingley, state legislators, and state officials. The keynote of the meeting was "to sell to the tourist world the 'paradise of northern New Mexico,' the only air-conditioned area in the west."[9]

While Governor Tingley promised to support the program proposed by the Santa Fe Chamber, he was not pleased with other political factors in the WPA road building program. In a letter to Harry Hopkins he complained bitterly about the inefficient construction of state highway 285 from Santa Fe to Taos. Claiming that two hundred men were working but accomplishing very little, Tingley put the blame squarely on administrator Fred Healy. Hopkins ordered an investigation which turned up the fact that the project involved what appeared to be an inordinate amount of hand labor. "While the appearance of the operations was terrible," the investigator noted, "the appearance of the completed work was very good. If I were to give the picture a title it would be 'Man with shovel versus earth with man finally conquering.'" In concluding the investigator asked Healy to secure heavy earth moving equipment or close the project.[10] While one can only guess at the story behind the official correspondence, it suggests that local politicians took advantage of the program to hand out quantities of jobs to unskilled laborers. The largess may have enhanced their political stature but it also fulfilled the intent of the road building program—that of giving work to laborers on relief—better than a program that employed large amounts of road building equipment. Whether this was, in fact, subverting the program, since the end result was, by testimony, very good, remains one of the perplexing contradictions of the New Deal.[11]

The state highway program had hardly gotten under way when the state turned its attentions to its severe educational problems. The first FERA teacher relief funds arrived in November 1933 and advanced money to rural schools which would otherwise have been unable to open. In some areas the need was so desperate that a second allotment, which arrived in February 1934, was earmarked specifically for rural schools in Taos, Rio Arriba, Union, and Sandoval counties. A third, much larger, grant for use by rural schools throughout the state followed in March 1935.

Other teacher relief funds were channeled into a variety of vocational, agricultural, and general education classes for adults, rehabilitation for the physically handicapped, and nursery schools. As would be expected, educational policies and programs followed directions already well established. In November 1933 the state embarked on an experimental emergency education program. Its stated purpose was to give relief to unemployed persons capable of doing educational work and to enrich the learning of those New Mexicans previously denied such opportunities. Directors of the program, all employees of the State Department of Education, were Brice Sewell, supervisor of Industrial Education and Rehabilitation; Rebecca Graham, supervisor of general Adult Education; and Birdie Adams, supervisor of Nursery Schools.[12]

The program under Sewell was a continuation of the vocational training in native New Mexican arts and crafts that he had begun in 1932 through the State Department of Vocational Education with federal vocational education Smith-Hughes funds. With the introduction of FERA funds, and later WPA funds, to pay teachers' salaries, Sewell established schools in many communities too poor to meet the fifty percent federal matching required for teachers under the Smith-Hughes Act. Classes were offered in spinning, weaving, ironwork, tinwork, leather tooling, and Spanish furniture making.[13] Beginning in January 1936 the National Youth Adminstration (NYA) enabled young people between the ages of sixteen and twenty-four from families on relief to participate as paid employees, learning the crafts and later helping to teach them, along with other vocational subjects, in other New Mexican communities.[14]

The first schools were located in Chupadero, La Cienega, and Galisteo in Santa Fe County, and in Taos and Peñasco in Taos County. The villagers of Chupadero had long been known for their extreme poverty and lack of agricultural resources. They had supported themselves for many years by bringing wood to Santa Fe on burros, but with the coming of natural gas the wood business became unprofitable. By 1933 almost the entire population was on direct relief.

Manuel Lujan, the Santa Fe County school superintendent, helped Chupadero get a vocational school and craft workshop and the community became an impressive case study in the benefits of handicraft production. Sales of its well made rawhide and wood furniture improved the economy to such an extent that the villagers added saddle and harness-making and weaving to their craft production. Soon most families were able to sustain themselves completely independently.[15]

Taos experienced a similar success story. A group called Taos Crafts raised funds and opened the first vocational school in September 1933 in an old pool hall. A proper school building was constructed in 1935 with FERA funds and donated labor. Moises Aragón taught the production of Spanish Colonial ornamental ironwork. He also showed his students how to be resourceful and economical by combing the countryside for junk piles from which to obtain materials for their work. Even parts of old cars were pressed into use. Aragón later added classes in woodworking, weaving, leather, and tinwork. Exhibits were held at the school and at the Harwood Foundation to publicize the student work and help them sell their products. The students also furnished the Harwood Foundation building with furniture, tin and ironwork, and woven draperies and rugs.[16]

Sewell called the vocational schools established under the Emergency Education Act "County Community Vocational Schools" to distinguish them from the vocational programs for the regular high schools. He envisioned them as cultural centers and cooperative workshops which would revitalize the community and, in time, become completely independent. Knowing the limited potential for industrial development in northern New Mexico, Sewell, like many other state officials, viewed this kind of vocational education as one of the only ways to bring much needed cash into the villages and equip the residents with a viable trade. The goals were very specific. To compete successfully with machine made products Sewell believed the craft products had to be both beautiful and durable. To appeal to tourists they had to have an aura of authenticity. But while Sewell sincerely expected handicrafts to restore financial independence to the villagers and put them once again in control of their own destinies, it is clear that he also severely limited their options. By contrast, the vocational classes he introduced into the Anglo American ranching communities in the eastern and southern parts of the state taught auto mechanics, welding, woodworking, the repair of farm equipment, commerce and finance—subjects far better designed to meet the needs of an industrializing economy.[17]

By 1936 there were vocational schools throughout most of Hispanic New Mexico. In the process of craft production students were taught to figure the costs of production, proper business correspondence, and selling methods. County agents trained boys and girls in farming and home economics, helped farmers to plan the leveling and terracing of fields, and showed them how to grade and pack fruit for market. In other classes farmers were taught how to make a living on small plots of land through the care of pigeons and rabbits for food and goats for milk. County Home Demonstration agents offered classes in home canning and county health officers and nurses cooperated in health work and in educating midwives. In a separate program individuals with physical handicaps were given special job training and placement and when necessary they were fitted and supplied with artificial limbs.[18]

The rapid development of the vocational school program highlighted the fact that most rural communities did not have adequate school houses. In June 1935 Governor Clyde Tingley proposed an extensive federal relief school construction program for rural areas. Schools built in New Mexico style architecture, he noted, would be show places for their districts and would fill a "long felt need" while providing work for more people than could be reached through any other project.[19] New school buildings were soon underway in many communities that had never before had them. In most villages local residents donated the land and the raw materials as their contribution while FERA, and later WPA, funds supplied the more costly manufactured items and paid the residents for their labor out of work relief funds. Men laid the adobe bricks and performed all of the carpentry, but the plastering, in traditional New Mexican fashion, was done by the women who, to their great delight, were also paid from federal funds.[20] Young people were paid through the National Youth Administration (NYA) to assist with these construction projects and to build school playgrounds. In communities with active vocational programs they also furnished the school buildings with handmade furniture and other native crafts.[21]

The new school buildings served the villages as community centers and provided facilities for a variety of adult education classes offered under the Emergency Education Act.[22] Classes were offered in elementary education, English, Spanish, homemaking, art, music, dancing, commerce, physical education, economics, and government, depending on the availability of teachers and the interests of the community. Literacy work, so important in New Mexico, was strongly emphasized and teachers managed to reach communities so small and remote that they had no other educational facilities or offerings. The classes were extremely popular with students of all ages. In one Hispanic community a grandfather and grandmother, father and mother, and their four children all enrolled in the same class to learn to read and write. In another a man past seventy learned to read so as not to be a burden on his grandchildren who had the task of entertaining him. In order to attend the students frequently had to travel many miles over almost impassable roads, on foot or on horseback. But they came, usually after a heavy day's work, lugging a chair to sit on and several logs for the fire.[23]

The students were not the only ones to endure hardships in the name of literacy. Nina Otero-Warren, now superintendent of the EEP Literacy Program, described her efforts and those of WPA teacher, Moises Romero, to reach students in the remote villages of Mora County. Romero taught classes in three small communities, traveling to them on horseback when the mountain passes were packed with snow. To observe one of his classes in late April 1939, Otero-Warren drove her 1937 Chevrolet over side roads and makeshift bridges, through wire gates and plowed fields. Twice she got stuck, once crossing an irrigation ditch, the other crossing a mud hole. When at last she met the teacher he informed her that she would have to climb the rest of the way up the mountain on foot.

The class, when she reached it, was held in a room loaned by one of the students. The room was cold because the owner's burro had died and the sixty-five-year-old man could haul only enough wood on his back for the kitchen stove. Romero taught his seventeen students, who ranged in age from seventeen to sixty-five, reading, writing, and arithmetic. He related their instruction to such practical questions as the quantity of seed needed for a particular field, the amount of hay that could be stored in a barn, and the prices of food and farm implements. While instruction was in English, class discussions were in Spanish and the evening concluded with the singing of Spanish folk songs.[24]

Such experiences gave both the teachers and the students an exhilarating sense of accomplishment. A midwife, after a week's concentrated effort at learning to write, was able to sign her name legibly to the birth and death certificates she was required to fill out for the State Health Department. She proudly added a note to her next report. "I have made this report unaided and please note: I have signed my name in ink."[25] In a class in Nambé in January 1940 a seventy-eight-year-old man who had never been to school, could not read in either English or Spanish, and knew no arithmetic, addressed his fellow students in Spanish:

> As a boy I worked an ox cart with my father. Poverty was bedmate to each new wed couple, and we knew little of the world about us. We *viejos* (old ones) in this class tonight, we have a chance which we never had before . . . to learn the things which we have needed for so long. . . . I have not long to live . . . yet I can learn and I do learn of words and numbers because the way of life is made complete by knowledge. He who can learn and will not learn is but a fool.

Another oldster in the same class added these words of wisdom:

> My friends and neighbors. I cannot read. I cannot write. But I can think and this is what I think. Through these night classes for the family heads the people of this country town who never had a chance for education are getting their first chance. And we must take it. We look for consolation in education, and for remedy for ills in truth. The scientist may tell us what is bad about our fields and crops but we, through moral growth and use of wisdom in ourselves must build new life for those who follow after.

When a speaker at this meeting remarked that America had been formed by men of the soil, and that in the great crises in American history one could always find the bulwark of defense to be men of the soil, a middle aged farmer in the group shouted, *"Verdad! Seguro! En Verdad, nos somos!"* (True! That's right! Truely, that is us!)

Dr. Thomas Calkins, supervisor of Education and Recreation under the EEP who attended this meeting, was so touched by the eloquence, simplicity, and sincerity of these statements that he penned a euphoric article entitled "I Heard America Singing—At Nambé." It read in part:

> I heard America sing the song that is America. A song of calm determination, love of truth, unstampedable confidence, eagerness for understanding, courage, simple honesty and appreciation, without a sign

of fear of the future. The spirit of America and the fiber of America was in
that crowd. . . . While Americans can do, and do, as those Americans did
last night, America need not fear. . . . All the blood-mad gangsters, self-
anointed political messiahs, and rabid-brained subversivists combined
cannot stop the song, or destroy the American way of life, nor kill the
spirit . . . of American courage, faith and the deep-rooted American belief
that each man has the unalienable right to have a chance to make a richer
fullness in life for himself and his neighbors. . . . The spirit heard and
felt among those Spanish-speaking villagers of Nambé is America's
guarantee.[26]

Such exuberant statements probably say a great deal more about the
state of mind of the writer than the nature of the program, but they
serve to illustrate the driving sense of mission that motivated many, and
possibly the majority, of the New Deal educators. Driven by the conviction that time was running out and that they had a unique opportunity
to right the wrongs of past generations and set America, and Americans,
on a bold new course, they mastered physical obstacles and bureaucratic
entanglements in a grand effort to achieve their goal.

"Women's Work" programs fell under the category of educational and
professional programs but for a time New Mexico relief officials found
it hard to fit their conception of the state's needs into the national rules
and expectations. When Margaret Reeves was asked by the national
administration to enumerate the kinds of women's programs being developed under FERA she sidestepped the issue by insisting that the state
did not really need such programs. Explaining that seventy-five percent
of the relief population was Spanish American from rural areas, she
argued with time honored conservative logic that if only one member of
a family could be employed on a work project it should be the man.
Women should be permitted to remain at home with their rather large
families. Women's projects, she concluded, were better adapted to Anglo
American communities and industrial areas.[27] Helen Dail Thomas, Director of Women's Work in New Mexico, continued the argument.
Women's projects were difficult to organize among New Mexico's rural
Hispanos because roads were bad and transportation difficult. During
the summer the women were occupied almost full time in their gardens
raising and preserving enough food for the winter. Not surprisingly,
when women's projects were finally organized in New Mexico they were
along very traditional lines. Hispanic women canned foodstuffs for commodity distribution and sewed workshirts, comforters, and clothing for

school children and community nursery schools. Women were also employed in the traditional Hispanic women's craft of adobe plastering.[28]

One of the major women's projects was, for a time, declared officially ineligible by Washington regulations because it involved the making of mattresses from surplus cotton. Pressure from commercial bedding manufacturers had forced the government to withdraw its support from the program but in New Mexico state relief officials continued to fund mattress-making surreptitiously. Arguing that Hispanic New Mexican villagers were unable to purchase commercial bedding, mattress-making was supported under such categories as "sanitation," "homework," and "commodity distribution." Both clothing and mattresses were distributed along with foodstuffs as direct relief in the WPA commodity distribution system.[29]

Nursery schools formed the third main division of the Emergency Education Program. Though nursery schools offered many unemployed women the opportunity to put their nurturing skills to a financially rewarding service, their main purpose was to introduce modern methods and concepts of child care, health, and nutrition to Hispanic women and to introduce Hispanic children to the English language at the earliest possible opportunity. Whenever possible nursery school teachers were native English-speakers and the children, exposed to the same teacher for as long as two years, picked up a fluent knowledge of the language.[30]

Much of the material prepared by the State Department of Public Health for use in the rural Hispanic communities was clearly based on middle class Anglo-American living standards. It was often inappropriate, even absurdly so, for villagers who lacked access to medical facilities and products and most of the household amenities taken for granted in the literature. While the information was undeniably useful, many of the concepts concerning proper health and social behavior must have seemed unnecessary, at best, or at worst, a denial of traditional Hispanic mores and values. Nevertheless, villagers appreciated and supported the program which became a model of federal, state, county, and community cooperation.[31] Local organizations donated food, clothing, and medical supplies. The Relief Administration furnished cod liver oil and milk. County health agents administered immunizations and vaccinations and checked the children for tonsillitis and other health problems. County Home Demonstration agents taught parents nutrition, sanitation, and child care. The local vocational school supplied furniture, blackboards, and play equipment, the Civilian Conservation Corps (CCC) donated surplus cots, and the women's sewing project donated mattresses. Local girls employed by the National Youth Administration assisted the WPA teachers, county health nurses, and County Home Demonstration agents. The local Red Cross gave instructions in First Aid.[32]

In a related program begun in 1940, Hispanic women were trained as Housekeeping Aides. Aides were instructed in bed-side care, child care, cooking, and all phases of housekeeping, and were placed in the homes of welfare families which needed such services. In 98 percent of the cases the families were also Hispanic. In most cases the mother was recuperating from childbirth or from a serious illness. In addition to caring for the patient and the family, aides provided instruction in hygiene and sanitation and, in general, whatever was necessary to overcome "native superstitions." The greatest problem, according to the health authorities, was the fear attached to bathing a mother during the first forty days after childbirth or exposing her to fresh air and sunshine.[33]

Both women and men were taught how to prepare and serve up hot lunches in a program carried on cooperatively between the WPA and the Farm Security Administration (FSA). Begun in one school in December 1939, the program expanded rapidly to include 124 units operating in all but two counties of the state by December 1940. Once again the purpose of the program, in addition to providing one solid, nutritionally balanced meal a day to children who might otherwise have gone hungry, was to provide both employment and instruction in nutrition, sanitation and social behavior. Those few units which operated during the summer also incorporated classes in canning fruits and vegetables. The effects of better nutrition on the children were gratifying. Teachers reported that their students had greater energy for work and play, missed fewer days of school due to illness, were more attentive and interested in learning, and got along better with their peers. When WPA programs closed in 1943 the hot lunch and nursery school programs were those most missed and bitterly lamented.[34]

Virtually every work and education program developed for New Mexico's Hispanic communities involved NYA boys and girls. Girls assisted in housekeeping, sewing, nursery school, hot lunch, clerical, and stenographic projects, most of the latter involving cataloging of library, public health, and other files in the larger communities. Boys worked on highway and street improvement projects, building construction, and handicrafts. To combat the problems encountered in serving a widespread and isolated rural population, the New Mexico NYA established several residence camps. Boys at the Las Vegas and Portales residence centers attended classes at Highlands University and Eastern New Mexico College, respectively, and assisted with the construction of college dormitories. Boys housed on the State Fair Grounds in Albuquerque assisted in the construction of fairground facilities, and those at a camp near Jemez Springs constructed stone buildings for a University of New Mexico Field School of Archaeology. Camp Capitan, located in south-central New Mexico, was considered to be the State's outstanding NYA project. Developed from an abandoned CCC camp, it housed 125 girls recruited from practically every county in the state. During their three month enrollment period the girls produced state flags for the public schools and furnishings for New Mexico's Crippled Children's Hospital. Their most extensive training, however, was in recreation since they were expected to act as leaders of recreational activities when they returned to their home communities. The monthly wages for young people in the program ranged from $22.18 in the Albuquerque area to $13.64 in the rural areas.[35]

Of all projects sponsored by the NYA in New Mexico, none was apparently more popular or widespread than that devoted to Rural Recreation. Based on the assumption that unemployed or under-employed people needed stimulating activities to keep them from becoming despondent, NYA workers constructed hundreds of recreational facilities throughout the state and conducted thousands of recreational programs. These programs included 4-H club work and such team sports as baseball, basketball, and track, but the heaviest emphasis was placed on the use of Hispanic cultural materials. In activities remarkably reminiscent of those of the Mexican popular culture revival of the 1920s, Hispanic NYA workers, usually in cooperation with WPA workers, organized "tipica" orchestras to play traditional Spanish folk music. They taught villagers to sing Spanish folk songs and perform Spanish dances, organized community festivals, and revived religious folk dramas. And, as always, they taught and encouraged the production of traditional arts and crafts for home use and personal satisfaction, if not for profit. While some villagers remained "passive" in the face of this onslaught of cultural awareness, most probably greeted the programs as another very welcome form of "relief" from the rigors of work and poverty.[36]

Thomas L. Popejoy, who served as State Director for the NYA throughout the entire program, was so concerned that it serve the needs of New

Mexico's Hispanic young people that his first request, upon being appointed, was for a Hispanic assistant. His second was for a project to introduce crafts training to remote communities and his third was for a "Coordination Project"—one that would coordinate vocational and recreational projects within each county so as to stimulate public interest and promote youth leadership in the establishment of community activities.[37]

Popejoy championed educational opportunities in a way sometimes considered puzzling to his superiors. In May 1938 the national director of NYA work projects questioned Popejoy on his tendency to turn residence projects into modified student aid programs. Since they were designed for out-of-school unemployed youth who did not plan to attend college, why, he was asked, were the students being encouraged to take college courses for credit? If the young people wanted to attend college, why weren't they transferred to the regular Student Aid Program? What the national director apparently did not understand was that in New Mexico the need was so great, and the total state allotment of 947 students for college aid (based on 12 percent of the total enrollment) so small, that such creative mixing of programs seemed quite justified. More than half of Popejoy's final report was devoted to a history of the state's Hispanic people and the many injustices they had suffered since annexation. Using George Sanchez's *Forgotten People* as his source, Popejoy argued that the so-called "youth problem" in New Mexico was attributable to handicaps that were products of the cultural gap separating Hispanic Americans from their fellow citizens.[38]

The other extremely popular program for the nation's youth was, of course, the Civilian Conservation Corps. More than any other depression program the CCC combined the appeal of the "agrarian myth" with relief and vocational education. Created by an Act of Congress on March 31, 1933, under its official title of Emergency Conservation Work (ECW) the CCC brought together two wasted resources—young men and the land, in an effort to save both. It was limited to single young men between the ages of eighteen and twenty-five, most of whose families were on relief. In New Mexico, as elsewhere, the young men worked in forest camps, on soil conservation projects, with the grazing service, and with the Bureau of Reclamation. For their work they received a salary of $30.00 a month but kept only $5.00 (or $2.50 at times) for their personal use. The remainder went directly to their families enabling many of them to withdraw from the relief rolls.[39]

Life in the CCC camps was simple but generally very satisfying. The food was plain but nourishing and served in large quantities. The work routine, which took place in an atmosphere of military discipline, was wholesome and most camps, at the end of the day, offered educational, recreation, and athletic programs. The enrollees gained weight, height, and vigor, learned useful skills and trades connected with their work, and broadened their horizons through various educational opportunities. Most of those who were illiterate learned to read and write. Others got their first introduction to higher education from camp classes and group discussions, and by being able to attend college classes while still enrolled in the corps. Many others learned vocational crafts and technical skills which later became their life work.[40]

True to the progressive pedagogy of the times, CCC educational programs grew out of the needs and wishes of the men. Courses centered around vocational trades, social problems, home relationships, hobbies, and in New Mexico, Hispanic folk culture. Every camp had its educational adviser who, together with the Corps Commander, was more or less free to devise programs within the areas of interest, talent, and facilities available to the camp. Teachers were garnered from the public schools, from FERA and WPA sources, and from the enrollees themselves. At a camp near Redlands, New Mexico, the men set up their own "college," which they called Yuma University, and exchanged whatever skills and knowledge they had from within their own ranks. Another camp located near Las Cruces offered qualified enrollees with high school diplomas the opportunity to attend courses at New Mexico State College. The matriculation fee was set at five dollars and tuition for the semester at ten dollars. The program, assisted by the Directors of the Bureau of Reclamation, the Soil Conservation Service, the Department of Grazing, and the Forest Service, created separate work projects for the men so that they could complete their corps work in the mornings and attend classes in the afternoons. A third camp, at Santa Fe, was the only CCC camp in the nation to incorporate a full-blown trade school. Classes were offered in weaving, woodcarving, carpentry, cabinet work, auto repair, and welding. As with other such vocational schools in the state, the students were permitted to sell part of whatever they made to buy materials. All educational programs, except for basic literacy classes, were completely voluntary, but there was such a hunger for education that attendance at evening classes was frequently over 70 percent.[41]

The CCC enrollees in New Mexico's forty-four camps did their share

of teaching as well—instructing farmers in such soil conservation practices as terracing, contour plowing, and crop rotation. They also built
roads, bridges, and fences; planted trees; built recreation facilities in
state and national parks; eradicated rodents; strung telephone lines; and
threw up thousands of check and diversion dams. Since the camps introduced money into the region they were eagerly sought after by local
politicians. In line with New Mexico's established priorities, most were
clustered within the heavily Hispanic Rio Grande watershed. However,
in spite of some bitter protests by residents in the eastern part of the
state concerning the unequal distribution of CCC camps, the program
apparently was relatively free from politics.[42]

Although New Mexican camps also seemed to be relatively free from
racial tensions, especially those in the northern counties which were 90
to 95 percent Hispanic, unpleasant incidents did occur. Camps in the
southern counties, which were more evenly integrated, experienced
problems when out-of-state enrollees complained about sharing tents
with "greasers." In one unfortunate episode an Anglo enrollee was beaten
to death when a boxing match degenerated into a riot. The investigation
which followed traced the cause of the outburst directly to race and
language difficulties, but the matter was quietly dropped when those
responsible deserted.[43] In Chaves County the director of Public Welfare
reported that complaints had been received from numerous recruits al-
leging failure of the camp authorities to pay them all the wages due
them, stealing and fighting in the camps, lack of proper medical care,
and racial discrimination against Spanish-Americans on the part of enrollees from Texas and eastern New Mexico. Apparently it infuriated the
Anglo men when the native New Mexicans spoke in Spanish among
themselves.[44]

In spite of these problems New Mexican camps must have been far
more comfortable for Hispanic recruits than camps in other states. Both
enrollees and state officials vigorously resisted attempts to transfer New
Mexican enrollees out of state. When they were transferred, New Mexican recruits tended to behave differently from Hispanic men from other
parts of the Southwest. They not only complained about discrimination
but they wrote letters—to the Chief of Police in Santa Fe, to the Governor, and to the director of the ECW in Washington.[45] In this regard
it may be significant that, even though the men spoke and understood
little English, they were confident that their petition, written in Span-

ish, would be read and received sympathetically by New Mexico state officials.

A petition that made its way to the Acting Director of the ECW in Washington in July 1936 concerned discrimination at a CCC camp in Duncan, Arizona. The first such complaint received by the office, it elicited a prompt investigation. According to the report the signers, all of whom classified themselves as "Spanish-speaking boys" from New Mexico, had been denied underwear, assigned disproportionately to K-P duty, and harassed in other ways by one of the camp officers. Since other Mexican men in the camp who were not from New Mexico declared themselves "extremely satisfied" with their treatment in camp, the investigating officer concluded, rather lamely, that the New Mexican men were unduly sensitive. He did admit that they were justified in complaining about the food.[46]

Paradoxically, while some federal, state, and local officials were striving mightily to relieve the symptoms of Hispanic poverty, and in the process extinguishing, so far as they were able, the remnants of a pre-industrial Hispanic life-style, others were striving ever so mightily to record and preserve its dying embers. The efforts were financed by a series of work relief projects for unemployed artists, writers, and musicians. Though the first project was initiated in December 1933, under the Civil Works of Art Project, the idea reached its greatest development in New Mexico under the famed Federal Project One of the WPA with its Federal Art Project, Federal Writers' Project, and Federal Music Project.[47]

While the principal aim of Federal Project One was to provide employment for destitute artists, writers, and musicians, New Mexicans seized upon the opportunity of federal funding to advance the Hispanic cultural agenda. Under the same local leadership that had initiated the Hispanic arts and crafts revival of the 1920s, the new federal projects devoted much of their money and effort to recording, preserving, and reviving interest in New Mexico's traditional Hispanic arts, folklore, music, and drama.

The first New Deal work relief program for artists, the Public Works of Art Project (PWAP), was initiated December 1933 under the direction of a committee consisting of archaeologists Jesse Nusbaum and Kenneth Chapman, artist Gustave Baumann, Senator Bronson Cutting, architect John Gaw Meem, and writers Mary Austin and Caroline Thompson. The PWAP hired fifty-one New Mexican artists, including a number of Indian and a few Hispanic craftsmen, to decorate public buildings and parks. Twenty-five works produced by New Mexican PWAP workers were later exhibited in a national PWAP exhibit at the Corcoran Gallery of Art in Washington, D.C.[48]

The PWAP's most famous, and best remembered successor, the WPA Federal Art Project, came under the direction of Russell Vernon Hunter, a noted New Mexican artist, and an advisory committee consisting of Paul A. F. Walter, Jr.; Mary Van Stone, Curator of the State Art Gallery; artists Raymond Jonson, Gustave Baumann, and Randall Davey, writer and art critic Paul Horgan; and Francis del Dosso, University of New Mexico art instructor. In a manner again reminiscent of the popular culture revival in Mexico in the 1920s, the national program emphasized the painting of murals on the walls of government buildings. Beyond that, much emphasis was placed upon easel work, graphics, and sculpture, much of which in New Mexico was based upon its regional subject matter.[49]

In the course of time two Hispanic New Mexican artists were "discovered"—Patrocino Barela and Juan Sanchez. Barela, a naive sculptor of enormous talent, rose to national prominence when several of his works were acquired for the collection of New York's Museum of Modern Art. Hispanic crafts were fostered primarily through the vocational program of the New Mexico State Department of Vocational Education but were used to decorate a number of WPA buildings, among them the Roswell Museum and the Albuquerque Municipal Airport terminal. However the most interesting project, from the standpoint of Hispanic cultural preservation, was the *Portfolio of Spanish Colonial Design,* an experimental research project aimed at recording a cross-section of traditional New Mexican crafts and folk arts.

Under the direction of E. Boyd Hall the project employed over forty-four artists and was completed in 1937. It became one of the immediate and important forerunners of the Federal Art Project's most widely discussed and best known activity, the *Index of American Design,* now housed at the National Gallery in Washington. In addition to making watercolor reproductions of traditional Hispanic designs, project workers compiled a complete list of craftsmen, and accompanied each drawing with a data sheet listing the type of object, the material from which it was made, the date and locality of its manufacture, and whenever possible, the name of the craftsman and the original owner. A limited edition of some two hundred copies of line woodblock and hand colored drawings was printed by FAP artists and distributed in 1938, apparently without the imprimatur of the federal director and without his approval of the final project.[50] While one can only guess at the circumstances behind this event, it strongly suggests that the determined New Mexicans were insisting, once again, on their own, very special, set of priorities.

New Mexico's Federal Music Project followed directly in the footsteps of its Federal Art Project in its emphasis on research and preservation. Instead of concentrating on the employment of professional musicians to play in community orchestras, as suggested by the national program, New Mexico's director, Helen Chandler Ryan, encouraged local musicians and musicologists to transcribe, record and revive elements of New Mexico's Hispanic musical heritage. She also emphasized music education and music recreation in the rural villages and CCC camps. Music teachers, working in a cooperative program with the University of New Mexico, began collecting New Mexican folk music as soon as the project was set up in 1935. After transcribing the melodies they cut stencils for the words and simple musical notation and mimeographed copies of the songs for use in the public schools. In cooperation with the NYA and WPA education and recreation programs and the League of Latin American Citizens (LULAC), they organized song fests and string orchestras and sponsored folk festivals. They also provided instruction in orchestral instruments and piano and, in communities too poor to have musical instruments, taught children to make music with water-filled glasses or bottles.

The project's most notable achievement was the publication in 1942 of its Spanish-American "Song and Game Book." Advertised as "the oldest folk music in America" (except for the music of the American Indian), the songbook included alabados and such traditional Hispanic musical forms as the *Decima,* the *Cuanda,* and the *Corrido.* Eager to preserve the original instruments as well as the music, the FMP revived interest in the old gut-stringed guitar of Spanish origin and published a collection of musical arrangements for its use in accompanying the old songs. In 1942 it also published "Spanish American Dance Tunes."[51]

The four hundredth anniversary of Coronado's arrival in the American Southwest provided an ideal opportunity for New Mexicans to use the musical materials collected by the FMP. The spectacular celebration, held in 1939 and called the Cuarto Centennial Coronado Festival, led Sara Gertrude Knott, FMP director of national folk festivals, to declare, "there is here in New Mexico a finer integration of music project activities with the life of the people than in any other part of the United States that I have visited."[52]

New Mexicans also brought their own priorities to the state's Federal Writers' Project which, like others in Federal Project One, gave them a chance to complete some long established goals. One of these was the translation of the state's Spanish documents. Begun in 1934 as a "white collar" project under the CWA, the project was transferred to FERA and finally to the WPA where it was included under the Federal Writer's Project, becoming the first such project in the national program.[53]

Two sets of archives needed translating: the Public Survey Office Archives and the Historical Society Archives. The first, part of the old Spanish archives, dated from 1682 to 1844 and consisted of wills, conveyances, grants of land, and land disputes. It was invaluable as a source for straightening out New Mexico's tangled land titles. The Historical Society archives contained correspondence between the Governor of New Mexico, the King of Spain, and the Viceroy of Old Mexico relating to legislative matters, relations with the Indians, and various matters of policy. These documents dated from 1621 to 1821. Of the ten people selected to work on the documents most were Hispanic scholars. Copies of the translations were supplied to the Historical Society of New Mexico and to the Laboratory of Anthropology of the Museum of New Mexico.[54]

The national director of the Federal Writers' Project, Henry G. Alsberg, apparently did not appreciate the importance of these documents and thus their great interest to New Mexicans. Alarmed by the number of writers on the project and the amount of material being turned out on the undertaking, he complained that work on the national project, an American Guidebook for each state, was being neglected.[55] Despite Alsberg's displeasure, the translation project continued and workers, temporarily or permanently assigned to the division, uncovered much useful historical data, provided translation services, and acted as a local review board for various Spanish-English, English-Spanish translations. The high point of the project was the discovery and translation of the famed Miera y Pacheco map of New Mexico made in 1779. The priceless document was found by a Hispanic shepherd carefully sealed in a tin can in a cave beside the Rio Grande near the old Valverde battlefield. The sheepherder suspected that it might be of some importance and took it to the local WPA office from whence it found its way to the headquarters of the translation project in Santa Fe. Harry Hopkins viewed the document upon a visit to New Mexico and was so impressed that he requested a copy of it for his office. Before sending it off, Ray Gomez, the document's translator, appended a note to the effect that the map was "proof that despite depressions times have been more hazardous in the Sunshine State."[56]

Director Alsberg had good reason to worry about New Mexico's compilation of a state guidebook. State workers were indeed very slow in getting started on the project and even slower in submitting the desired tour descriptions and essays on the state's history, "racial elements," literature, music, art, architecture, and folklore. The problem lay not in a lack of interest, for the project was recognized as being of immense value to the state. It lay, rather, in the enormous size of the job. Most of the material had first to be collected and checked for historical accuracy—a formidable task under the best of circumstances given the length and diversity of New Mexico's history and archaeology. The state lacked trained writers and researchers among its field workers, all of whom had to be chosen from the relief rolls. It also lacked travel funds to enable them to cover the vast, largely inaccessible, areas in the northern part of the state.[57]

From the outset the state's director, Ina Sizer Cassidy, believed the strength of the project lay in the collection of Hispanic folklore. Since other federal programs dealt with Indian matters she and her staff concentrated on the collection of Hispanic customs, legends, folk beliefs, and oral histories, and cooperated with workers on the federal art and music projects in the collection and recording of Hispanic musical and art forms. Aurora Lucero-White, the writer-educator chosen to supervise the collection of native New Mexican materials, had already amassed, prior to 1934, a considerable volume of folklore from her native San Miguel county. This she edited, translated, and later published, bringing national recognition to the New Mexico FWP. Her recordings and translations of "Romances and Corridos of New Mexico" appeared as "Americana Number 7" in the FWP's publication *American Stuff: An Anthology of Prose and Verse*. Many of the field workers Lucero-White supervised were themselves participants in the folk traditions they recorded.[58]

But if New Mexicans were sure of their priorities, they were once again at odds with the national administration. The first version of the folklore chapter of the New Mexico Guide, written by Eustaquio Garcia, a National Youth Administration student at the University of New Mexico, was entitled "Introductory Essay: New Mexican Spanish Folklore

and Provincialisms." Sent back for revision by the national editorial
review board, it was condensed and rewritten by Robert Young of the
University, and entitled "Early Folklore Legends—Introductory Essay."
This revision and a third rewrite were criticized by John Lomax, American folklore specialist, for their heavy emphasis on Indian and Spanish-
American contributions, and their neglect of Anglo-American folklore.
The national administration had the final word. The brief chapter that
finally appeared in the 1940 volume entitled *New Mexico: A Guide to the
Colorful State* contained only a short overview of Spanish lore and concentrated on Pueblo Indian tales and Anglo-American stories of buried
treasure, outlaws, and cowboys.[59]

In 1939 the Works Progress Administration, together with several
other agencies, was reorganized into a new agency called the Federal
Works Administration. Under the new Work Projects Administration,
projects sponsored solely by the WPA were forbidden and in New Mexico
the Coronado Cuarto Centennial Commission became the statewide sponsor
of the Writers' Project with the University of New Mexico assisting in
sponsoring the state guide. Even before this reorganization was put into
effect, however, the international situation had begun to influence national policy in respect to domestic issues. From 1939 to the close of
the WPA in June 1943, an unsympathetic Congress desirous of reducing
relief expenditures cut appropriations to all agencies not directly concerned with national defense. In February 1942 all community service
programs were reorganized into a new Service Division. The art, music,
and writing projects survived only because they changed their emphasis
from research and professional performance to recreational and educational activities in support of defense and wartime service. The prevailing
hourly wage was abandoned and, except for veterans, all WPA employees
with more than eighteen months tenure were laid off and declared ineligible for reemployment for a period of thirty days. The provision
immediately removed all experienced workers from the various programs, seriously undermining their efforts and effectiveness.[60]

As the United States edged ever closer to war, the educational programs shifted emphasis from vocational preparation and modernization
to patriotic citizenship and national preparedness. In New Mexico the
literacy classes became classes in war information, bringing news of the
war effort translated into Spanish to the rural villages. Teachers held
appointments from the State War Board as local Victory Council men
and women. County agricultural agents also served as Victory Council-

men. Their duties were to carry information vital to the war effort to farmers and ranchers in remote areas, conduct War Stamp and Bond campaigns, and engage in a statewide registration of farm labor. Special classes were developed for draftees rejected for illiteracy, especially in the CCC camps which often were the repository for such rejects. The entire WPA education program was, in fact, put at the service of the United States Army. Even nursery schools were involved in an Americanization program which put even greater emphasis on the teaching of English. The Community Service programs conducted naturalization classes for Mexican aliens using English and Spanish reading materials taken from the Preamble to the Constitution, the Pledge of Allegiance, and other patriotic and historic texts.[61]

Wartime concern for Latin American allies led to a new emphasis on the teaching of Spanish. New Mexico, along with Puerto Rico, was an important source for Spanish teachers and Nina Otero-Warren transferred from the Literacy Program to a Spanish language program for the army and navy.[62]

New Mexico's WPA vocational education program and its affiliates in the NYA and the CCC also shifted emphasis from traditional crafts to such defense related trades as arc welding, commercial and aircraft sheet metal work, automotive repair, general mechanics, and radio operation. New Mexico's Hispanic young people responded enthusiastically to the establishment of the War Production program, and their numbers increased as they saw the hope of material gain, as well as national service, from their studies. Hispanic enrollment in the NYA program increased from 75 to 85 percent in 1941 and when 1942 brought an exodus of males to industrial areas and the Selective Service, Hispanic girls rushed in to take their place, soon making up 70 percent of the total enrollment.[63]

An imaginative suggestion for improving the wages and security of New Mexico's farm workers came in December 1941 in the form of a confidential memorandum from the State Director of the WPA Training and Employment Division to a Bureau of Agricultural Economics–New Mexico State College Subcommittee on Farm Labor. In New Mexico, as elsewhere, the rush of American men to join the armed forces following the Japanese attack on Pearl Harbor precipitated a labor crisis. Relief rolls shrank as workers found employment in defense plants and as other industries expanded their activities to meet the demands of a wartime economy. One of the first and most critical industries to be affected by the labor shortage was the farm industry, whose workers were among the lowest paid in the United States. They also had the most physically demanding jobs and the least job security. The confidential memorandum was directed to the problem of securing an adequate supply of farm laborers while continuing New Deal efforts to improve labor relations and modernize the local agricultural economy.

According to the memorandum, state efforts to recruit farm labor were hampered by a number of problems. Among them were a lack of information concerning employer and employee needs, a lack of adequate housing, adequate transportation, and adequate facilities for training skilled and semiskilled workers. The requirement that all workers possess a New Mexico automobile license was an additional deterrent to out-of-state workers.

The memorandum suggested a number of solutions. The state should conduct a survey of the types of work available and the amount and kinds of labor required by establishing a labor subcommittee in each county. The Farm Security Administration should provide labor camps wherever needed and should assist in recruiting farm labor. The vocational schools should cooperate in training students in the needed job classification, and the government should make vacant CCC camps available for seasonal labor. [64]

On a confidential level the memorandum noted the fact of legal discrimination on the part of governmental units that failed to extend the benefits of Social Security, Workmen's Compensation, and wage and hour control to farm labor, leaving it the most disadvantaged group in the United States. Because farm workers lacked definite wage rates, adequate shelter, food, and transportation and suffered loss of time and income due to inclement weather, temporary labor surpluses, and the need to travel long distances between jobs, they tended to migrate to industrial centers. The government could stem the tide, the memo noted, by encouraging more family farms that would cooperatively pool and exchange work and machinery. It could also help by developing a combined public and private work program that would dovetail seasonal agricultural needs with public works in such a way as to provide farm labor with guaranteed full employment throughout the year. Examples of the public works proposed were soil conservation, road construction, repair and maintenance, fencing, and construction of agricultural housing. A later memorandum enlarged on the idea and suggested the development of a rotation cycle between the beet workers in Colorado and the cotton pickers in Arizona and the lower Rio Grande Valley in New Mexico.[65]

This innovative government plan was never implemented. It was, in fact, all the federal agencies could do to prod New Mexico farmers to bring their wages up to a competitive level with agricultural employers in Arizona, Texas, and Colorado. The minutes of a State Farm Labor Subcommittee meeting held in May 1942 reported that Colorado beet farmers paid considerably better wages than New Mexico farmers. Noting the availability of cheap labor from Mexico, the chairman of the meeting declared, "We can't force laborers to accept work. Farmers must set reasonable wage standards comparable with wages paid in other agricultural areas. No Mexican aliens can (or will) be imported as long as there is available labor in the State and if the purpose of imported labor is to hold down wages. Mexico will not consent to it."[66] Apparently the New Deal agents did not intend to consent to it either.

According to the subcommittee minutes, its members believed that workers were reluctant to leave the WPA because it paid better wages than local farmers. The minutes reported that the WPA, in order to force workers into taking jobs, took them off the rolls during the harvest season and signed them on again only after they had submitted a card signed by their employer to the effect that their work had been satisfactory. The subcommittee, aware that there were strong pressures within the state resisting federal efforts to bring up farm wages, recommended that the State Agricultural Planning Committee and the State War Board hold educational meetings in the cotton producing counties to discuss better farm labor relations.[67]

Clearly the phasing out of most programs by February 1943 was hard on unskilled farm workers, as it was on women who had depended upon WPA employment to support themselves and their dependents, and on the elderly and the handicapped who could not qualify for jobs in industry. However the opening up of new vocational opportunities in defense plants and in the selective service was generally beneficial to Hispanic workers.[68] For the first time in over a decade a labor shortage existed throughout the nation. As the demands of a wartime economy increased so did wages and the Southwest entered a new era of relative prosperity.

# EIGHT

# Restoring Village Lands

In June 1933, when John Collier, the newly appointed Commissioner of Indian Affairs, singled out the Navajos to be a showcase for his reforms in Indian policy, he set forces in motion which led within two years to plans for a New Deal land reform program for New Mexican Hispanos. The Hispanic program, like the Indian program, envisioned restoring large sections of New Mexico's old Hispanic grant lands to the exclusive use of its native inhabitants. It also intended to restore the fertility of the disastrously eroded lands. Unfortunately both programs fell considerably short of their intended goals. That they did so was due in part to the controversial nature of the programs themselves and their threatened impact upon the Anglo ranching economy. It was also due to the intense friction generated within and outside the Hispanic and Indian communities by Collier's rigid and often ill-considered methods. [1]

The New Deal land program for New Mexico's Hispanos received its major impetus from the almost universal reaction to Collier's efforts to expand Indian lands at the expense of the state's Hispanic and Anglo ranchers. With the Anglo ranchers representing one of New Mexico's wealthiest and most politically influential power blocs, a vigorous opposition was assured. In the three way struggle the Hispanic ranchers, individually, through their livestock associations, or through their employer or political patrons, became the swing factor. Spurred by the state's politicians as well as by their own concerns, other New Deal agencies tried to iron out inequities in the land program by coming up with programs especially designed for the Hispanic villagers. Most Hispanos threw their weight in with their employers, the commercial livestock interests, for reasons of job security and because of their distrust of the federal government. Frustrated by the tide of protest that he, and

his colleagues in the Soil Conservation Service had generated, Collier
then tried to outflank his critics by incorporating the poorest Hispanic
ranchers into the land reform program. At that point Hispanic land
reform, as well as Indian land policy, became the subject of conservative
reaction.

Collier's decision to begin his reforms with the Navajos derived from
two important considerations. Overgrazing on the reservation had so
eroded the land that it endangered the future welfare of the tribe; and
Congress had voted funds for erosion control as part of the National
Industrial Recovery Act of 1933. Erosion on the Navajo reservation was
responsible for the heavy load of silt that flowed annually into the Colorado River, threatening the life-span of Boulder Dam, one of the nation's
most ambitious and expensive reclamation projects. Collier therefore
determined to use his new influence in the Roosevelt administration,
and the concern for Boulder Dam, to direct a significant proportion of
federal erosion control funds into a dramatic program of land and social
reform on the Navajo reservation.[2]

Collier consulted with Secretary of Agriculture Henry Wallace and,
at his suggestion, contacted Hugh Hammond Bennett in the Bureau of
Chemistry and Soils. Bennett had already won nationwide attention for
his studies in soil erosion and had been granted funds for research by
Congress. Bennett was convinced, however, that more than research was
needed. Farmers had to be shown how to control soil erosion. At Collier's
urging he visited the Navajo reservation and was appalled at the dev-
astation of the land. Convinced of the urgency of the problem he identified the area as a prime target for erosion control experimentation and
demonstration. The Navajos, though they surely did not understand all
the implications of the proposal, agreed to let it proceed.[3]

With Navajo cooperation apparently assured, Bennett returned to
Washington to convince his superior, Assistant Secretary of Agriculture
Rexford G. Tugwell, of the merits of the project. Collier penned a
memorandum to his old associate and new boss, secretary of the Interior
Harold Ickes, recommending the creation of a nationwide erosion control
program with Bennett in charge. The powerful Ickes arranged for Bennett's transfer to the Department of the Interior and on September 13,
1933, the Soil Erosion Service was created within his department. Ickes
gave Bennett five million dollars from Public Works Administration
funds, one million of which was specifically dedicated for work on the
Navajo reservation; together with a labor force of CCC workers. The

decision to allot one-fifth of the total SES budget to the Navajos permitted Bennett to carry out his long-stated dream of implementing soil conservation on a watershed basis, something far easier done on government-owned lands than on private lands.[4]

Collier apparently played a key role in the selection of some of the staff for the newly created SES. He personally recruited Hugh G. Calkins, a former chief of operations of the Forest Service in New Mexico and Arizona, for the largest of the demonstration projects on the reservation, and in 1934 he persuaded the SES to employ his old friend, Eshref Shevky, to perform the functions of a "sociologist" and gather information about Navajo population, property concepts, land use, and sources of income. A Turkish national with a Ph.D. in experimental medicine from Stanford University, Shevky had an impressive self-taught knowledge of anthropology, sociology, economics, and colonial administration. Collier assigned him the job of designing what became known as "human dependency surveys."[5]

Shevky soon discovered that he was pioneering new ground. Little data existed concerning the Navajo reservation. There were few maps, no accurate statistics concerning the Navajo and their herds, and little comparative information on the extent and progress of soil erosion. There was even less information on Navajo culture and its relation to the land. To gather this information Shevky devised two types of surveys. One gathered data on range, soils, fauna, vegetation, and agriculture. The other combined the methodology of the "hard sciences" with economics, sociology, and anthropology. Directed by Shevky, interdisciplinary teams interviewed family leaders concerning the functioning of Navajo institutions, the distribution of livestock, concepts about property and land use, credit relations with traders, and housing, diet, and clothing.[6]

The core of the Navajo conservation program was a gigantic stock reduction to relieve the pressure on the range and allow the land to recover. Collier possessed statutory power to compel the Navajos to reduce their herds but, being committed to Indian self-rule, he asked the Navajo Council to give its consent to the program. To offset the loss of income represented by the removal of some four hundred thousand sheep and goats, Collier promised the Navajos that the FERA would purchase one hundred thousand head of stock for its commodity distribution program. He also promised them wage work through the CCC, the PWA, and other federal programs. The Navajos welcomed the idea of wage work and the introduction of a wage economy onto the reservation but wealth to them was not money. It was livestock. They were extremely reluctant to part with any of their beloved animals but, after an evening executive session with Commissioner Collier, the delegates gave their consent. It became apparent only later that Collier had elicited their agreement by promising them something that they desperately wanted—legislation to expand the boundaries of the reservation and the acquisition of more grazing land.[7]

In 1934 in fulfillment of his promise to the Navajos Collier acquired 425,000 acres of eroded land in several of the old Spanish land grants. The Land Division of the Indian Service bought the land through the submarginal retirement program of the Bureau of Agricultural Economics (BAE) using Agricultural Adjustment Administration (AAA) funds. In 1935 Collier also worked out an agreement with Hugh Bennett whereby the newly established Soil Conservation Service would begin erosion control work on those lands with Indian CCC labor. Concern over another expensive reclamation project lay behind consent for the land purchase. In this case severe erosion in the Rio Puerco drainage threatened the life-span of the Elephant Butte Reservoir.[8]

The acquisition of these public domain lands for exclusive Indian use aroused immediate concern among New Mexico's commercial livestock operators and its state and municipal authorities. Early in 1935 the Bureau of Agricultural Economics also received several petitions from Hispanic villages affected by the purchase projects—one from Peña Blanca with 500 signatures, another from the Española area with 1,425 and one from the Cuba Valley with 250. The latter area, already 50 percent abandoned due to the loss of virtually all of its agricultural resources, was in the most desperate need of help. The flooding and erosion on the Rio Puerco had lowered the water table to such an extent that irrigation was impossible. With Collier's purchase of the Espiritu Santo and Montaño land grants for the Laguna, Zia, and Jemez Indians, the Rio Puerco villagers faced the loss of their traditional grazing lands as well.[9]

The newly formed New Mexico State Planning Board responded to the clamor by protesting Collier's actions to the National Resources Committee in Washington in the summer of 1935. State officials also set about developing their own land use plan for the state, expanding the preliminary report made a year earlier under the joint direction of the State Agricultural College and the Land Policy Section of the BAE. In this revised report they argued that the purchase of the grant lands by the Indian Service would work a hardship on the Spanish-American communities that had long used them. They concluded that unless the state had some say over the use of these grant lands the "problems involving the Spanish-American communities, small homesteaders, and stockmen will be much more serious than the Indian problem is at the present time."[10]

A group of wealthy ranchers, led by Floyd Lee from San Mateo in northwestern New Mexico, directed their protests to the state's Congressional delegation. Speaking through the Wool Growers and Cattle Growers Associations, and the Land Use Committee of the State Planning Board, they purported to represent the many Hispanic partido sharecroppers as well as the large commercial livestock interests. If the Hispanic sheepmen had doubts about throwing in their lot with their employers, these doubts must have been overshadowed by the realization that without the political and legal support of the large ranchers they could lose all rights to their traditional grazing lands to the Indians and Collier's Bureau of Indian Affairs.[11]

Both Dennis Chavez, appointed in early 1935 to fill the senatorial seat vacated by the death of Bronson Cutting, and Senator Carl Hatch responded to their pleas. Chavez, in particular, was concerned for the welfare of the Hispanic Rio Puerco communities. He and Hatch worried as well that private land was being removed from the state tax rolls and that the "multiple purpose" public lands were being usurped for the exclusive use of one special group. Chavez passed these concerns along to the Resettlement Adminstration (RA), the agency created in the spring of 1935 to supervise the submarginal land program. He also used his seat on the Senate Indian Affairs Committee to demand an equitable federal land policy and to block legislation to extend the boundaries of the Navajo reservation.[12]

The chorus of protest was successful insofar as it persuaded Rexford Tugwell, the RA administrator, and Lewis Gray, chief of the agency's Land Utilization Section, to maintain legal control over the disputed lands instead of transferring them to the BIA. It also led L. H. Hauter and his colleagues in the Resettlement Administration's New Mexico field office to work actively for the interests of the Hispano communities most effected by the BIA threat. Collier completely misinterpreted their motives. While he should have understood that the politicians would represent the state's different ethnic and economic interests, and that the Resettlement Administration field workers would feel some sympathy for the destitute Hispanic villagers, he described Chavez's actions as a sell-out to the large stockmen, and accused the Resettlement Administration of a power play within the agriculture department.[13]

In the meantime the BIA and the Soil Conservation Service pressed ahead with their efforts to acquire more land. In what may have been an attempt by Collier to counter efforts by state and other agency officials to gain control of the land program, Collier's old associate Hugh Calkins, now director of the regional SCS office in Albuquerque, organized the Rio Grande Advisory Committee. He included in this group representatives of each of the federal agencies involved with land use including L. H. Hauter, representing the Resettlement Administration. Hauter insisted from the beginning that proper consideration had to be given to the Hispanic villagers in the allocation of use rights on the federally purchased lands, but Collier apparently dominated the meetings and the matter remained unresolved. He argued that most of the Hispanic sheepmen were partido sharecroppers for the wealthy and powerful Bond family and refused to consider allocating any portion of the newly acquired lands to their use until a study of the entire watershed documented their need.[14]

Fortunately for the Hispanos, such a study was not long in coming. In April 1935 at the request of both Bennett and Henry Wallace, and with the support of the Indian Service, all activities bearing on erosion control were consolidated into the Soil Conservation Service (SCS), a permanent agency within the Department of Agriculture. Hugh Calkins was named director of the regional SCS office in Albuquerque, and both he and Shevky left the Navajo project. Shortly thereafter the Indian Land Research Unit was transferred to their care in the Soil Conservation Service.

The change was opportune because Shevky was in the midst of a human dependency survey of the northern Rio Grande watershed known as the Tewa Basin Study. By this time both Calkins and Shevky must have been aware that no survey or program for the area could be complete that did not include its rural Hispanos. Working from his new base as head of the Conservation Economics Section of the SCS, Shevky expanded his study to include the Hispanic villages of the Tewa Basin. Along with other concerns he expressly intended to gather data for an allocation of the newly acquired federal lands based on need. Both Shevky and Calkins had learned a great deal from the Navajo experiment. They now turned their knowledge and much of the zeal of Collier's Indian program into a controversial land reform program for New Mexican Hispanos.[15]

In his Tewa Basin Study, Shevky revealed the acute suffering of the Hispanic villagers, their extremely limited agricultural resources, and the extent to which they had depended upon wage labor to sustain themselves.[16] Another study, circulated in December 1936 reported specifically on the Espiritu Santo Grant. It noted that while the range represented a significant source of income for the area, the village population had the use of only one-half of its carrying capacity. The other half was used by large commercial, and in some cases nonresident, stock owners. Since the range was 50 to 75 percent overstocked, a stock reduction was essential. However, if the villagers, who were already unable to support themselves, were required to reduce *their* stock, the situation would become even more desperate. "If the rights of a person to a livelihood are primary rights," the study concluded, then "the national interest would be best served by protecting the indigenous noncommercial rural population in the possession of its land and in making available to it the feasible maximum of use-rights to renewable resources controlled and administered by the federal government."[17]

The Tewa Basin study was but the first of a series of monographs, most of them apparently authored by Shevky, which were published by the SCS in mimeographed form as regional bulletins in its Conservation Economics Series. These monographs, which set forth the terms and dimensions of the Hispanic New Deal land program, document the geography, demography, history, land use, and economics of the Rio Grande watershed from Colorado to the New Mexico–Texas border. Based on an ecological approach to land-use planning, they provided much of the information and many of the insights upon which the New Deal Department of Agriculture action programs in New Mexico were based. They also provided some of the sharpest criticism of the early Resettlement Administration programs.[18]

Bold and controversial in his thinking, Shevky was the prototypical social engineer. As idealistic as his old friend and colleague, Collier, he sought to right the wrongs and abuses of the world by governmental fiat. Like Collier he also tended to see the immensely difficult problems of the region, and of its native peoples, as a two-dimensional struggle between right and wrong, rich and poor, exploiter and exploited. More a social theoretician than a social worker, he was, if anything, even more naive than Collier concerning the state's political realities. His studies were keenly insightful, cutting deftly to the heart of problems, but the solutions he proposed treated people as if they had no wills of their own.

He surely must have been surprised and disheartened when his programs met with opposition, not only from the people they intended to displace, but from the people they intended to help.

That the Shevky monographs threatened some of New Mexico's most powerful economic interests cannot be doubted. Rumor has it that they were ordered destroyed during the conservative, McCarthyite backlash of the 1950s. It appears that a number of the SCS monographs, and others published by the Farm Security Administration, no longer exist. Of those that do exist, very few copies remain. Fortunately for the historian, these few have been preserved in the libraries of several Southwestern institutions.[19]

The New Deal programs that affected New Mexican Hispanic land use were almost all funded and directed either by or through the Soil Conservation Service (April 1935 onward) or the Farm Security Administration (FSA) (September 1937–August 1946) and its predecessors, the Resettlement Administration (RA) (April 1935–August 1937) and the Rural Rehabilitation Division of the FERA (April 1934–June 1935). Their programs divided along two general lines, those of the SCS dedicated to conservation research, demonstration, application, and land-use planning; and those of the FSA directed toward aid to destitute or low income rural families, farm tenants, sharecroppers, and migratory workers.[20] Both RA and FSA programs assumed that rural poverty could, and should, be cured, not just relieved. It was essential to the future of *all* Americans because rural poverty resulted in human suffering, inadequate purchasing power, overused and eroded land, disease, and costly social services.[21]

Both agencies were heavily involved in education; the SCS concentrating upon conservation education, the FSA and its predecessors devoting its energies and funds to farm and home education related to health, nutrition, food processing and preservation, family budgeting, and cooperative buying and marketing. Field representatives of both agencies had, of necessity, to work out a *modus vivendi* with other federal, state, and county agents who assisted and supplemented their efforts. They did this despite high-level struggles for control. Since many of them had begun their careers as county extension agents they had a firm basis for rapport with their local counterparts. Federal guidelines inevitably limited agency interaction and there was a tendency for each agency to defend its turf but, considering the complexity of the operations, the amount of cooperation appears to have been, if anything, exemplary.[22]

A major reason for close federal and state agency interaction and cooperation was the fact that responsibility for many programs was divided among several agencies. The interweaving of activities often became quite complex. The SCS, for example, was assigned both CCC and WPA relief labor to carry out its conservation work. Within the CCC camps assigned to the Soil Conservation Service, both SCS and WPA instructors conducted technical and general education classes. After February 1936 funding for villagers to participate in soil conservation efforts was provided through the Agricultural Adjustment Administration (AAA), the administration of which was largely through the State Agricultural College. Legislation, in the form of the Soil Conservation and Domestic Allotment Act, provided payments or grants-in-aid to farmers for approved soil conservation practices and related purposes.[23] Under the Omnibus Flood Control Act of June 1936, the SCS was directed to work in cooperation with the Forest Service and the Bureau of Agricultural Economics (BAE) to conduct investigations and apply measures to retard runoff and soil erosion on specific watersheds.[24] Under the provisions of the Pope-Jones Water Facilities Act of 1937 it was directed to work with the BAE and the FSA to provide technical and financial help to farmers and ranchers in the development of water supplies, primarily for irrigation.[25]

The most complex, and frequently frustrating, agency interaction in New Mexico was, however, that related to land use and acquisition. Submarginal land was purchased first under the Rural Rehabilitation programs of the FERA and the Resettlement Administration. Beginning in 1937 it was purchased or leased under the provisions of the Bankhead-Jones Farm Tenant Act. Administration of these lands was at different times in the hands of the Federal Emergency Relief Administration, the Soil Conservation Service, the Resettlement Administration-Farm Security Administration, the Bureau of Agricultural Economics, the Indian Service, and the Forest Service.[26] Programs involving the use and disposition of these lands became so complicated and sensitive that they necessitated the creation of various planning boards and committees. Not surprisingly, John Collier was at the center of the action and the focus of controversy.

Inspired, no doubt, by Collier's challenge, Hauter and his colleagues in the Resettlement Administration addressed the matter of Hispanic rights through a study of their history and land titles. Their report reviewed the terms of the Treaty of Guadalupe-Hidalgo and the more recent confirmation of Hispanic land titles under the Pueblo Lands Board Act of 1924 and concluded that the Hispanic peoples had as much right to the use of New Mexico's old Spanish and Mexican grant lands as the Indians. A related report suggested that they had an even greater need for them. As proof for this contention the writer of the report called attention to the many free services provided by the Indian Service that had no counterpart among non-Indian groups. Indians paid no taxes, received free hospitalization and medical service, free access to "higher" education, free legal service, free agricultural and livestock service, free protection of their ranges, and free use of government owned heavy equipment for leveling and clearing irrigable land and developing water resources. Since a far greater portion of non-Indian resources had to be used to maintain the same standard of living, Resettlement Administration officials estimated that Hispanic resources would have to be increased by 25 percent to make them comparable with Indian resources.[27]

By late 1936 even Collier was convinced that the problem of allocating use rights to the federal grazing lands was not so much a contest between Indians and non-Indians, as it was a conflict between the noncommercial "subsistence" populations of the region and the large commercial stock growers. He even agreed to allow state and federal officials to negotiate a temporary allocation of use-rights to the Indian Purchase area, but not without an effort to strengthen his hold over the submarginal land program. Using Shevky's monograph on the land resources of the Española Valley to demonstrate the need for action, Collier urged Ickes and Wallace to reconstitute the old Rio Grande Committee and assign "prime responsibility" in the reorganized body to representatives of the BIA. The two secretaries acceded to his wishes and in January 1937 they signed a memorandum of understanding creating a new entity entitled the Interdepartmental Rio Grande Advisory Committee. The new Committee, like the old Advisory Board, was made up of representatives from the Forest Service, the Grazing Service, the General Land Office, the Soil Conservation Service, and the Resettlement Administration. Walter Woehlke of the Bureau of Indian Affairs served as chairman. The committee was officially charged with mediating and resolving the land problems of the area for the benefit of the noncommercial rural population and of devising ways and means of protecting and enlarging their basic agricultural resources. Its first report, circulated in October 1937, recommended land purchases closely correlated with the provisions of the Bankhead-Jones Farm Tenant Act which had become law in July.[28]

In February 1937 the Interdepartmental Rio Grande Committee began to plan its "attack" on what it called the "Rio Grande Problem." Acknowledging that both the native Hispanic and Indian populations of the Rio Grande Basin were undersupplied with renewable natural resources, the committee declared its intention of allocating use rights to the federal lands so as to make up as far as possible for the resource deficit. The populations throughout the area were heavily dependent upon grazing so no sudden stock reductions were contemplated. Such an action, the committee declared, would throw the inhabitants onto public charity, demoralize them, and introduce them to a cash economy and a higher standard of living through relief than they were accustomed to having on their own resources. The committee requested the Forest and Soil Conservation Services to stretch their stocking limits to the utmost, and the Grazing Service was asked to refrain from allocating public domain permits until a proper procedure was developed.[29]

The committee further declared its intention of encouraging the development of cash employment through such measures as craft production and coal mining. In order to free Hispanos from exploitative partido share-cropping relationships it suggested that the government step into the role of landlord on federally leased lands. Finally, it urged the creation of a new federal agency which would oversee the welfare of all underprivileged families in a unified program irrespective of race or color.[30] A later report expanded the areas of committee responsibility to include the development of new cultivated land, the improvement of existing cultivated lands, and the redistribution of grazing lands to the subsistence populations through the acquisition of both the lands and the livestock of large commercial operators.[31]

The Interdepartmental Rio Grande Committee recommended two areas for priority action: the Rio Puerco drainage and the Santa Cruz Valley of the Upper Rio Grande. Of the two, the Rio Puerco area took precedence because of its threat to the Elephant Butte Reservoir and the desperate condition of its subsistence populations.[32]

According to two historical studies of the Rio Puerco drainage, one written by Ernest Maes of the Soil Conservation Service, the other by Morris Evans of the Bureau of Agricultural Economics, the area had once been a garden spot. Beginning about 1848 several Hispanic ranchers began running sheep on the Ojo del Espiritu Santo Grant, and shortly thereafter a number of Hispanic farmers moved out from the village of Peña Blanca to establish the community of Cabezon. They constructed extensive irrigation facilities, finding it a simple matter to divert water from the Rio Puerco, which had not yet cut a deep channel. In 1905 Frank Bond, the sheepman from Rio Arriba County, began operations in the Cuba area as a dealer in wool, hides, and lambs. After the disastrous winter of 1928, during which the Hispanic ranchers lost nearly one-half of their sheep, Bond virtually monopolized the range, renting out sheep on shares to the destitute Hispanos.[33]

Heavy grazing led to soil denudation and erosion. The water table fell due to the cutting of arroyos. In less than twenty years a one-time spring became a twenty foot well. Water could no longer be diverted for irrigation, and after 1922 farming became a subsidiary activity. The villagers depended upon their livestock and on wage labor for a cash income. With the onset of the depression, which virtually eliminated opportunities for wage labor, and the acquisition of the Espiritu Santo Grant by the Indian Service, the population was left bereft and almost completely dependent upon relief.[34]

In 1935 and 1936 the federal government issued loans in the amount of seventy-five thousand dollars to the distressed farmers through the Rural Rehabilitation Division of the Resettlement Adminstration. Most of the loans were due in the fall or winter of the year in which they were issued. By December 1936 delinquency on the loans reached an estimated 90 percent. Shevky and his colleagues in the SCS who studied the situation realized that the loans could never be repaid, for lack of resources with which to repay them, and reasoned that the delinquency was not the result of individual failure but of a complex of problems pertaining to the area as a whole. WPA wage work was, at best, a temporary solution. Only an extensive development program could bring the relief population back to its former level of subsistence. As a joint undertaking of several different agencies it presented an exciting challenge.[35]

Throughout 1937 and 1938 the Interdepartmental Rio Grande Committee debated and eventually approved a number of specific action programs. These programs were made possible by two major legislative acts: the Bankhead-Jones Farm Tenant Act, passed in July 1937 and the Pope-Jones Water Facilities Act of August 1937. Title I and part of Title IV of the Bankhead-Jones Act were administered by the Farm Security Administration and provided loans to tenants to enable them to buy farms. The same program provided grants to extremely low-income farmers to help them get off relief, and permitted the federal government to buy land to lease to individuals or associations for the grazing of livestock. Title III of the Act provided for the utilization and retirement of submarginal land. Responsibility for administering the Land Utilization Program passed from the Resettlement Administration (reconstituted in August 1937 as the Farm Security Administration) to the Bureau of Agricultural Economics and, in November 1938, came to rest in the Soil Conservation Service. The Pope-Jones Water Facilities Act was assigned to the Farm Security Administration. Under this program the FSA made loans to farmers, ranchers, and incorporated water associations in seventeen western states to enable them to build, improve, or repair wells, ponds, windmills, and small irrigation systems. In July 1938 the Soil Conservation Service and the Bureau of Agricultural Economics were given responsibility for developing conservation management plans for, and rendering technical assistance to, farms and ranches where water facilities programs were being carried out.[36]

By September 1937 three soil conservation grants had been allocated to the use of Indians, covering an area of 174,000 acres with a carrying capacity of 1,656 cattle. Three grants had also been allocated to non-Indian, primarily Hispanic, use with an area of 187,000 acres and a carrying capacity of 1,601 cattle. Despite efforts by the Resettlement Adminstration/Farm Security Administration to assure Hispanic rights, however, the Indian Service continued to dominate decisions. According to FSA records, Indian lands received five times the expenditures for soil conservation work as non-Indian lands. With these improvements, Indians were permitted to graze livestock equal to the full carrying capacity of the land, whereas non-Indians were limited to a bare 59 percent of the carrying capacity of theirs.[37]

While the Interdepartmental Rio Grande Advisory Committee debated the terms of the land program, the struggle between the commercial ranching interests, the Resettlement Administration/Farm Security Administration and the Bureau of Indian Affairs raged on. Backed by RA/FSA agents the small stock farmers, most but not all Hispanic, formed livestock associations and through them demanded access to the Espiritu Santo range. They were ably led by Bernardino Hovey, president of the Cabezon Livestock Association and one of the more prosperous ranchers of the region. Hovey added his voice, and the weight of his followers, to the protests of the commercial livestock interests who demanded that the grazing system and the land purchase policy preserve a mixed occupation by all groups.[38]

The alliance of the small ranchers with the commercial stockmen in this instance was in reaction to the conservation policies of the Soil Conservation Service. That agency, charged with restoring the desperately eroded Rio Puerco grass lands, had had to impose severe limits on the number of sheep and cattle it would permit on the unimproved range. With Hispanic use-rights limited to little more than half the carrying capacity of the land, the average of fifteen head of sheep per family was insufficient for family subsistence. Worse, not all needy applicants could be accommodated. But most significantly for the success of the program, the decision of the SCS to permit use by only the poorest ranchers had the effect of excluding entirely all mid-size operations, like those of Bernardino Hovey. Hovey, who had painstakingly built up his herds to a profitable level after returning from army service in World War I, simply refused to accept such limitations on land he considered part of his ethnic heritage. On more than one occasion he and other Hispano stockmen ignored the SCS regulations and drove their livestock onto the disputed lands.[39]

In late November 1937 Hovey also joined Floyd Lee, several other big ranchers, and New Mexico's Representative, John Dempsey in a face-to-face confrontation with Collier in his BIA office. They had heard about the plan to assign more lands in the northwest corner of the state to the BIA and informed Collier that action would be taken to sponsor a bill turning over all the Rio Grande Project lands to the Grazing Service. A month later Hovey and other stock farmers from Cabezon again demonstrated their frustration with the government's land policies by ripping down a section of government fence and driving several hundred head of cattle onto the Espiritu Santo range.[40]

The escalating level of Hispanic protest, and the alliance of small ranchers with the powerful commercial livestock interests, not only undercut the Interdepartmental Rio Grande Committee's land reform program, it also threatened to derail Collier's Navajo boundary extension bill. Frustrated by the continuing opposition to him and the BIA, Collier embarked on a truly remarkable course of action. Hoping to effect a political separation of the poor "subsistence" Hispanic ranchers from the commercial ranchers, and to divide the constituency of his nemesis, Senator Dennis Chavez, Collier tried quietly to organize a counter "grass roots" Hispanic land reform movement. Knowing that he could not lead it himself, he asked George Sanchez to do so. Sanchez, engaged in his study of the Taos area, demurred on the basis that the Hispanic villagers were not ready to take such organized action. Collier then turned to a group of supporters in Santa Fe and Albuquerque and suggested that they form a Spanish American Affairs Committee and back the land reform campaign being waged by the Hispanic labor union, the *Liga Obrera*.[41]

The proposed alliance between the BIA and the Liga Obrera was nothing short of political dynamite. The Liga had been involved in numerous labor disputes and was regarded by state administrative leaders as a subversive body with communist leadership. When the Archbishop of Santa Fe heard about Collier's plan he expressed his opposition in such decided terms that Collier backed away and turned the organizing effort over to the Catholic Church. The Archbishop's attempts to establish a network of church-controlled bodies in the Rio Puerco area only succeeded in further antagonizing Hovey and his followers.[42]

In March 1938 a joint action by Secretaries Wallace and Ickes changed the Interdepartmental Rio Grande Advisory Committee into the Interdepartmental Rio Grande Board. No longer limited to an advisory capacity, the new Board was empowered to carry land, social, and economic reform well beyond the earlier division of lands. Under its new terms both the Agriculture and Interior departments could purchase land under Title III of the Bankhead-Jones Act to correct land-use patterns in the Rio Puerco area. Unfortunately, by this time so much interagency friction had been created that board action was severely limited.[43] It did manage to effect a few important transactions, however.

Concerned about the Hispanos' invasion of the Espiritu Santo Grant, the BAE planners in charge of the land program modified the Collier-Woehlke plans. Instead of purchasing more land for the Indians in the western Rio Puerco region they urged the purchase of several grants for the use of Hispanos as well as the transfer of the Espiritu Santo Grant from Pueblo to Hispanic use. Catching Collier at a time when he still hoped to mobilize the Hispanic ranchers behind his land reform program, the board persuaded him to accept the purchase of the Antonio Sedillo Grant in exchange for the Espiritu Santo, which reverted to the primary use of the Rio Puerco villagers. The board also worked out an agreement between Frank Bond, the Santa Fe Railroad, and the Soil Conservation Service whereby all railroad lands within the project area would be exchanged for federal lands outside. To complete the intended elimination of all commercial use of the Rio Puerco lands, the two secretaries agreed to create a new grazing district with special rules and regulations limiting use of the range to the noncommercial rural population. Eventually some 270,000 acres were purchased for the exclusive use of "subsistence" Hispanos.[44]

In August 1938 the Soil Conservation Service published a justification for the actions taken and pending in the Rio Puerco and elsewhere. The report, most likely authored by Shevky, was entitled "The Rio Grande Watershed in Colorado and New Mexico." It explained the reasons for the Hispanic land reform program, and noted that the population of the Rio Grande Valley constituted one of the outstanding rural poverty areas in the United States.[45] According to the report, that poverty stemmed to some degree from a scarcity of available resources but even more from the high concentration of control of those resources; the water by a few commercial growers in the San Luis Valley of Colorado, and the range lands by a few commercial livestock operators in the Upper Rio Grande Valley. Any efforts to achieve conservative use of the land would have to take into consideration the welfare of the dependent population or leave the federal government with a permanent and very expensive relief load.[46]

Although the destructive overstocking of the range derived from both commercial and noncommercial users, the report continued, the native noncommercial population depended heavily on its livestock for survival. The commercial operators, on the other hand, were in the business for quick and large profits. Since the federal government owned 48 percent of the land in the watershed, it controlled the economic future of the major part of the agricultural population as well as the future of the range resources. In spite of this it had permitted a concentration of control to endanger the livelihood of the native population, destroy the resources, and threaten its fifteen million dollar investment in the watershed's two major reclamation areas—the Elephant Butte Dam and Reservoir, and the Middle Rio Grande Conservancy District. A subsidy of this sort for the commercial livestock industry was, the report concluded, an expensive luxury that neither the people of the watershed nor the nation could afford.[47]

The Interdepartmental Rio Grande Board's findings concerning the Rio Puerco applied equally to its second area of priority concern, the Santa Cruz Valley of the Upper Rio Grande. Based on Shevky's surveys, which had begun with the 1935 Tewa Basin Study, the Soil Conservation

Service had much to say about what was needed in the way of federal action in the area. As in the Rio Puerco area, the first rehabilitation programs in the Santa Cruz Valley had provided low interest loans to farm families. These loans were also soon outstanding. Eshref Shevky judged such federal programs to be not only totally inappropriate but potentially disastrous for the traditional, noncommercial economy, a fact which he had pointed out in a second 1935 monograph entitled "Proposals for the Santa Cruz Valley." According to his studies, 85 percent of the population in the area lived on a bare subsistence level, yet clients were urged to switch from subsistence crops to cash crops. Those who did soon found themselves dependent upon storekeepers for their basic food supplies. They not only had to pay the middleman's profit, but the 10 percent surcharge for credit. Their crops, when they came in, brought them little or no profit because of problems with transportation and limited markets. To make matters worse, the Rural Rehabilitation agents in their eagerness to help them had grossly overestimated their cash profits and underestimated their expenditures. With insufficient cash to repay the loans as they came due, the farmers were in danger of losing both their homes and their land. There was no alternative, Shevky concluded, but for the federal government to write off the loans as uncollectible debts.[48]

Rural Rehabilitation, working under the philosophy of "solid banking," Shevky argued, could do nothing to solve the problems of the valley. Loans could not make up for insufficient agricultural resources. Since outside wage labor would not likely regain its dominant position as the chief source of livelihood for the Valley people, Shevky had proposed a public subsidy in the form of a government sponsored regional production and marketing association. The association, which would have operated under the old barter system, would have excluded the few large landholders who, Shevky reasoned, would not want to be part of a noncommercial system. It would also have excluded the families with too little or no land who would have placed an unfair burden upon the rest. They would be helped through government relief, Shevky argued, while the large landowners could get loans from the Rural Rehabilitation Corporation.[49]

Shevky had been so enthusiastic about his cooperative marketing association that he had worked out a table of equivalencies for the barter exchange of various foodstuffs. He envisioned wheat being grown in the high country and fruit, onions, chiles, and beans in the lower valley. He even urged a renewal of the old Hispanic trade connection with the San Luis Valley of Colorado.[50]

Although Shevky's proposals were never seriously implemented, his insights profoundly influenced the thinking of local SCS, FSA, and BAE administrators and field personnel. Convinced that a population so poor that it could not maintain itself could never bear the burden of repayable loans, these agencies, individually or through the Interdepartmental Rio Grande Board, concentrated on programs that would restore the region's resources through outright grants. The SCS water facilities program, which operated through grants from the AAA, was particularly effective in the Santa Cruz Valley. Under the program many small but significant improvements were made in the irrigation systems and community water supplies. Ditches cut by arroyos were repaired so that water would not be wasted. Sanitary wells were dug to reduce the incidence of typhoid and dysentery. New Deal officials justified the channeling of the "lion's share" of water facilities funds into these small, grant supported projects on the basis that maintenance of the large, stable, Hispanic population upon the land was in the best possible interests of the state and nation. Judging from the extant correspondence, their views were shared widely throughout the state.[51]

Outright grants to extremely low-income farmers for rural rehabilitation were also available through the Farm Security Administration Tenant Purchase Program. To protect Hispanic pride, the cash advances were referred to as "benefit payments" and compared to the payments provided larger operators through the AAA. According to Ralph Will, the Assistant Regional Director of the FSA, the supervised grant program was the only effort in the Department of Agriculture that could reach New Mexico's Hispanic farm families but it was "no more than a drop in the bucket." In June 1941 the entire Tenant Purchase Program was discontinued allegedly for reasons of the wartime economy.[52]

Land acquisition in the Upper Rio Grande Valley began in 1935 when the Resettlement Administration began purchasing grazing lands for the area's Indian population. The Soil Conservation Service, given responsibility for administering the lands, removed all large commercial operators. In early 1936, after surveying the extent to which non-Indians as well as Indians were dependent upon the grants, it began to issue temporary grazing permits to local Hispanic subsistence families on the basis of need. By September 1937 agreements had been reached between the Secretaries of Agriculture and the Interior allocating certain of these lands to exclusive non-Indian (Hispanic) use. The lands so designated were the south half of the Juan Jose Lobato Grant, the Polvadera Grant, the Sebastian Martin Grant in the Tewa Basin, and the Caja del Rio Grant and the La Majada Grant in the Cochiti area. With the smaller Cuyamungue Grant in the Tewa Basin they constituted a total of 241,339 acres. Lands transferred to the Forest Service for the primary use of Hispanic subsistence families included the San Jose Grant in the Jemez area and the Gabaldon and Ramon Vigil Grants in the Tewa Basin. By 1942 the Farm Security Administration had acquired another 125,000 acres for the Northern New Mexico Grant Lands Project by buying the north half of the Lobato Grant, the Abiquiu Grant, and the Ortiz Mine Grant.[53] For the location of these grants see Map 3.

Calkin's and Shevky's interest in area wide studies and a sociological/ecological approach to solving the problems of New Mexico's subsistence populations led not only to the interdepartmental approach used in the land adjustment programs in the Rio Puerco and northern Rio Grande Valleys, but also to a project known as the New Mexican experiment in village rehabilitation. Although a natural outgrowth of the human dependency and anthropological studies carried out after 1935 by the Soil Conservation Service, the establishment of the ten county New Mexico Special Area was part of a broader Farm Security Administration program to rehabilitate noncommercial farmers throughout the United States. Since there had long been considerable opposition nationally to SCS involvement in human dependency and anthropological studies, and none were conducted in New Mexico after 1939, the initiation of the New Mexico village rehabilitation project in 1940 amounted to a fortuitous bit of timing. The project's rationale, according to the FSA regional director, Wilson Cowen, was that problems of poverty were areawide and therefore rehabilitation could be carried out better on a community basis than through individuals. Moreover, because of the similarity in culture between one Hispanic village and another, lessons learned from the experiment could be aimed at the rehabilitation of hundreds of other such villages in the Southwest and even in the Spanish-speaking countries of Latin America.[54]

The experimental program was approved in February 1941, and the FSA was authorized to provide loans to individuals and associations within the new Rural Rehabilitation District for health and medical programs, the renting or leasing of land, and the payment of back taxes or liens. It could make grants for such specified purposes as the purchase of garden seeds and supplies, household supplies, essential home furnishings, and subsistence livestock.[55]

Four tiny villages in the Upper Pecos Valley were selected for the program. Known collectively as El Pueblo, they were thought to represent a typical rural New Mexican, Hispanic community. They also resembled the nearby village of El Cerrito, which had been studied intensively by anthropologists and economists in the BAE for the express purpose of planning such rehabilitation projects as the one proposed for El Pueblo. Since investigators had begun working in the community as early as 1938 there was a substantial basis for planning the program.[56]

The intent of the program was to make the people independent of relief and outside labor and to develop techniques for accomplishing the same in other Hispanic villages. Activities included the usual efforts to improve community health, sanitation, food preservation, and nutrition; to improve its irrigation system and water supplies; and to increase agricultural production. The FSA oversaw the building of a community center and bought 26,400 acres of grazing land in the Anton Chico Land Grant to lease to the El Pueblo Livestock Association. Members of the association worked with the Soil Conservation Service to fence the land and initiate erosion control and water conservation. In 1943 when the program ended and accomplishments and failures were assessed, the program supervisor pointed with pride to a definite increase in the production of food and crops, to an increase in the net worth of participating families, and to improved sanitation and medical care.[57]

The supervisor had also learned a lot about directing change in a traditional Hispanic community. His most important insight, perhaps, was that villagers had to really *want* change before they would cooperate in bringing it about. The villagers, he reported, were extremely suspicious of Anglo and government motives due to decades of injustice. Supervisors had to work slowly and within the culture to gain their trust. Their job was made more difficult by the fact that higher-ups in the agency frequently changed the rules in ways that the supervisors could neither control nor explain satisfactorily to their clients. The villagers were particularly fearful of paper work that required signatures, and programs that required monetary commitments, since past experience had shown them to be traps through which they, and others, had lost their land. Most of all, the El Pueblo experiment demonstrated that an understanding of language, culture, and social organization was essential to the success of rehabilitation work.[58]

The other major rehabilitation project in the New Mexico Special Area was the Taos County Project. Work had begun in the Taos area in 1936 when the University of New Mexico made the Harwood family's gift of a house and endowment in Taos the occasion for an experimental education program. In 1938 the Carnegie Corporation of New York granted the University four thousand dollars for the countywide survey made by George I. Sanchez and published as *Forgotten People.* In April 1940 it followed up this grant with another totaling forty-three thousand dollars to cover the three-year action phase of the program. Its director, J. T. Reid of the University Extension Service, made it his goal to coordinate the work of all governmental agencies, federal, state, and local, in a single cultural and ecological attack on the problems of the Taos area. It was, in many ways, the philosophical and practical culmination of the Hispanic New Deal.[59]

Seventeen agencies formed the charter membership of the Taos County Project when it opened in June 1940. Eventually thirty-six agencies and twenty-two communities in Taos County participated in the project. Their representatives met in committee to plan land use programs, school hot lunches, libraries, roads, water facilities projects, land acquisitions, and the Taos County Cooperative Health Association. Specifically, the project helped the communities of Amalia and Costilla buy back their communal grazing lands. It protested the sale of the Antonio Martinez Grant to the Indian Service on behalf of the communities of Arroyo Seco, Colonias, and Las Córdovas and, when this was unsuccessful, worked out a leasing arrangement with the Indians. It endeavored to lease other grant lands for grazing purposes; negotiated, unsuccessfully, to acquire land for a demonstration farm for NYA youth; helped the community of Cerro get a new irrigation system; and mediated a water litigation suit between the community of Costilla and the San Luis Water and Power Company.[60]

The Taos Project coordinated vocational arts and crafts classes and sponsored a visual education program which brought motion pictures for the first time to many mountain villages. The subject matter ranged from cartoons and short subjects to programs on health, nutrition, soil conservation, and agricultural production. Through the project community centers were built in a great number of outlying villages. Many were used for adult education classes, village recreational activities, and town meetings and contained branch libraries. A county bookmobile brought new books and periodicals on a regular basis to outlying villages from the main library in Taos.[61]

To relieve the shortage of grazing lands the Project encouraged families to combine their small flocks of sheep into herds of one thousand or more so that they could qualify for better grazing permits in the National Forest and for better private grazing leases. It encouraged them to limit the number and improve the quality of their sheep and to vote in the first Hispanic soil conservation district in the state. It also helped the Taoseños to set up a successful cooperative marketing association. The most elaborate accomplishment, however, was the Taos County Cooperative Health Association which brought modern medical care to thousands who had never had it before. Subsidized by the Farm Security Administration on the theory that healthy farmers would be better able to make a go of rehabilitation and, therefore, pay back their loans, the Association provided quality medical care for as little as thirty dollars per family, per year.[62]

In his book, *It Happened in Taos,* Reid described the great sense of accomplishment and pride he and his colleagues felt. "The people have done most of the jobs themselves," he wrote. They "spontaneously" accepted "the grueling task of carrying the heavy end of their own rehabilitation." Before this they had lived "among their peaks with their handicaps—poverty, sickness, superstitions, and ignorance—a challenge to every red-blooded fellow citizen of this great democracy of ours."[63]

Reid's boastfully euphoric description of the Taos Project was a fitting climax to a decade of feverish activity and utopian scheming. In 1943 the programs seemed to be on the threshold of major accomplishments with the necessary interruption caused by World War II nothing more than an interlude. As the New Dealers departed the programs for wartime service they were convinced that they had left New Mexico a better place for their efforts. With the end of the global struggle they fully expected to pick up the programs where they had left them and carry them to new heights.

# NINE

# The Final Years and Later

Driving across northern New Mexico in the late 1980s one sees few signs to justify the efforts and the high hopes of the Hispanic New Deal. The land is still badly overgrazed and eroded. Agricultural production has, if anything diminished.[1] The industrious weavers of Chimayo, whose craft production long predated the New Deal, and successfully survived it, are hard, and successfully, at work, but except for them and one or two notable exceptions there are no bustling village industries.[2]

The Hispanic villages survive, but they are no more able to support their populations solely with their agricultural resources than in the past. With very few forms of industrial development, and with very limited employment opportunities, the predominantly Hispanic counties of northern New Mexico continue to represent one of the most intransigent pockets of poverty in the United States. Of the six poorest counties in the state, five range from 69 to 87 percent Hispanic. The sixth is 66 percent Indian. Within these counties, 32 percent of the population live below the poverty line. Twenty-seven percent of them receive food stamps and other forms of welfare.[3]

While many of New Mexico's Hispanos have left the villages in search of greater economic opportunity, those who remain do not, in general, regard such a move as either easy or particularly desirable. Poorly prepared educationally and with linguistic handicaps that make assimilation into the mainstream of United States society difficult, they have suffered job and wage discrimination and the loss of highly valued cultural ties. Those who can effect a partial transition do so by living within the village and commuting to jobs in Albuquerque, Santa Fe, Española, or Los Alamos. Others sustain themselves marginally by performing multiple small-scale entrepreneurial activities reminiscent, in a way, of the multi-resource economy of the nineteenth century. Often both husband and wife hold jobs and raise a garden. Other activities may consist of gathering and selling local products such as firewood and flagstones, cultivating small amounts of fruit and vegetables for sale as well as for family consumption, and performing odd jobs and services.

Even with these activities, and financial assistance from relatives who have made good elsewhere, chronic welfare dependence has clearly become both a fact and a way of life for a great many of New Mexico's Hispanic villagers. Non-villagers may argue, with considerable justification, that they are paying a high price in lost productivity and wasted talent for the retention of cultural traditions, village and kinship ties, and a clear sense of ethnic identity. The villagers contend simply that the villages are *home,* and where they belong. While most would like to have some form of productive work if it were available, they accept such federal subsidies as Aid for Dependent Children, Medicaid, and food stamps as little enough compensation for the loss of their old grant lands and no more than their due.[4] Meanwhile, life in the villages, though never the idyll imagined by romantics, has clearly lost the sense of corporate community that carried its people so vigorously and resourcefully into the twentieth century. Anglo sociologists and historians, who generally deplore Hispanic welfare dependence, trace it to New Deal origins.

So what went wrong? With so much money and planning, so much hope and energy expended, why were the results so transitory? The easiest explanation, and the one most often cited, is that it was too big a job to accomplish in the time allotted—that the war cut off programs which, had they been allowed to continue, would have resulted in substantial and lasting gains.

The time was undeniably short. Most of the cultural programs were only getting underway by 1936. The most significant agricultural programs got an even later start, after legislation enacted in late 1937 provided the necessary federal funds. Like most government programs, they started on a small scale in special targeted areas. Real momentum, and a broader response to the needs of the state, was not achieved until 1941 when United States entry into World War II changed national priorities, cut off funds, and reduced personnel. Five years is certainly not enough time to effect change on the scale intended in New Mexico, but the question remains, had the war not intervened would these programs have changed the subsequent history of the area? To find the answer we must look at the continuing history of the New Deal and at the post War years, both in New Mexico and on the national level.

Some federal programs involved in the Hispanic New Deal, such as the Reconstruction Finance Corporation which bailed out the bankrupt Middle Rio Grande Conservancy District and averted the immediate foreclosure of thousands of acres of Hispanic lands, were founded on such conservative principles that failure was built in from the beginning. The problems of the Middle Rio Grande Valley derived from the devastating overuse and abuse of the Rio Grande watershed. They could not be helped merely by an infusion of solid banking principles. By the time the conservancy repairs had been put into effect great numbers of Hispanic farmers had lost the productive use of their lands through waterlogging and flooding. They lacked the machinery to reclaim them and, in the meantime, were in danger of losing their land titles because of their inability to pay the exorbitant conservancy assessments. Since the conservancy fees were attached to, and inseparable from, the property taxes, inability to pay the one led automatically to tax delinquency and eventual foreclosure by the state.[3]

To further complicate matters, Conservancy assessments were based on an appraisal of future benefits. A Board of Appraisers, appointed by the county, had placed the highest appraisals on waterlogged and over-grown lands on the theory that they would benefit the most from the conservancy repairs and improvements. So, with a skewed kind of logic, the farmers with the least productive lands and the fewest cash resources were required to pay the heaviest assessments. The so-called rescue by the Reconstruction Finance Corporation, since it did nothing but defer the debt, was no rescue at all. By late 1937 over two thousand properties had been deeded to the state for tax delinquencies and another nine thousand were about to be sold. Eighty-five percent of the delinquent tracts were under ten acres and 89 percent of the owners were Hispanic.[4]

Hispanos were not the only farmers in the middle valley affected by the conservancy's financial problems, however. Numerous groups mobilized to urge the state legislature to provide some relief. One solution proposed was a reappraisal of assessment levies based on actual rather than potential and unrealized productivity. Another was the separation of conservancy taxes from state and county taxes. But while all land-owners agreed on these issues there was a notable area of disagreement between the larger landowners, who had to carry the entire cost of the conservancy because the smaller landowners could not pay their assessments, and the smaller landowners who felt that they were in danger of losing their lands for benefits that they had never received and had not requested. Both groups were disheartened by what they perceived as an inequitable burden imposed by the other. The large landowners, in particular, were very vocal about the poorer farmers who, they believed, were being confirmed in their attitude of "not trying to pay anything." Led by their chief spokesman, Clinton Anderson, who in 1945 would be named Secretary of Agriculture under Harry Truman, they were represented by the New Mexico Farm Bureau and the Middle Rio Grande Farmers' Association. The *Liga Obrera* and Collier's Committee for Spanish-American Affairs, chaired by Rabbi A. L. Krohn from Santa Fe, represented the Hispanic farmers. The Board of the Conservancy District took a third position condemned by both groups—that any farmer who could not pay his taxes should be promptly dispossessed and his land sold to newcomers who would "recolonize" the District.[5]

The press and the New Mexico Congressional delegation, represented by Senators Dennis Chavez and John Dempsey, once again supported the cause of the small Hispanic landholders, in part because of historical and humanitarian reasons, but also because they feared their dispossession would add enormously to the already overburdened state relief rolls. It was far better, they argued, for the state to forego the taxes on the lower bracket lands and leave the small farmers to support themselves, as they had for the past 250 years, than to have them become dependent upon public tax money. Newcomers would be just as hard pressed to make the lands productive given the same set of circumstances, a fact they believed was demonstrated by the lack of interest in the lands already acquired by the state.[6]

Rabbi Krohn and the *Liga Obrera* advanced a more radical argument. They contended that the government had acted illegally when it allotted water to Colorado, Texas, and Mexico. Krohn urged Hispanic landowners to file suit against the government on the basis that their ancient and vested prior rights, granted under the Treaty of Guadalupe-Hidalgo, took precedence over the Rio Grande Tri-State Compact.[7]

While nothing came of the *Liga Obrera's* and Krohn's argument, Chavez and Dempsey tried to find federal funds to relieve the beleaguered Hispanic farmers. Declaring that a minority of bondholders demanding "their pound of flesh" was causing suffering to thousands of citizens of the middle valley, they suggested removing the small farm owners from the jurisdiction of the Conservancy District altogether and establishing them in a new district under the jurisdiction of the Bureau of Reclamation. The Reclamation Service, they argued, could take over the debt, allow the farmers to retain their homes, and permit them to pay their tax obligations separately from their Conservancy assessments. The proposal was supported, and may have been initiated, by representatives Walter Woehlke of the Indian Service, Eshref Shevky of the Soil Conservation Service, and John Adams of the Forest Service, who met privately with Governor Clyde Tingley in late November 1937, shortly before all three were appointed to positions on the newly created Interdepartmental Rio Grande Advisory Committee. However, this plan also fell by the way when Tingley informed them that the Conservancy District, since it had been established by the state legislature, would have to be completely restructured before it could be eligible for federal assistance.[8]

A compromise of sorts was reached when the Conservancy Board accepted $600,000 from the Reconstruction Finance Corporation and cancelled the $2,500,000 district bond interest charges. The RFC extended the maturity date for the payment of principal to five years and reduced the bond interest from $5\frac{1}{2}$ percent to 4 percent, making it retroactive for three years. It also permitted the district to buy back the land titles lost due to tax delinquency from the state and to sell them back to their former owners under a ten-year contract during which they could pay back their debts and rehabilitate themselves free of further taxation. The Middle Rio Grande Farmers' Association declared itself well pleased with the arrangement. Not so the *Liga Obrera* and Rabbi Krohn, who declared that, "we would be merely buying back a bad debt. The landowners never got the benefits promised in . . . the construction of the District."[9]

All farm groups continued to fight for a reappraisal of their benefits based on actual, rather than potential, productivity, and the separation of conservancy levies from state and county property taxes, but nothing came of their efforts. The small landowners requested the opportunity to work off their tax indebtedness by repairing the ditches but were turned down on a technicality. Because the RFC had granted the money to finance the work, WPA workers had to do it, and few men in the district qualified for WPA labor.[10] In August 1942 the New Mexico legislature passed a "Relief Act" that suspended the payment of interest and principal on inactive agricultural lands for a period of fifteen years and capitalized the interest on the debt as part of the principal, but the Act was declared unconstitutional and was rescinded. When the Conservancy District was finally taken over by the Bureau of Reclamation in 1947 a new "Plan for the Development for the Middle Rio Grande Project" noted that there appeared to be "no remedy to relieve the district from the effect of its original economically unsound basis of assessment of benefits . . . short of cancellation of the existing debt." By this time the poorest lands had all reverted to the state. Most of these lands— those most damaged by the backing up of waters behind the Elephant Butte dam—were in Socorro and Valencia counties.[11]

This is not to say that all Hispanic lands were served badly by the conservancy. Some, particularly those to the north of Albuquerque, were made considerably more productive. However the small size of most Hispanic farms made it virtually impossible for the owners to raise enough produce to feed the family and still provide a profit. Those farmers whose lands were close enough to Albuquerque to permit them to commute to the city for wage work held on to their small farms and made them an asset to the region.[12] Others, not so fortunate, were forced off the land. As their tracts came on the market the better ones were bought up by the wealthier farmers and consolidated into larger, more economically competitive tracts. The poorer lands were turned into bird and wildlife refuges or developed for recreational purposes by various state and federal agencies. But even those who had lost their lands continued to love them unabashedly. As one old man, interviewed in 1948, commented: "It is good to be able to see our old lands produce more with all that machinery!"[13]

Many of the dispossessed Middle Rio Grande Valley farmers drifted into the community of San Jose on the southern edge of Albuquerque. Here they found "cheap rents" in run down houses with broken, dilapidated, and inadequate furnishings. A fortunate few found jobs in the expanding national defense activities clustered around the municipal airport. Others depended upon WPA wage work to support their families. In an ironic footnote to the pre-New Deal educational experiment that had launched the Hispanic New Deal cultural agenda, a graduate student who studied the community in 1941 found virtually no trace of the San Jose Experimental School and was, apparently, only dimly aware that such a program had ever existed. She reported that San Jose parents were apathetic and resigned to a life of extreme poverty and economic insecurity. They had no hope of sending their children to high school. They did not even have resources sufficient to provide them with adequate clothing and transportation. San Jose parents had once supported school activities eagerly, she noted, contributing food and attending programs, but in 1941, six years after the end of the experiment, they had lost all hope that education could help them solve their economic problems. [14]

While some New Deal programs failed to help Hispanic farmers because they did not change any of the existing economic relationships, others failed precisely because they threatened to do so. In the Rio Puerco area, the negotiations initiated by the Interdepartmental Rio Grande Board to buy out the commercial livestock growers and establish a special grazing district for the exclusive use of the subsistence populations broke down during the latter half of 1940. At about the same time the Interdepartmental Rio Grande Board ceased to function as an administrative organization. [15] In February 1941 the Rio Puerco Land Use Planning Committee, composed of residents of the San Luis, Casa Salazar, Cabezon, and Guadalupe communities, met with BAE representative Andrew Cordova to find out what had happened to the land purchase and distribution program. Cordova informed them that, even though no legal or procedural problems prohibited the creation of a special grazing district, such a district would not be formed. Instead, the Rio Puerco area would become a precinct in a much larger district and would be subject to the same rules and regulations that governed other western grazing districts. As for the needed diversion dams, they were prohibitively expensive. The smaller project which called for the storage of surplus water for irrigation had still to be cleared through the State Engineer and the Rio Grande Compact Commission. [16] Pertinent to the irrigation problem, though Cordova did not mention it, was the fact that all such projects would soon have to be self-liquidating—an impossible requirement for the impoverished Rio Puerco communities.

Without a special grazing district most Rio Puerco sheepmen were limited to partido sharecropping. The Grazing Service, in awarding permits, emphasized prior or past use and commensurate property or water rights. The poorer sheepmen did not qualify on either count except for their use of the adjoining public or private lands as trespassers without leases. Unless rules and regulations were especially tailored to their circumstances they were effectively barred from using the federal grazing lands. [17]

They could, of course, still use the 260,000 acres of federally owned grant lands acquired specifically for their benefit by the Soil Conservation Service. These lands, however, were scattered throughout a total area of

715,000 acres of mixed ownership including private and railroad lands, public domain lands under the Department of the Interior's Grazing Service, state lands, Indian reservation lands, and the large area called "Indian Withdrawal Lands" that were without administration of any kind. Since none of the lands were fenced, all were subject to trespass by large commercial livestock operations. Besides the fact that the lands acquired by the Department of Agriculture for the so-called "subsistence" populations were entirely insufficient to meet their needs, even without stock reduction, there was no effective way to restrict them to noncommercial use.[18]

In the meantime, the Farm Security Administration subsistence grant program was being phased out in anticipation of its official termination in June of 1941. Because the Rio Puerco sheepmen could give the FSA no assurance that they would ever have adequate grazing resources to become economically independent they were ineligible for loans. Since they had, in the recent past, received FSA grants they were also ineligible for employment on the WPA-SCS road project. As a last resort the Rio Puerco villagers turned to the State Welfare Board. It denied their request for assistance for lack of funds. In the meantime, the families in the area were so poor that the children had to attend school with their feet wrapped in burlap sacks for lack of shoes.[19]

In February 1941 fifty angry and disillusioned Rio Puerco farmers piled into trucks and carried a petition for emergency aid directly to Governor John Miles. He ordered an investigation of the problem and in March held a special meeting to discuss its findings. The meeting included the representatives of all agencies on the Interdepartmental Rio Grande Board, the WPA, the State Department of Public Welfare, Miles's two investigators, and two members of Senator McCarran's public lands subcommittee. The transcript of the meeting revealed that Frank Bond, in accordance with the written agreement signed with the SCS in April 1940, had indeed removed many sheep from the area but, since he controlled the "checkerboard" railroad lands, he continued to use the alternating sections of federal land. As a result very little pressure had been removed from the range and the success of the plan hinged upon the government's ability to buy back the railroad property. Governor Miles concluded the conference by asking that a transcript be sent to each member of New Mexico's congressional delegation with the request that they, with the help of Senator McCarran's subcommittee, do all in their power to achieve a just solution to the Rio Puerco problem.[20]

The hoped for solution never came, though numerous state and federal officials attempted to mediate in favor of the dependent population. In 1942 the Soil Conservation Service proposed that all federally owned land in the eastern half of the Cuba–Rio Puerco area be consolidated under its administration. Arguing that the official demise of the Interdepartmental Rio Grande Board in the spring had left the area without any effective regulation, it declared itself to be the only federal agency with policies designed to benefit the resident subsistence population— policies which would allocate grazing use-rights strictly according to need. Since Soil Conservation Districts already existed, or were being formed throughout the area, consolidation of these lands would eliminate inefficient overlapping of jurisdiction and personnel.[21] Despite the forceful logic behind the proposal the exchange did not take place.

Early in 1943 the New Mexico Legislature tried to force a solution. A Senate Joint Memorial incorporated several resolutions to the effect that small cattlemen should be permitted more extensive grazing on the federally owned grant lands and that these grants should be dedicated exclusively to their use. The State action put the new regional director of the SCS, Cyril Luker, on the defensive. In a letter to Hugh Bennett he explained that the area was supporting all the livestock it could handle. If more operators were permitted on the range the SCS would have to reduce the number of animal units per family below the current average of fifteen head, further endangering the ability of any one family to derive a subsistence livelihood from livestock. Fifteen animal units per family, Luker declared, was already below the minimum needed for subsistence.[22]

Luker explained that, since the state action also affected Forest Service lands, he had discussed the problem at length with Frank Pooler, Regional Forester, and found that their views and findings coincided exactly. A month earlier Pooler had written about the matter to his superior in Washington, Earle H. Clapp, associate chief of the Forest Service. Clapp had just finished reading Sanchez's *Forgotten People* and Pooler outlined for him Forest Service efforts to help the Hispanic farmers and ranchers of northern New Mexico. The Bond case had finally been settled, Pooler declared, and the Bond Company permit in the Santa Fe National Forest had been reduced from 12,000 head of sheep in 1934 to 4,100 head in 1943. This reduction had enabled the Forest Service to increase small permittee use.

Timber in the forests went largely to small mill operations, Pooler continued, and there was a large volume of free use. Efforts were underway to acquire more land for the dependent populations through purchase or exchange, including sixteen thousand acres in the Tierra Amarilla and F. M. Vigil Grants. A great deal more land should be acquired for this purpose, Pooler explained, but public discussion of the matter would make consolidation of the forest holdings more difficult.[23]

The Forest Service, he continued, was currently attempting to exchange alternate sections of railroad land for Forest Service property in the area north of Mount Taylor. For over twenty-five years the Forest Service had managed the grazing use of these lands for the Railroad Company, but now the Railroad had decided to sell them to a large livestock owner. Fearing that this would dislocate the many small Spanish-American permittees who used these lands, Pooler had persuaded the purchaser to accept the division least harmful to them.[24]

Pooler explained that the Forest Service had provided employment and "desperately needed" transportation facilities for the Spanish American communities through its road program. While he was sure that there were more ways in which the Forest Service could help the rural population, such as helping the Farm Security Administration with its efforts to improve herd quality, Pooler was convinced that no complete solution was possible if the growing population continued to rely primarily on the region's limited natural resources. He hoped that better schooling, vocational training, and wartime travel would break down the isolationism of New Mexico's young people and enable them to seek opportunities elsewhere in the years ahead.[25]

It seems clear that the interest of New Mexico's intellectual and business elites in preserving the village population in the irrigated Upper Valley was not shared by the state's commercial ranching interests—at least not to the extent that it interfered with their use of the public lands. The reaction of the commercial wool and cattle growers to the decision of the Interdepartmental Rio Grande Board to evict them from the Rio Puerco lands in favor of the so-called subsistence peoples can only be imagined. They had little sympathy for the small and, to their mind, inefficiently run, Hispanic operations and their inability to pay taxes. Instead they fought for a consolidation of these holdings into commercial-sized units. And, while they claimed to understand the importance of not overgrazing, many were convinced that the soil erosion was simply the result of a cycle of aridity and that man was helpless in the face of a natural and inevitable process. Insisting that irreparable damage had already been inflicted upon the land during the Spanish and Mexican period, they concluded that it was useless for governmental agencies to undertake deliberate and expensive measures of resource control. Moreover, they were indebted to banks which had loaned them money and argued that they could not afford to reduce their herds.[26]

Resistance, first to Collier's, then to Calkins's and Shevky's, efforts to purchase grant lands for the exclusive use of the native population quickly became enmeshed in both a statewide and nationwide struggle for power between the United States Department of Agriculture, the Agricultural Extension Service, and the commercial farmers and ranchers represented by the American Farm Bureau.

The heart of the conflict, in New Mexico as elsewhere, concerned the concept of centralized planning and the communal use of land. While the former sounded to many farmers more like a bureaucracy than a democracy, the latter challenged the American assumption that the best possible use of land was in private, individual ownership. By late 1940 the American Farm Bureau was providing national leadership in a concerted attack upon the social scientists of the Department of Agriculture and their policies.[27]

The commercial farmers and ranchers in New Mexico found a ready ally in Director George M. Quesenberry of the State Agricultural Extension Service. Quesenberry, like other Extension Directors, had reason to resent USDA efforts to usurp his position of leadership in matters of state agricultural policy, and he shared the rancher's distaste for the policies of the Soil Conservation Service and the Farm Security Adminstration.[28]

The struggle for power found expression during 1937 and 1938 through the administration of New Mexico's Agricultural Conservation Program which was directed by a politically elected state committee. According to a report submitted to Governor John Miles by members of the De Baca County AAA Committee, the State Committee, with the tacit consent of Quesenberry, had encouraged farmers to carry out practices contrary to the rules and regulations set forth by the federal government. To regain control of the Agricultural Conservation Program, the AAA in 1939 eliminated the politically elected committee and gave the power to appoint state committeemen to the director of its Western Division. Retaliating, the Farm Bureau criticized the 1939 Agricultural Adminstration program for waste and inefficiency. It also passed a resolution at its state convention to the effect that state committeemen should be appointed by representative groups of farmers and ranchers throughout the state. The Farm Bureau resolution was widely interpreted as having been instigated by Director of Extension Quesenberry.[29]

Shortly after the Farm Bureau Convention the AAA presented an ultimatum to President Arthur Starr of the New Mexico State College Board of Regents. It would remove its offices to Albuquerque, it declared, unless the Board fired Quesenberry and appointed a new head of Extension Services. Starr called a meeting of prominent businessmen from the area who advised him to take whatever actions were necessary to prevent the removal of the AAA office from the State College. Quesenberry was fired and an acting director appointed to the position. Shortly thereafter a new man by the name of A. A. Fite was named head of the Extension Division. The Presidents of the State Farm Bureau, the New Mexico Cattle Growers' Association, the State Wool Growers' Association, and the New Mexico Crop Improvement Association, as well as various farmers from across the state, protested the action as politically motivated and unfair to Quesenberry.[30]

Quesenberry was out, but the end result may not have been without a margin of victory for New Mexico's commercial farmers and ranchers. One of the first tasks of the new State College–BAE committee, created in July 1940, was to review and revise on a county by county basis all land use planning maps and recommendations made in 1938, 1939, and 1940.[31] Shortly thereafter the Interdepartmental Rio Grande Board was ordered to suspend active operations, allegedly because of conditions created by the war. Although the Board was officially abolished only in spring 1942, no further publications were put out under either its aegis or that of the Soil Conservation Service Conservation Economics Series after August 1940.[32]

The concern of the commercial/ranching interests over federal land policies at the local level was echoed strongly at the national level where the powerful Western livestock and commercial farming interests lobbied effectively and were supported by such institutions as the United States Chamber of Commerce.[33] The commercial ranching interests had, in fact, won a partial victory over the New Deal in 1934 with the passage of the Taylor Grazing Act. The Act gave considerable control over the grazing lands to the states along with 50 percent of the grazing receipts, which were to be used by the state legislatures for the benefit of the counties in which the grazing districts were located. Another 25 percent of the receipts, when appropriated by Congress, was set aside for range improvement and management.[34] Since it was clearly to their advantage, many state interests supported the livestock lobby in urging an increase in grazing fees. Although no action was taken during the war years pressure on Congress continued and by 1947 Congress had voted to starve the Grazing Service into compliance by reducing its annual appropriations by 55 percent. The cut in funds had the desired effect of forcing the Grazing Service to increase grazing fees and reduce the allocated percentage of such fees to local communities. An amendment to the Department of the Interior Appropriations Act in August 1947 legalized the stockmen's claim that fees should be based on the cost of administration.[35]

Pressures were also applied to the Department of Agriculture to force it to release its control over the public lands administered by the Farm Security Adminstration, the Soil Conservation Service, and the Forest Service. Since most of these lands had been acquired under the Land Utilization program for the benefit of the dependent local population, the agencies resisted efforts to put the lands up for public sale. In 1943 when the Farm Security Administration was advised to liquidate its land holdings in the El Pueblo Experimental area and on the north half of the Juan Jose Lobato Grant, it sought to transfer them to another agency in the Department of Agriculture. Cyril Luker, Regional Conservator of the SCS in Albuquerque, was quick to apply on the basis that the SCS had been party to the cooperative agreement signed between the two agencies when the projects were initiated. He insisted, once again, that the SCS had policies better able to preserve the rights of the subsistence ranchers than any other agency. Glen Grisham, the Farm Security Administration's Special Area Supervisor, apparently thought otherwise. He had discussed the matter with Regional Forester, Frank Pooler, and concluded that the Forest Service was the agency best able to serve the interests of the local people. Grisham hoped, Pooler noted in a letter to his chief in Washington, that within one or two years the Forest Service would release control of the El Pueblo lands to a cooperative of local El Pueblo farmers which would manage the grazing lands along with a small sawmill operation.[36]

Three years passed while the FSA held up actual relinquishment of its lands and the stockmen escalated their campaign against the Department of Agriculture. In July 1946 Congress ordered the FSA to transfer its lands to another agency or sell them to the highest bidder. With time running out the FSA passed its lands on to the Forest Service which signed a Memorandum of Understanding to the effect that it would uphold the Land Utilization policies and the terms of the Bankhead-Jones Farm Tenant Act under which the lands had been acquired. Although aware at the time that the grazing receipts would not equal the costs of operation, the Forest Service agreed to subsidize them in the public interest. The transaction was completed in May 1950 under Secretary of Agriculture Clinton Anderson of New Mexico. Although all FSA properties were transferred to the Forest Service at that time, actual jurisdiction of the lands remained the responsibility of the Soil Conservation Service until November 1953, when that, too, was transferred to the Forest Service.[37]

Transfer of the FSA and SCS lands to the Forest Service may have mollified the commercial grazing interests but it did not satisfy their desire to regain control over the use of these lands. The lands had, after all, been acquired in trust to be used specifically for the purposes authorized—namely, the furtherance of rural rehabilitation in the State of New Mexico. The Forest Service, though less than totally enthusiastic with these terms, had agreed to them. Finally, Public Law 419, passed June 28, 1952, which incorporated the El Pueblo and north half of the Lobato Grants into the National Forest system, provided for their administration "with due regard to the purposes for which the land was originally acquired by the United States in its program of rural rehabilitation." It is not surprising then that pressure now shifted to the Forest Service to get it to dispose of its Rio Puerco and Northern New Mexico Grant lands.[38]

In August 1954 the Forest Service established a set of criteria to be used in determining whether its Land Utilization properties should be kept in federal ownership. Significantly, no mention was made of the government responsibility for the welfare of the dependent populations. The Department of the Interior requested, and was granted, transfer of the Cuba–Rio Puerco lands to the Bureau of Land Management, where they became subject to the rules of all western grazing districts. The Department of the Interior also requested, but was denied, the Rio Majada Grant. The greater part of the Northern New Mexico Grant lands remained under the management of the Forest Service.[39]

To the many New Mexicans, Hispanic and otherwise, who have come to see United States forest rangers as uniformed occupational troopers guarding the spoils of the Treaty of Guadalupe-Hidalgo, it will come as no surprise that the Forest Service subverted so soon the intentions of the Land Utilization program in whose trust its new lands had been acquired. It may more likely come as a surprise to know that these lands were taken into the Forest Service in full good faith by such men as Regional Forester Frank Pooler. The correspondence leaves no doubt that he sincerely believed that the lands would be dedicated to the continued benefit of the dependent Hispanic farmers. But Pooler, with the rest of New Mexico's New Deal reformers, passed from the scene and his influence, along with that of other colleagues of like mind in the Forest Service, was no longer felt. As early as March 1947 the Acting Forest Ranger at Vallecitos suggested that the policy of favoring local residents when allotting grazing and timber resources was a fallacy and should be changed in favor of the large operator. His superior, the Assistant Regional Forester in Albuquerque, apparently agreed, but warned against too rapid a change, stating:

> I wonder if we would not be charged with lack of faith in [not] continuing the policy objective of the Farmers' Home Administration [the new name given the Farm Security Administration]. At least any major change should be a slow process rather than to discontinue consideration of the poorer dependents.[40]

Among the many people who expressed concern over the future of the Land Utilization properties, Senator Dennis Chavez was one who favored their transfer to the Forest Service as preferable to their outright sale. He was assured in March 1952 that the Forest Service had carried out the trust conditions faithfully and that, if the properties were given full national forest status, the recommendations and needs of the local communities would be given careful consideration before any changes were effected. At the same time the Chief of the Forest Service informed the president of the New Mexico Cattle Growers Association that:

> No policies have been contemplated which would do other than take care of present small permittees. The proposed legislation itself provides for the administration of the Lobato and El Pueblo tracts in accordance with the objectives for which they were originally acquired by the Federal Government.

Whether these assurances were written in good faith or not, policies within the Forest Service during the 1960s shifted from a major concern with range management and soil conservation to profits from timber and recreation. In the process grazing fees were raised and the local inhabitants gradually displaced by larger commercial livestock and timber operations. In September 1962 the terms of Title III of the Bankhead-Jones Farm Tenant Act were amended to bring the administration of all Land Utilization properties in line with the rules and regulations applying to other National Forest lands.[42] This act of Congress effectively dismantled the last remnants of the Hispanic New Deal.

Plans to aid the subsistence farmers of the Upper Rio Grande Valley during the 1930s and early 1940s suffered from the same delays and obstacles as those of the Rio Puerco area and the Middle Rio Grande Valley but, since the population was more stable and the economy more diversified, the villagers did not suffer the same degree of dislocation. One incident from late in the period reveals another aspect of the political climate in the state. It concerns the village of Amalia near the Colorado–New Mexico border.

During the late 1930s land speculation reached the Amalia Valley in the person of Thomas B. Campbell, referred to in the press as the "Montana Wheat King." Campbell determined to buy up 128,000 acres of tax delinquent land at auction for the bargain price of $55,000—the amount owed for back taxes. According to the August 7, 1941 edition of the *Taoseño and Taos Review* he planned to bring in "the latest scientific farming machinery" and turn the area into a vast sugar beet farm. He also planned to build a refinery for processing the beets in the neighboring village of Costilla.[43]

The Amalia and Costilla families organized against the threat to their lands and appealed for political help to Senator Dennis Chavez. They also set up the Rio Costilla Livestock Association and applied to the Farm Security Administration for a tenant purchase loan with which to buy back their land from the state for the taxes owed on it. The FSA, in its report recommending the loan, stated that: "The trend of agricultural resources falling into the hands of large commercial operators is not regarded as conducive to a sound agricultural economy, or a virile citizenship." It urged government at all levels to "assist in the acquisition of land resources for the resident population who are dependent on those resources for a livelihood." The report recommended that the people of the Amalia Valley be given loans and grants to allow for the purchase of necessary equipment and noted that the valley farmers had been able to survive before they were deprived of their grazing lands by the large commercial enterprises on the national forests.[44]

The aid from the Farm Security Administration enabled the Amalia farmers to pay their taxes and forestall Campbell's grandiose plans. His reaction can only be imagined, but a month later George Quesenberry, the ousted State Extension Director, now living in Taos, reported what he considered to be suspicious political behavior on the part of an Amalia resident to the El Paso field office of the Federal Bureau of Investigation. FBI Director J. Edgar Hoover took up the matter and, in a letter to Matthew F. McGuire, assistant to the Attorney General, declared that:

> Mr. Quesenberry said that the entire [FSA] program appeared to be one that was Communistically inspired with the idea in mind of obtaining control of large tracts of land and operating them on the Communistic idea of property being held by the state. . . .

Shortly thereafter FBI agents visited the home of Alex Ortega, one of the leaders of the Amalia community who had applied for the FSA loan, and ransacked his house in search of incriminating evidence. Needless to say, they found none.[45]

The fear that many state and federal programs, especially those concerned with land and welfare programs for low-income families, were communistically inspired was apparently widespread throughout New Mexico in the final years of the New Deal. In 1938 when professors Arthur Campa and George Sanchez announced plans to hold the First National Congress of Spanish-Speaking Peoples in the United States at the University of New Mexico, they were vilified as radicals and communists. The matter eventually came to the attention of the House Un-American Activities Committee, which forced the University to withdraw its support. According to Allan Harper, the executive director of the defunct Interdepartmental Rio Grande Board, and two of his colleagues in the BAE, Andrew Cordova and Kalervo Oberg, state and federal agents were often caught in a difficult bind. Those who pushed for the rights of the underprivileged people of New Mexico were labeled "Reds," while those who expressed concern for the interests of the businessman, the commercial farmer, or the livestock man, were accused of being "reactionaries." Most federal officials, in Harper's opinion, were independent of mind and able to resist the kinds of political pressures that restricted the activities of state officials.[46]

Thus a variety of forces at both the national and local level in the early 1940s brought a change of direction to the programs that had been aimed at helping the poorest farmers and solving the problems of regional rural poverty. In New Mexico the demise of the Interdepartmental Rio

Grande Board was symptomatic of the change in political climate. It signaled the end of the ideological fervor of the early New Deal and the decline of influence of the state's intellectual elites. It is perhaps not surprising that the change coincided with the expiration of the Santa Fe and Taos art colonies.

By the early 1940s many of the colonies' leaders, especially those whose intellectual and political roots lay in the pre–World War I progressive movement, were dead. Those who were left found their vigor and enthusiasm sapped by the intransigency of the depression and United States involvement in World War II. However even those who continued to speak for the old values discovered that they no longer wielded the same influence. Their fellow citizens, who had long tolerated and indulged them because of their economic value, primarily as tourist attractions, came to resent this collective dictatorship, particularly when it appeared to impinge upon their own welfare. Instead of dominating local politics and Chamber of Commerce activities, the artist/intellectuals were excluded from planning commissions and other decision-making bodies. Unable to play their preferred role as a social action force and group conscience directing and influencing change, they withdrew from social and political involvement and retreated to the safe haven of artistic and professional circles.[47]

If the Hispanic New Deal broke down due to the withdrawal of federal funding, the decline of local support, and a strongly conservative backlash at both the state and national levels, the question remains: would it have succeeded had these factors not interfered? Again, we can get some insights by examining the continuing history of the New Deal projects.

The Amalia Valley of the Upper Rio Grande appeared to be a New Deal success story. Through the FSA the small subsistence farmers bought back their communal grazing lands on the Sangre de Cristo Grant in spite of the efforts of "Montana Wheat King" Campbell to dispossess them. But the end of FSA support brought renewed problems. The small farms were still unable to supply all of the needs of their owners. Without the supplemental wage labor that had been provided prior to the depression by a local sawmill, the farmers were forced to migrate in search of work. The farms continued to be a source of stability keeping families together and providing a sense of home, but they deteriorated for lack of consistent attention. Nor could the Amalia farmers compete during the late 1940s and 1950s with the commercial farmers in the area. They could neither afford the new efficient machinery nor produce on the same scale. Falling farther and farther behind, many families left the Valley permanently. As they sold out more commercial farmers moved in. The core of families left behind to guard the village patrimony lacked both the numbers and the vitality to maintain cohesive and communal village life.[48]

The New Mexico Special Area project at El Pueblo was another apparent New Deal success story, but after 1947 permits on the El Pueblo allotment were reduced by 31 percent. Still later the Forest Service moved the allotment from well-watered pasture to an area with no water, with the result that the villagers had to reduce their stock even further or lose them through death. As grazing fees increased the members of the local grazing association were unable to pay the fee for their full allotment of permits. Still they continued to graze a few cows on their range, which permitted them to eat if not derive a cash income.[49]

The Taos County Project was surely the Hispanic New Deal's greatest success with its ambitious and important Taos County Cooperative Health Association. Incorporated in June 1942, the association got off to an auspicious start. The medical director was respected by Anglos and Hispanos alike. He and his nurses liked the Hispanic people with whom they worked and were willing to make house calls in any kind of weather. The nurses were accepted with pride by the communities in which they worked and, in general, there was a warm feeling of good will throughout the program.[50]

However Taos County decreased 7.5 percent in population between 1940 and 1950 as almost 50 percent of the adult Hispanic males left in search of employment. When the Farm Security Administration terminated its grant funding of the association there were not enough members to support it. Charges had always been minimal but those who had signed up first paid the least. Those who joined later were assessed at a higher rate and these differences became a source of controversy.[51]

There were other problems as well. The medical personnel in Taos opposed the association as the start of socialized medicine. The Hispanos were not only suspicious of any Anglo introduced scheme because of bitter past experience, but they had different attitudes toward illness and medical care. Many distrusted hospitals where they were subjected to impersonal treatment, strange food, and immodest procedures, and put their faith in the people whose cures had often worked in the past— the local *curanderos* and *albolarios* whom they knew personally. Most, however, dropped out of the association for purely pragmatic reasons. With so little disposable income they could not afford to pay for medical care, especially when it was required in advance of any illness. Those who lived far from the available facilities knew that they would not likely benefit from them. The association was dissolved in August 1947, and in 1949 the Clinic closed its doors for good. Founded with such high hopes, it foundered upon the utter poverty of the people it served, and because it had never been integrated into their everyday lives. Without funding and support from the outside it could not sustain itself.[52]

Unquestionably, many of the reasons for failure lay in the ways the programs were perceived by the Hispanic villagers. In Taos, as elsewhere in northern New Mexico, the Hispanic population was highly selective in its acceptance or rejection of New Deal programs. When they met well-defined needs and were free of onerous and suspicious obligations they were welcomed. The teaching of English and the skills of conducting business operations with the Anglo population were *always* well received because of their immediate practical application. In communities where Anglo efforts to revive Hispanic arts and crafts, songs, stories, and religious plays fitted into a growing consciousness of Hispanic ethnicity, these programs were greeted as a visible sign of Hispanic cultural worth and equality. When, as in more economically distressed communities, they seemed to be little more than a distraction from the more vital concerns of physical survival and the preservation of family and village lands, they were dismissed as essentially irrelevant. The CCC, NYA, and WPA programs, which replaced wage labor and provided a vitally needed source of cash, were extremely popular. Without them it is doubtful whether many communities could have survived the crisis of the depression as nearly intact as they did.

The benefits of the WPA were the best known and most sought after of all government programs, and Hispanos used both regular procedures and unethical means to gain certification on a project. WPA projects enabled workers to receive livable wages and families to return to something like the old pattern of living. Best of all, WPA labor entailed no obligations that could threaten personal or family possessions. In contrast, most Hispanos considered farmers who had borrowed money for feed and seeds to be examples of what not to do. Despite public opinion, workers did not make more money on WPA projects than they did in private industry or doing farm work, especially when such work involved two or more members of the family. As one worker explained:

> WPA jobs just let you live. I can only work about three months at a time, then I am turned off for awhile. All of my money has gone for clothes and to buy something to eat. I have tried to save, and we have tried to reduce the food bill, but with a large family we can't do either.

While Hispanos were often reluctant to accept seasonal work from private sources, their hesitation usually derived from a fear of not being reemployed on a WPA project when the seasonal work ended. Under different circumstances they were willing to travel long distances to localities where wages in private industry were better than the wages offered locally in order to improve their financial condition.[53]

In general Hispanos appreciated the opportunities to conserve and improve the land, just as they appreciated aid to older people and incapacitated dependents, but they knew that when the aid was discontinued they would be no better off than when the aid began. Most would have preferred, by far, to return to their old independent status. They worried that things given free would sap all initiative, particularly among their young people, but feared to criticize the government programs because of the general feeling that they were expected to be humbly accepting and appreciative. In the meantime, since true independence was impossible, they pragmatically did everything possible to keep in power those who promised government grants and jobs.[54]

Anacleto Garcia Apodaca, a Farm Security Administration field agent in the Tewa Basin, studied Hispanic perceptions of the New Deal agricultural programs in 1951 as part of a doctoral study for Cornell University. He found that most Hispanic farmers considered them to be good to excellent. Many had received outright grants during the years such grants were available. Others had received loans and, although they accepted them as emergency measures only, were grateful because they had helped them through hard times, enabled them to buy needed equipment, and had low interest rates with a long pay-out period. Farmers who had participated in soil conservation programs saw the benefits to their farms and appreciated the fact that they were able to do work that they could not otherwise have afforded. They wanted to do more but lacked the means to buy or rent the necessary equipment—and wished that loans or grants would have been available for this purpose. Without these resources many had no choice but to continue to use older, less efficient methods which did not tax their meager cash resources. In all of the programs the farmers would have preferred less paper work and more convenient evening hours for those who could not visit agency offices during the day.[55]

A major reason for the failure of the federal programs to accomplish what they intended undoubtedly lay in the ways that the programs were administered, and Apodaca had a number of criticisms on this account. The federal agricultural programs, he believed, had failed to reach the poorest farmers just as they had failed to take into consideration cultural differences. Anglo field agents unfamiliar with Hispanic culture often interpreted resistance to programs as a sign of ignorance. They failed to adjust their activities to the interests and schedules of the people or consider how the changes they wished to introduce might affect traditional status relationships. The only concession made to Hispanic culture by any of the federal agencies, he declared, was the employment of persons, like himself, who knew the Spanish language and understood the local culture. Agency heads assumed that such employees would make whatever modifications they deemed necessary but, since these modifications were never institutionalized, or even officially incorporated into the program, they were of limited value. New agents, who came to New Mexico from other parts of the country still picked up deleterious generalizations concerning Hispanos from other Anglos and carried them into their work without question. The most common generalizations were that Hispanos were not interested in their own betterment, as evidenced by their poor attendance at meetings and demonstrations; that Hispanos had to break away completely from their culture to be successful; and that they wanted so much to live as their forefathers did that they would not accept modern improvements. Once having accepted these generalizations, Apodaca contended, the agents made fewer efforts to reach and help Hispanos than they did to help Anglos.[56]

Field personnel who wanted sincerely to help the poorer farmers often had to do so at a sacrifice to their careers. Low income Hispanic farmers were beset with limitations that left them powerless to follow recommended practices even when they completely agreed with them. Since field personnel were judged solely on their ability to increase agricultural productivity, time spent with them yielded few professional or financial rewards. Not surprisingly most agents preferred to work with higher income groups where their efforts resulted in measurable improvements. The Hispanic farmers, sensitive and resentful of the obvious inequalities in the programs, tended to suspect the depth and sincerity of the federal commitment and withheld full acceptance and cooperation.[57]

Finally, and most importantly, Apodaca argued, the programs for Hispanos in New Mexico failed to address the major problem of the area—the lack of real opportunity. Recommendations made by investigators were not followed, especially those calling for a long-range program of economic rehabilitation. In spite of demonstrated need, he believed that much too little had been done to increase the land base, improve the irrigation systems, and record the titles to ditch community systems.[58]

Glen Grisham, FSA Supervisor for New Mexico's ten-county special experimental area, echoed many of Apodaca'a criticisms and added a few more in an April 1942 report to the FSA Area Director. Grisham objected to the fact that the methods used by the FSA failed to develop community and individual responsibility.

> In our impatience to get the job done we push our goals so strongly that even though they [the Hispanic farmers] generally cooperate, they see themselves as helping *us* with *our* program. Furthermore, we have so many regulations and directives it is strange that we expect people to believe that *they* are directing and operating the program.

The local leaders in Taos County, Grisham noted, knew that the Health Program had to develop slowly. They preferred to postpone action for two to three or four years and get something sound that would continue indefinitely rather than pressing too hard and "turning the thing sour."[59]

Supervisors, Grisham reported, spent so much time filling out paper work with their clients that the clients got the impression that the FSA's sole interest was to keep its papers in order. No county supervisor could convince a native farmer that the paper work required for his loan was for *his* protection and not ultimately to take his land.

> We spend too much time on details like the number of sanitary toilets rather than on the total picture and long range effectiveness of our program. If our job is to restore ranching opportunities to people despoiled of their grazing lands and crowded onto small irrigated patches we haven't found that way yet and until we do, many of our efforts in this area will continue to yield superficial results.

Grisham's letter was forwarded to C. B. Baldwin, the national administrator of the Farm Security Administration in Washington, D.C. with a memorandum praising his work and commending his observations, but, as Grisham, himself, might have predicted, nothing came of his recommendations.

Finally, the programs failed because they did not, and probably could not, anticipate the complex ways in which American rural life was changing, and the ways it would be affected by the post-War technology. What happened in Taos and Amalia was true throughout northern New Mexico. In a general sense it was true as well throughout much of the rest of rural America.

When the sudden curtailment of supplementary wage labor brought home the full impact of the undermining of the Hispanic community land base, the implementation of government relief programs did no more than postpone the inevitable adjustments required of the local population. By replacing wages for migrant labor with wages for public works projects, the programs averted widespread starvation, and introduced a number of welcome amenities into the villages. Some programs even promised to return parts of the old grant lands to their Hispanic owners. However neither the control of the programs nor the free ownership of the lands was turned over to the farmers themselves. They, perforce, remained dependent upon agents and agencies they could neither direct nor fully understand, and upon a money economy in which they could not fully participate. Even more seriously, the money for the wages and the programs did not derive from any development intrinsic to northern New Mexico. It was, by its very nature, no more than an artificial and temporary infusion.

In the meantime, the stress of the New Deal programs upon the individualization of achievement and security completed the undermining of the old communal patterns that had stood the villagers in such good stead during their previous two hundred-odd years of residence in the Southwest. Anthropologist Charles Briggs has argued persuasively that the productivity of the Hispano system was predicated upon its corporate nature, expressed in an obligation to share. The individualization and secularization of production, the individual acquisition of wealth, and the market regulation of land and labor delivered the *coup de grace* to Hispanic self-sufficiency. When, during the latter days of the New Deal and especially during World War II, great numbers of men and boys of working age left rural New Mexico, the future of Hispanic village agriculture was all but sealed. The women and children left at home to tend the fields and livestock had either to hire assistance in the fields with cash wages or reduce production. In either event productivity, and cash resources, suffered. Unable to make their small farms pay, countless families sold out and moved on to cities where opportunities existed for wage labor. Other families, reluctant to give up family lands, or unable to sell them for lack of a clear title, abandoned them to the weeds.[61]

After 1940, in New Mexico and elsewhere throughout the United States, there was a massive increase in agricultural technology. Since it was very costly and could only be incorporated profitably into the production processes of the larger farms, small farmers found it almost impossible to compete. Those who tried were often wiped out by their own debts. Their difficulties, added to the fact that many veterans of wartime service and defense industry had become accustomed to a life of greater affluence and excitement than that offered in the rural countryside, led many to seek employment in other, primarily urban, areas. Between 1940 and 1960 the number of individuals employed in agricultural production in New Mexico fell from 40 percent to less than 10 percent, while the total rural population declined almost 30 percent. During the same years nearly twenty thousand New Mexico farms "vanished," most of them swallowed up in the process of consolidation, as indicated by the threefold increase in the size of the average farm.[62]

At the same time that an increase in agricultural technology was putting small farmers out of business, an increase in the mechanization of farm industry reduced much of the need for seasonal migrant labor. Spurred by the manpower shortages and technological developments of World War II, many farmers turned to machines to do the work of men. For those jobs in the Southwest that still required arduous hand labor there was, as before, a pool of workers in Mexico willing to work at the lowest wages and under the most deplorable conditions. In either case New Mexico's Hispanic villagers found their employment options severely limited.[63]

The exodus of New Deal money from the Upper Rio Grande Valley, unaccompanied by a renewed demand for supplementary wage labor, left the area as poor as it had been at the beginning of the Depression. Just as in the 1920s, taxes remained high in proportion to income and tax revenues were entirely inadequate to the job of providing public services, particularly in the impoverished northern counties.[64] With the old multisource economy irreparably gone and Hispanic corporate community and independence shattered, the society that remained was far from the revitalized traditional one envisioned by the New Deal reformers.

What emerged in New Mexico in its stead was a dependent society heavily converted to and desirous of the material conveniences of a twentieth-century life-style, residing in a pocket of regional poverty that provided very few opportunities for its residents to earn these benefits for themselves. In the end, nothing had been done to change the fact that northern New Mexico was, as it had been from the beginning of the seventeenth century, a colony tangential to and economically dependent upon the industrially developed world. Fortunately for the employment situation in the northern counties, the United States government provided a continuing source of federal employment in the Los Alamos weapons research laboratory, a burgeoning institution offering a variety of manual, clerical, technical, and professional jobs.

Having seen what went wrong, it is time, at last, to ask *why* it went so wrong and if, in the final analysis, there were any gains. Quite simply, the Hispanic New Deal failed because it cut across the grain of American social and economic orthodoxy. It was cut off at the source, along with other Department of Agriculture community programs, when the nation became aware that to have the benefits of organization and centralization it had to be willing to sacrifice a measure of individual opportunity and open competition. The reluctance to make this sacrifice, as historian Ellis Hawley has pointed out, has forever plagued American reform.[65]

The Hispanic New Deal was cut off at the state level because there it even more strongly threatened the capitalist ethic and New Mexico's established sources of economic power. Only Utopian idealists like Collier, Shevky, and Calkins could have imagined that the powerful, Anglo-dominated cattle and sheep industry would allow itself to be displaced and "bought out" in favor of "subsistence" Hispanic villagers—or that ambitious entrepreneurs like Bernardino Hovey would accept conditions that limited Hispanic participation in the American free enterprise system. That they did so can only mean that they assumed a false homogeneity in the Hispanic community, and that they failed utterly to take into consideration New Mexico's complex social and political history—mistakes they made as well in the Indian New Deal.[66]

The Hispanic New Deal failed because it tried to turn back the clock and reverse the dominant trends in American history. Despite its claims to being liberal it was actually very conservative. Where the consistent long-term trend in American agriculture had been toward private ownership and land speculation, the Hispanic New Deal sought to institute communalism. Where it had been toward the consolidation of land holdings in the cause of greater productivity and efficiency, the Hispanic New Deal endeavored to preserve New Mexico's small, subsistence farms and family herds. Where the trend had been toward the centralization and mechanization of industry, the Hispanic New Deal tried to revive village hand crafts. Where the trend had been toward individual initiative, the Hispanic New Deal urged centralized planning.

The Hispanic New Deal failed because, true to its romantic origins, it was Janus-faced. It endeavored to preserve a preindustrial, nineteenth-century life-style based upon village values for Hispanic farmers while it tried to convert them to the twentieth-century cult of industrial efficiency. While it argued mistakenly that New Mexico's Hispanic farmers could remain economically independent if they were permitted and, in fact, required to live on a subsistence level, it successfully introduced and educated them to a more abundant life-style. While it intended to keep Hispanos "down on the farm" it gave them the education and the experiences that would make rural life for many less and less attractive and satisfying.

In short, the Hispanic New Deal tried to produce an "economic man" who would not desire profits; one who was independent and resourceful enough to assume responsibility for his own "rehabilitation," but who would not make decisions contrary to the plans of the federal agents who controlled his destiny; one who would draw upon his "native creativity" but who would not develop his own ideas; one who would strive to improve himself but who would remain content with little.

Most of all, the Hispanic New Deal failed to come to grips with the realities of a changing world. It could not stabilize Hispanic subsistence farmers on the land when a technological revolution in agriculture would soon make all but the largest and most mechanized farms obsolete. Neither could it hold Hispanic farmers in a nineteenth-century village existence once it had introduced a revolution of rising expectations through its own efforts at social engineering. It was extremely unrealistic to expect the Anglo mainstream to approve the subsidized, collective farms and policies which were intended to sustain Hispanic farmers at a subsistence level of living, but it was even more unrealistic to expect the farmers, themselves, to forfeit control over their lives for the well meaning but paternalistic and Utopian schemes of the government planners. Far more practical than the sociological reformers, they regarded the New Deal programs with the skepticism that they deserved.

The New Deal, criticized from the 1930s through the 1950s as a radical, un-American experiment in government intervention bordering dangerously on communism, has been more recently damned as the ploy of a conservative administration to give just enough aid to the poor to avoid social upheaval while preserving the basic tenets of capitalism. The Hispanic New Deal has been subject to the same general criticisms, and has been charged specifically with enclosing and perpetuating a distinct Hispanic culture within its village heartland in order to keep Hispanic workers in a seasonal laboring class. Was it then, as suggested, the "ultimate Anglo conquest"?[67]

There is no doubt that the programs were paternalistic, anachronistic, and Utopian. They were no more than "a drop in the bucket," and they halted neither the steady loss of Hispanic lands nor their steady depletion by erosion, for more than a moment in time. They certainly did not restore prosperity to northern New Mexico, revitalize its traditional culture, or restore economic independence to its people. But it would be naive to suppose that any program could have righted wrongs, stopped processes, and changed attitudes that had been generations in forming in the space of less than a decade. What they did do was to make an honest effort to understand and correct the causes of chronic rural poverty, and they did, at the very least, save New Mexico's Hispanic farmers from outright starvation during the worst crisis in their history.

In the implementation of its cultural agenda the Hispanic New Deal introduced many villagers, not only to English and business arithmetic, but to the prospects and potentialities of formal education. It provided many villages which had never had them with school buildings and teachers, giving their resident adults a second chance to learn the skills essential to survival in twentieth-century society. In the process these villagers were gratified to discover that they were no longer "forgotten people" but had, in fact, acquired a special value in the eyes of the dominant Anglo culture—for why else would so many Anglos make such a concerted effort to reach them, teach them, and learn from them? Not only they, but their culture had acquired a new acceptance. Their Spanish language was pronounced beautiful. So were their traditional songs and stories and crafts, which were briefly made a part of the new village school curriculum. Their historic religious arts, so long denigrated as crude and ugly, were praised as expressions of great sensitivity. Though paternalistically inspired to be sure, these efforts, while they lasted, must have brought a healthy message of cultural acceptance and collective worth to a people who had too long been treated as the spoils of conquest.

The Hispanic New Deal contributed in other, unanticipated, ways to the growth of Hispanic ethnic awareness. By giving the Hispanic villagers better communication skills and a sympathetic hearing it encouraged them to articulate their needs in the form of letters, petitions, and demonstrations. By giving them programs unsuited to their needs or denying them equal access to their benefits, it contributed to their sense of group identity and strengthened their long tradition of standing up forcefully for their rights within the American system.

On a more pragmatic level, the Hispanic New Deal introduced the knowledge and the facilities necessary to combat the problems of endemic disease among humans, and of soil erosion on the land. It provided villagers with practical new methods of farming and introduced their young people to skills which, during and after the war, translated into broadened opportunities for economic advancement, if not in New Mexico, then beyond the state's boundaries. Most of all, it helped the villagers to complete their transition to a money economy and a modernized life-style based upon competition and market values—not a desired or desirable outcome from the point of view of the New Deal planners, or of many of the Hispanic elders, but an essential one given the direction of mainstream American society.[68]

The New Deal agricultural planners in New Mexico, though they failed to accomplish their goal of a new and more equitable relationship between human and natural resources, must certainly be numbered among the more innovative and humanistic thinkers of their time. It is an enduring testimony to their vision that many of the remedies they proposed were revived almost intact during the 1960s federal War on Poverty. Such New Deal agency officials as the Farm Security Administration's Glen Grisham could only have been gratified to see the extent to which the 1960s reformers involved local residents in the planning, direction, and implementation of their community action programs in this second New Deal go-around.[69]

Finally, the Hispanic New Deal helped to preserve the physical existence of many Hispanic villages in northern New Mexico. Let there be no doubt that the villages survived the depression, and the social and economic changes in the years following, because of the determination of the villagers to preserve their historic patrimony. No amount of federal funding could have accomplished that goal without their dedication to the cause. However even this amount of dedication might have been insufficient had their residents not been enabled to remain in their homes and on their lands through the timely introduction of federal relief programs. These programs brought a morale building source of employment rather than charity and an infusion of cash and credit. They introduced the opportunity and the resources to repair and upgrade irrigation systems, improve land and livestock, and revitalize village life. They provided roads and transportation, and eventually even electricity, to link the villages socially and economically to the urban centers and pave the way, quite literally, for the commuter society of today. By doing so these programs averted the widespread social disorganization and abandonment of village lands that almost certainly would have occurred otherwise.

These villages survive today as a continuing focus of Hispanic ethnic identity, for those who remain to tend the land, for those who commute daily to jobs in Los Alamos, Santa Fe, and Albuquerque, and for those who, though separated from their ancestral home by time and space, continue to support it with gifts and money, and return to it for visits and for family and community celebrations.

The regional community, despite its temporary collapse during the dark years of the Great Depression, also survives, but in changed form from its late nineteenth- and early twentieth-century origins. No longer a strategy of autonomous cultural survival, it has become a means by which today's Hispanos, no matter how long removed and distant from their village origins, retain a sense of cultural/ethnic identity. As before, it is largely the Hispanic women who sustain the regional community. Through a regular pattern of visiting within the extended family, and by encouraging family attendance at special village functions, they maintain the kinship ties that unite Hispanos from as far away as Wyoming and California with their New Mexican villages of origin.[70]

To the extent that the New Deal helped preserve, and even foster, this sense of ethnic identity, either through its programs or through its confrontations, that may be its most enduring legacy. For all its failings, it must be regarded as a uniquely humanistic moment in the history of Hispanic American relations in the American Southwest.

# Notes

## Introduction

1. John Higham, *Strangers in the Land: Patterns of American Nativism, 1860–1925* (New York: Atheneum, 1963); John Higham, *Send These to Me: Jews and Other Immigrants in Urban America* (New York: Atheneum, 1975).

2. Higham, *Send These to Me,* 232–36.

3. George I. Sanchez, *Forgotten People: A Study of New Mexicans* (Albuquerque: University of New Mexico Press, 1940).

4. Carlos E. Cortés, "New Chicano Historiography" in Ellwyn P. Stoddard, Richard L. Nostrand, and Jonathan P. West, eds., *Borderlands Sourcebook: A Guide to the Literature on Northern Mexico and the American Southwest* (Norman: University of Oklahoma Press, 1983), 60–63.

5. Otis L. Graham, Jr., "The Age of the Great Depression, 1929–1940," in William Holmes Cartwright and Richard L. Watson, eds., *The Reinterpretation of American History and Culture* (Washington, D.C.: National Council for the Social Studies, 1973), 497, 500.

6. Ibid., 502.

## Chapter One

1. John Francis Bannon, *The Spanish Borderlands Frontier, 1513–1821* (Albuquerque: University of New Mexico Press, 1979), 79–85.

2. Although no statistical study has been made of the decline of the native Indian population in the Southwest following first European contact, enough evidence exists to suggest that the area suffered a demographic collapse similar to that experienced, and amply documented, in Mexico and on the Eastern seaboard.

3. Michael C. Meyer, *Water in the Hispanic Southwest: A Social and Legal History, 1550–1850* (Tucson: University of Arizona Press, 1984), 47–55, 145–57, 161–64; John Van Ness, "Hispanos in Northern New Mexico: The Development of Corporate Community and Multicommunity" (Ph.D. dissertation, University of Pennsylvania, 1979), 166–70.

4. National Resources Committee, "Regional Planning, Part IV—Upper Rio Grande," February 1938, 7, Land and Water Facilities Reports, NMSRCA.

5. D. W. Meinig, *Southwest: Three Peoples in Geographical Change, 1600–1970* (New York: Oxford University Press, 1971), 103.

6. Kenneth R. Weber, "Rural Hispanic Village Viability from an Economic and Historic Perspective" in Paul Kutsche, ed., *The Survival of Spanish American Villages* (Colorado Springs: Colorado College, Research Committee Series No. 15, Spring, 1979), 79–84, argues that the villages lack economic viability. Paul Kutsche and John Van Ness, *Cañones: Values, Crises, and Survival in a Northern New Mexico Village* (Albuquerque: University of New Mexico Press, 1981) disagree. They found Cañones in 1967 to be very much intact, socially and economically. Some villages have obviously fared better than others due to such factors as the degree of isolation, the desirability and accessibility of their lands to Anglo farmers and land speculators, and the proximity of opportunities or wage labor.

7. David J. Weber, "Editor's Introduction," in David J. Weber, ed., *Foreigners in Their Native Land: Historical Roots of the Mexican Americans* (Albuquerque: University of New Mexico Press, 1973), 141–42.

8. Stephen Watts Kearny, "Their property, their persons, their religion," "All the rights of citizens—The Treaty of Guadalupe-Hidalgo, 1848" in Weber, *Foreigners*, 161–68.

9. Weber, "Editor's Introduction," 142; Malcolm Ebright, "New Mexican Land Grants: The Legal Background," in Charles L. Briggs and John Van Ness, eds., *Land, Water, and Culture* (Albuquerque: University of New Mexico Press, 1987), 16–64, provides an excellent legal analysis of land grant litigation and concludes that the United States failed to discharge its obligations under the Treaty of Guadalupe-Hidalgo for lack of a clear and consistent standard for adjudicating the validity of Spanish and Mexican land grants.

10. U.S., Department of Agriculture, Soil Conservation Service, "Population of the Upper Rio Grande Watershed," Regional Bulletin No. 43, Conservation Economics Series, No. 16, July 1937, 1. Mimeographed monograph, MNM-LA.

11. Ibid., 1–3, 6–7. Seven population groups were listed in the 1930 Census: Native White, native parentage; Native White, foreign or mixed parentage; Foreign-born White; Negro; Mexican; Indian; and Japanese, Chinese, Filipino, etc. This was the first year in which "Mexican" was listed as a separate, nonwhite category and, judging from an editorial in *La Bandera Americana* (20 March 1930), a Spanish-language newspaper published in Albuquerque, New Mexico, Hispanos were highly incensed at the implied slight to their "whiteness." The editorial declared that:

> Those who enumerate the people of this region should be given to understand that our "race," the Spanish American, is Caucasian, and should thus be listed in taking the Census. They [the census takers] should be permitted to classify us in no other way. We are as white as the whitest of our late-arriving cousins [the Anglo Americans] who now wish to be our superiors.

The issue was such a touchy one in New Mexico that census takers asked to have the category removed from the census forms. A space was left vacant and was filled in later by the census taker according to his or her personal judgment (see Chapter Six). Because New Mexican Hispanos resisted being listed separately from Anglo Americans it was very difficult to determine their numbers in the total state population. Several surveys made by the Soil Conservation Service calculated their numbers based on estimates prepared by the State Health Bureau which, in turn, had based them upon county school censuses made in 1932 and 1933.

12. David J. Weber, "Editor's Introduction," 145, 155–56; Rodolfo Acuña, *Occupied America: A History of Chicanos,* 2nd ed. (New York: Harper and Row, 1981), 40.

13. Acuña, *Occupied America,* 31, 40.

14. Weber, "Editor's Introduction," 148–52. Leonard Pitt, *The Decline of the Californios: A Social History of the Spanish Speaking Californians, 1846–1869* (Berkeley: University of California Press, 1968), Chapter 3.

15. Acuña, *Occupied America,* 98–104.

16. Weber, "Editor's Introduction," 144; Acuña, *Occupied America,* 73–83.

17. Reuben W. Heflin, "The New Mexico Constitutional Convention," *NMHR,* 21 (January 1946): 60–68; Constitution of New Mexico, Article II, Sec. 5, Article VII, Sec. 3, and Article VII, Sec. 8 and 10, in *Constitutions of the United States: National and State* (New York: 1962), 7, 25–26, 37.

18. Sarah Deutsch, *No Separate Refuge: Culture, Class, and Gender on an Anglo-Hispanic Frontier in the American Southwest, 1880–1940* (New York: Oxford University Press, 1987), 31–39.

19. Ibid., 60–62.

20. U.S., Department of Agriculture, Soil Conservation Service, "The Rio Grande Watershed in Colorado and New Mexico: A Report on the Condition and Use of the Land and Water Resources Together with a General Program for Soil and Water Conservation," August 1939, mimeographed monograph in the collection of the Laboratory of Anthropology, Museum of New Mexico, Santa Fe, New Mexico, 105 (hereafter MNM-LA).

21. SCS, "Population of the Upper Rio Grande," 8.

22. John E. Russell, "State Regionalism in New Mexico" (Ph.D. dissertation, Stanford University, 1938), 267.

23. Marta Weigle, ed., *Hispanic Villages of Northern New Mexico: A Reprint of Volume II of the 1935 Tewa Basin Study, with Supplementary Materials* (Santa Fe: The Lightning Tree, Jene Lyon Publisher, 1975), viii.

24. Ibid., 227.

25. U.S., Department of Agriculture, Forest Service, "Material on the Partido System" (Albuquerque: 1937).

26. Wesley R. Hurt, "Manzano, a Study of Community Disorganization" (M.A. thesis, University of New Mexico, 1941), 180; U.S., Department of Agriculture, Soil Conservation Service, "Reconnaissance Survey of Human Dependency on Resources in the Rio Grande Watershed," Regional Bulletin No. 33, Conservation Economics Series No. 6, December, 1936.

27. SCS, "Reconnaissance Survey," 138.

28. Russell, "State Regionalism," 248.

29. J. T. Reid, *It Happened in Taos* (Albuquerque: University of New Mexico Press, 1946), 68.

30. Sanchez, *Forgotten People,* 65–66.

31. Sanchez, *Forgotten People,* 64.

32. Thomas C. Donnelly, "The State Educational System," Division of Research, Department of Government, University of New Mexico, *Bulletin* 1 (1946): 33.

33. R. J. Mullins and E. H. Fixley, "Public School Attendance and School Costs in New Mexico," Division of Research, Department of Government, University of New Mexico *Bulletin* 6 (1946): 7–8.

34. John E. Seyfried, "Illiteracy Trends in New Mexico," New Mexico University, Education Series, *Bulletin* 4 (1934): 9, 17–18.

35. Ibid., 14, 23–24.

36. Lawrence Cardoso, *Mexican Emigration to the United States, 1897–1931* (Tucson: University of Arizona Press, 1980), 120–34, 143; Abraham Hoffman, *Unwanted Mexican Americans in the Great Depression: Repatriation Pressures, 1929–1939* (Tucson: University of Arizona, 1974), 9–10.

37. Hoffman, *Unwanted Mexican Americans,* 6–9.

38. Hoffman, *Unwanted Mexican Americans,* 6–9, 13.

39. Hoffman, *Unwanted Mexican Americans,* ix, 2, 126; Cardoso, *Mexican Emigration,* 143–47; Frances Swadesh, *Los Primeros Pobladores: Hispanic Americans of the Ute Frontier* (Notre Dame: University of Notre Dame Press, 1974), 205–6. According to an article in the *Albuquerque Journal* of 23 November 1937, a worker deported to Mexico during a WPA crackdown had been a resident of New Mexico for thirty-seven years. He had entered the United States at the age of nine and, under the impression that he was an American citizen, had voted regularly since statehood. His eight American-born children presumably accompanied him into exile. On 28 November 1937 the *Albuquerque Journal* reported that, according to a law passed 22 September 1922, an American-born woman married to an alien before this date was considered to be an alien and liable to deportation. Paradoxically, an alien woman married to an American citizen after this date retained her original citizenship and so was also subject to deportation and exclusion from the relief rolls. The article concluded that American women married to alien husbands prior to 22 September 1922 should divorce them in order to reinstate themselves and their children as United States citizens.

40. James B. Swayne, "A Survey of the Economic Political, and Legal Aspects of the Labor Problem in New Mexico" (M.A. thesis, University of New

Mexico, 1936), 47–50; John Richard Chavez, *The Lost Land: The Chicano Image of the Southwest* (Albuquerque: University of New Mexico Press, 1984), 93–94.

## Chapter Two

1. For a discussion of Dependency Theory see Immanuel Wallerstein, *Modern World Systems,* 2 vols. (New York: Academic Press, 1974). Richard White, *The Roots of Dependency: Subsistence, Environment, and Social Change Among the Choctaws, Pawnees, and Navajos* (Lincoln: University of Nebraska Press, 1983), xvii–xix, uses the definition of dependency most often cited, by Theotorios Dos Santos: "By dependency we mean a situation in which the economy of certain countries is conditioned by the development and expansion of another economy to which the former is subjected." Clark Knowlton, "Development Theory and the Rural Spanish Americans of San Miguel County, New Mexico," a paper presented before the Rural Sociological Society Annual Meeting, Burlington, Vermont, 24–26 August 1979, discusses various dependency theory models and concludes that, while none of them fit the situation in New Mexico perfectly, northern New Mexico can be described as an internal colony of Albuquerque, and Albuquerque as fully dependent upon the federal government and outside corporations. According to John Bodley, *Victims of Progress* (Menlo Park, California: Cummings Publishing Co., 1975), 25, dependency occurs when a modern, industrial civilization based on a culture of consumption co-opts the land base of a "tribal" or "primitive" society and consumes its resources to the extent that the simpler society is no longer able to exist on its own. The process inevitably leads to depopulation, apathy, dependence, and detribalization.

2. The bounty of New Mexico was widely publicized through *The Land of Sunshine: A Handbook of the Resources, Products, Industries and Climate of New Mexico,* by Max Frost and Paul A. F. Walter, eds. (Santa Fe, New Mexico Territory: Bureau of Immigration, New Mexico Printing Co., 1906).

3. W. W. H. Davis, *El Gringo* (Santa Fe: The Rydal Press, 1938, Reprint of the 1857 edition), 195. Wherever Western Civilization encroached upon subsistence people their apparent failure to take full advantage of the natural resources provided the justification for seizing control of the land and ignoring prior ownership rights, cf. Bodley, *Victims of Progress,* 25.

4. There is considerable disagreement concerning the extent of trade in livestock with Mexico. Hubert Howe Bancroft, *History of Arizona and New Mexico, 1530–1888, 50th Anniversary of 1889 edition* (Albuquerque: Horn and Wallace, 1962), 301, reports that twenty-five to thirty thousand sheep were exported yearly, whereas Alvar W. Carlson, "New Mexico's Sheep Industry, 1850–1900: Its Role in the History of the Territory," *NMHR,* 44 (1969), 27, quotes sources that report annual drives of two hundred thousand to over half a million sheep; and D. W. Meinig, *Southwest: Three Peoples in Geographical Change,* believes that the New Mexican economy remained on a subsistence level throughout the Spanish and Mexican periods. A recent authoritative and well-documented study by John O. Baxter, *Las Carneradas: Sheep Trade in New Mexico,*

*1700–1860* (Albuquerque: University of New Mexico Press, 1987), 11, 63, 101–4, traces the beginnings of the sheep export trade to the mid-seventeenth century. Baxter suggests that the eighty thousand sheep exported to Mexico in 1835 was not only a pre-Territorial peak, but that the region could not sustain annual deliveries at such a high level, since in 1836 exports shrank by more than 90 percent. Earlier reports of shipments ranging from between fifteen to twenty-five thousand were probably closer to the norm.

5. Alvar Ward Carlson, "New Mexico's Sheep Industry," 27. Alvin R. Sunseri, *Seeds of Discord: New Mexico in the Aftermath of the American Conquest, 1846–1861* (Chicago: Nelson-Hall, Inc., 1979), 31. According to Charles L. Briggs, "Our Strength Is in the Land: The Expression of Hierarchical and Egalitarian Principles in Hispano Society, 1750–1929" (Ph.D. dissertation, University of Chicago, 1980), 184, the number of sheep jumped from 619,000 in 1870 to 3,939,000 in 1880.

6. Meinig, *Southwest,* 34.

7. Carlson, "Sheep Industry," 27.

8. Robert W. Frazer, "The Army and New Mexico Agriculture, 1848–1861," *El Palacio,* 89 (Spring, 1983): 27.

9. Alvar Ward Carlson, "El Rancho and Vadito: Spanish Settlements on Indian Lands," *El Palacio,* 85 (Spring, 1979): 32.

10. SCS, "Population of the Upper Rio Grande Watershed," 4.

11. Ibid., 3–4. According to this study, presumably written by Eshref Shevky, head of the Soil Conservation Service Conservation Economics department, by 1850 the agricultural resources available to the rural village population were already supporting the maximum population. His calculation of the area's "carrying capacity" was based on the fact that after this date numerous new settlements were established outside the area to draw off excess population, and that the rural villagers began at this time to seek wage labor. Shevky did not, apparently, take into consideration other factors that must enter any such calculation. The introduction of new trade goods had made a source of cash, available primarily through wage labor, highly desirable. According to John Van Ness, who has more recently explored the wage labor versus farming phenomenon, it is more complicated than Shevky, or most other writers, have understood. The establishment of new communities, made newly possible by the presence of the United States Army, and the turn to wage labor, which brought a new degree of affluence, may have *caused,* rather than resulted from, an increased population. More importantly, the principal cause of growing poverty in the Hispanic uplands was the gradual alienation and spoilation of the communal grazing areas and woodlands that were essential to the Hispanic cultural ecology. John R. Van Ness, "Hispanic Land Grants: Ecology and Subsistence in the Uplands of Northern New Mexico and Southern Colorado," in Briggs and Van Ness, *Land, Water, and Culture,* 141–214.

12. Warren Beck, *New Mexico: A History of Four Centuries* (Norman: University of Oklahoma Press, 1962), 262. In one year John Chisum, who claimed a range 150 miles up and down the Pecos from the Texas border to Fort Sumner, sold thirty thousand head of cattle to the commission house in Kansas City.

13. Ralph E. Twitchell, *The Leading Facts of New Mexican History, Volume II* (Cedar Rapids, Iowa: The Torch Press, 1911–1917), 467.

14. Bancroft, *History of New Mexico,* 769.

15. Allen F. Harper, A. R. Cordova, and Kalervo Oberg, *Man and Resources in the Middle Rio Grande Valley* (Albuquerque: University of New Mexico Press, 1943), 29–30.

16. John Van Ness and Christine Van Ness, *Spanish and Mexican Land Grants in New Mexico and California* (Manhattan, Kansas: Sunflower University Press, 1980), 8–10.

17. Ibid.

18. Charles T. Du Mars and Malcolm Ebright, "Problems of Spanish and Mexican Land Grants in the Southwest: Their Origin and Extent," *The Southwestern Review: Management and Economics* 1 (Summer, 1981): 185. Surveyor-general Clark summed it up in 1867 in a letter to his superior in Washington as follows:

> The Surveyor-general is not permitted to incur any expense in calling witnesses, no notice is required to be given to any party of interest by publication or otherwise, and as a consequence almost all investigation has been ex parte . . . I have, therefore, again to urge that Congress will make provision for the better security of the rights of individuals in the settlement of these claims.

Surveyor-general's Report, 19 July 1867, 40th Congress, 2nd Session, HED No. 1, 372. A more general discussion is contained in Malcolm Ebright, "New Mexican Land Grants," 15–64. Interesting histories of New Mexican land grants are contained in Malcolm Ebright, "Report on chain of title—Northern portion—Juan Jose Lobato Grant," testimony in *United States versus Moises Archuleta,* Santa Fe, 1977; Malcolm Ebright, *The Tierra Amarilla Grant: A History of Chicanery* (Santa Fe: Center for Land Grant Studies, 1980); Malcolm Ebright, "The Embudo Grant: A Case Study of Justice and the Court of Private Land Claims," *Journal of the West,* 9 (1980): 74–85; and Myra Ellen Jenkins, "The Baltasar Baca 'Grant': History of an Encroachment," *El Palacio,* 68 (1961): 47–64, 87–105. Van Ness, "Hispanos in Northern New Mexico," provides an extensive and excellent history of land grant adjudication.

19. Carey McWilliams, *Brothers Under the Skin* (Boston: Little, Brown & Co., 1943), 136. It is clear that upper class Hispanos were quick to take advantage of the new economic opportunities offered by the changing power structure. By allying themselves with Anglos they essentially abandoned their traditional patron-client relationship with lower class Hispanos, leaving them highly vulnerable to exploitation. According to Frances Swadesh, "The Social and Philosophical Context of Creativity in Hispanic New Mexico," *Rocky Mountain Social Science Journal,* 9 (1972): 12, the emergence of patrons as a distinct social class appears to date from the mercantile development stimulated by the Santa Fe Trail. They owed much of their power to the junior partnership status to which they were elevated during the Yankee military occupation.

20. Van Ness, *Spanish Land Grants,* 10; U.S., Department of Agriculture, Soil Conservation Service, "Notes on Community-Owned Land Grants in New

Mexico," Regional Bulletin, No. 48, Conservation Economics Series No. 21, August 1937, p. 7; William A. Keleher, "Law of the New Mexican Land Grant," *NMHR*, 4 (1929): 35–39; Stan Steiner, *La Raza* (New York: Harper and Row, 1969), 59.

21.  G. Emlen Hall, *The Four Leagues of Pecos* (Albuquerque: University of New Mexico Press, 1984) documents many such transactions in the history of the Pecos Grant.

22.  Keleher, "Law of the New Mexican Land Grant," 350–71; Hall, *Pecos;* Frances Leon Swadesh, *Los Primeros Pobladores,* 80–86; George W. Julian, "Land Stealing in New Mexico," *North American Review,* 145 (1887): 31. Julian's widely publicized report revealed the wholesale plunder of the public domain but expressed no concern for the rights of Spanish Americans. Instead, Julian was outraged that five million acres had been surrendered to monopolists that should have been reserved for "the influx of an intelligent and enterprising population . . . to ensure the development of the vast mineral wealth of the Territory, as well as the settlement of her lands." Victor Westphall, "Fraud and Implications of Fraud in the Land Grants of New Mexico," *NMHR,* 49 (1974): 311–22, argues that the practice of enlarging grant boundaries, together with abundant infighting among grant applicants, can better be described as "greed" rather than "fraud." He also argues that the greater crime was the apathy of Congress in allowing grants to remain for so long in an unsettled condition. Fraud is more easily detected and corrected.

23.  Van Ness, *Spanish Land Grants,* 10; SCS "Notes on Community-Owned Land Grants," 2, 3; Victor Westphall, *Mercedes Reales: Hispanic Land Grants of the Upper Rio Grande Region* (Albuquerque: University of New Mexico Press, 1983), 269–71.

24.  Swadesh, *Primeros Pobladores,* 85–86, cites the case of the Tierra Amarilla Grant which was acquired by Thomas Catron using several kinds of fraud. When he introduced his spurious documents as evidence in the district court at Santa Fe the Tierra Amarilla residents did not even know that title suit had been filed and that they had lost their land.

25.  Harper et al., *Man and Resources,* 63.

26.  Briggs, "Our Strength," 230–37; Frank Grubbs, "Frank Bond: Gentlemen Sheepherder of Northern New Mexico, 1883–1915," *NMHR,* 36 (1961): 288, 300.

27.  Harold H. Dunham, *Government Handout* (Ann Arbor: Edwards Brothers, 1941), 3; Harper et al., *Man and Resources,* 61–63; Lynn Perrigo, *Texas and Our Spanish Southwest* (Dallas: Banks Upshaw & Co., 1960), 320.

28.  G. Emlen Hall, "The Pueblo Grant Labyrinth," in Charles Briggs and John Van Ness, eds., *Land, Water, and Culture,* 67–138, provides an extensive discussion of this issue.

29.  Daniel Tyler, "Looking for the Law: Pueblo Land Alienation in New Mexico During the Mexican Period," paper delivered before the Pacific Coast Branch of the American Historical Association, San Diego, August 1976, 4–13; Alvar Carlson, "El Rancho and Vadito," 28–30, 38; Carlson, "Spanish-American Acquisition," 95.

30. Lawrence C. Kelly, *The Assault on Assimilation: John Collier and the Origins of Indian Policy Reform* (Albuquerque: University of New Mexico Press, 1983), 190–91; Hall, "Pueblo Grant Labyrinth," 94–126; *U.S. vs. Joseph,* 94 U.S. 618.

31. Carlson, "Spanish-American Acquisition," 95.

32. Kelly, *Assault,* 192–94; Hall, "Pueblo Grant Labyrinth," 113–15; *U.S. vs. Sandoval,* 231 U.S. 28; "Pueblo Land Problems," Bulletin No. 1, New Mexico Association on Indian Affairs, Santa Fe, New Mexico, n.d., Pueblo Land Files, History Library, Museum of New Mexico, Santa Fe, New Mexico (hereafter MNM-HL); Kenneth Philp, "Albert B. Fall and the Protest from the Pueblos," *Arizona and the West,* 12 (1970): 239–40.

33. Baxter, *Las Carneradas,* 28–30. Descriptions of traditional Hispanic partido relationships are to be found in Fabiola Cabeza de Baca Gilbert, *We Fed Them Cactus* (Albuquerque: University of New Mexico Press, 1954) and Oliver La Farge, *Behind the Mountains* (Boston: Houghton, Mifflin, 1956).

34. Marta Weigle, *Hispanic Villages,* 217; Grubbs, "Frank Bond," 11, 172; and Carlson, "New Mexico's Sheep Industry," 36.

35. Briggs, "Our Strength," 191–200; Forest Service, "Material on the Partido System," 1937.

36. Briggs, "Our Strength," 203.

37. Weigle, *Hispanic Villages,* 230–31.

38. Deutsch, *No Separate Refuge,* 19; Marianne L. Stoller, "Spanish-Americans, Their Servants and Sheep: A Culture History of Weaving in Southern Colorado," in *Spanish Textile Tradition of New Mexico and Colorado* (Santa Fe: Museum of New Mexico Press, 1979), 51; Swadesh, *Primeros Pobladores,* 109; Harper et al., *Man and Resources,* 64.

39. Briggs, "Our Strength," 203.

40. Robert J. Rosenbaum, *Mexicano Resistance in the Southwest: "The Sacred Right of Self-Preservation"* (Austin: University of Texas Press, 1981), 86–87. Lawrence C. Goodwyn, *The Populist Moment: A Short History of the Agrarian Revolt in America* (New York: Oxford University Press, 1979) provides a national perspective to these Populist protests, and Robert W. Larson, *New Mexico Populism: A Study of Radical Protest in a Western Territory* (Boulder: Colorado Association of Universities Press, 1974) puts them into the context of New Mexico territorial history. The outbreaks of violence in New Mexico fall into what Eric Hobsbawm has termed "peasant" or "primitive" rebellion, most specifically, into his categories of Social Banditry (when one individual refuses to submit and is supported by the general community) and community upheavals (when tensions precipitate a "spontaneous" outbreak). According to Hobsbawm, "Social banditry of this kind is one of the most universal social phenomena known to history." It is "not a programme for peasant society but a form of self-help to escape it in particular circumstances." Since "peasant" rebellions tend to be conservative, seeking to restore things to their proper balance, not to end injustice, their effectiveness is limited. Eric Hobsbawm, *Social Bandits and Primitive Rebels* (New York: Free Press, 1959), 14, 20, 24–25.

41. Rosenbaum, *Mexicano Resistance,* 90–94; Perrigo, *Spanish Southwest,* 279;

Rodolfo Acuña, *Occupied America,* 64; David Weber, "Editor's Introduction," 213.

42. "Neustra Plataforma, 1890," *Las Vegas Daily Optic,* 12 March 1890; "Felix Martinez, 1890," *Las Vegas Daily Optic,* 18 August 1890; reprinted in David Weber, *Foreigners,* 234–38.

43. Rosenbaum, *Mexicano Resistance,* 125–39; Robert Rankin White, "Felix Martinez: A Borderlands Success Story," *El Palacio,* 87 (Winter, 1981–82): 13–17. White, like Larson, *New Mexico Populism,* equates El Partido del Pueblo with the Populists. Rosenbaum disagrees but sees the two movements as reinforcing each other to some degree, Rosenbaum, *Mexicano Resistance,* 214.

44. Swadesh, *Primeros Pobladores,* 231 footnote; Hurt, "Manzano," 49.

45. Kutsche, *Cañones,* 84, lists other mutual aid societies as Los Esclavos de Santiago and the Cofradia de San José de Mora; Van Ness, "Hispanos in Northern New Mexico," 290.

46. Warren A. Beck, "The Penitentes of New Mexico," in Renato Rosaldo, Robert A. Calvert, and Gustav L. Seligmann, Jr., eds., *Chicano: The Evolution of a People* (San Francisco: Winston Press, 1973), 139–43; Paul Horgan, *Lamy of Santa Fe, His Life and Times* (New York: Farrar, Strauss and Giroux, 1975) provides the fullest account of the Anglo domination of the Catholic Church.

47. Beck, *New Mexico,* 205.

48. José Amado Hernandez, *Mutual Aid for Survival: The Case of the Mexican American* (Malabar, Florida: Robert S. Krieger Publishing Company, 1983), 16; William Wallrich, "Auxiliadoras de la Morada," *Southwestern Lore,* 16 (1950): 9.

49. Beck, *New Mexico,* 222, 223; Hernandez, *Mutual Aid,* 22–24; Marta Weigle, *Brothers of Light, Brothers of Blood* (Albuquerque: University of New Mexico Press, 1976), 81.

50. Jack E. Holmes, *Politics in New Mexico* (Albuquerque: University of New Mexico Press, 1967), 20–24; Briggs, "Our Strength," 12–16, 32–33; Jack E. Holmes, "Success and Failure: The Limits of New Mexico's Hispanic Politics," in Renato Rosaldo, Robert A. Calvert, and Gustav L. Seligmann, Jr., eds., *Chicano: The Evolution of a People* (San Francisco: Winston Press, 1973) blames the writings of many sociologists and anthropologists for the "somewhat Procrustean" synthesis that describes Hispanic villagers as passively dependent and blindly deferent. Holmes maintains that the villages selected for some of the early studies comprised a statistical oddity. The skewed results, which suggested the existence of great social inequality within the Hispanic rural community, gave rise to the concept of a passive, one-sided, patron-peon relationship. Once in the literature, the idea gained strength through repetition, especially after Florence Kluckhohn's 1941 dissertation "Los Atarqueños, a Study of Patterns and Configurations in a New Mexico Village" (Ph.D. dissertation, Radcliffe College), was revised, in collaboration with Fred Strodtbeck and republished as *Variations in Value Orientations* (Evanston, Illinois: Row, Peterson and Co., 1961). Briggs, "Our Strength," agrees with Holmes and argues that hierarchy and equality coexisted in traditional Hispanic society in a set of paired and shared duties and obligations. One might also argue that this tendency to

impose stereotypical values on Hispanic villagers is part of the 1930s and 1940s intellectual search for the primitive (Audrey Shalinsky, personal communication, July 1985).

51. Beck, *New Mexico,* 223; Holmes, *Politics,* 27–33.

52. Beck, *New Mexico,* 223–24.

53. Maurilio E. Vigil, *Los Patrones: Profiles of Hispanic Political Leaders in New Mexico* (Washington, D.C.: University Press of America, 1980), 166–68. For a contemporary account of patron politics see Harvey Fergusson, "Out Where Bureaucracy Begins," *The Nation,* 121 (July 1925): 112–14.

54. William B. Taylor and Elliot West, "Patron Leadership at the Crossroads: Southern Colorado in the Nineteenth Century," in Norris Hundley, ed., *The Chicano* (Santa Barbara and Oxford: Clio Press, 1975), 80; Vigil, *Los Patrones;* Kutsche, *Cañones,* 97.

55. Frances Leon (Swadesh) Quintana, "Structure of Hispanic-Indian Relations in New Mexico," in Kutsche, *Survival of Spanish American Villages,* 54.

56. Twitchell, *Leading Facts II,* 323–24; George I. Sanchez, "New Mexicans and Acculturation," *New Mexico Quarterly Review,* 2 (February 1941): 32.

57. Deutsch, *No Separate Refuge,* 27; Zeleny, *Relations Between the Spanish-Americans and Anglo-Americans in New Mexico* (New York: Arno Press, 1974), 273.

58. Deutsch, *No Separate Refuge,* 28; Lorin W. Brown, Charles L. Briggs, and Marta Weigle, *Hispano Folklife of New Mexico: The Lorin W. Brown Federal Writers' Project Manuscripts* (Albuquerque: University of New Mexico Press, 1978), 195.

59. Briggs, "Our Strength," 246.

60. Deutsch, *No Separate Refuge,* 33.

61. Briggs, "Our Strength," 236, 241, 277–78. While women customarily tended home gardens, the heavier jobs of plowing, planting, and irrigating the larger fields were done by men.

62. Briggs, "Our Strength," 238–39.

63. Briggs, "Our Strength," 254–55; Sigurd Johansen, *Rural Social Organization in a Spanish American Culture Area* (Albuquerque: University of New Mexico Press, 1948), 133–35.

64. Timothy John Rickard, "Perceptions and Results of the Irrigation Movement in the Western United States, 1891–1914" (Ph.D. dissertation, University of Kansas, 1974), 10–11, maintains that the primary motive of irrigationists was the economic development of the West by any means. The advocates were primarily western politicians and businessmen who had a financial stake in the swift economic development of their section. In a geographic context, the irrigation movement was a series of campaigns to remove the arid West from the control of cattlemen whose methods of resource control were alien to the American small farmer tradition. However, the reclamation program encountered severe financial problems so that the main result of the movement was to commit the federal government to a program of subsidies that persists today.

65. P. M. Baldwin, "A Short History of the Mesilla Valley," *NMHR,* 13 (July 1938): 314–44; Ruth Laughlin, "Coronado's Country and Its People,"

*Survey Graphic,* 29 (1940): 280; R. G. Hosea, "The Middle Rio Grande Conservancy District," *New Mexico Highway Journal,* 7 (May 1928): 6–9; SCS, "Reconnaissance Survey"; Swadesh, *Primeros Pobladores,* 80–86.

66. Harper et al., *Man and Resources,* 35–39.

## Chapter Three

1. James M. Gaither, "A Return to the Village: A Study of Santa Fe and Taos as Cultural Centers, 1900–1934" (Ph.D. dissertation, University of Minnesota, 1957), 16–17; Arthur A. Lovejoy, *A Documentary History of Cultural Primitivism and Related Ideas* (Baltimore: Johns Hopkins Press, 1935), 7.

2. Horace M. Kallen, "Democracy Versus the Melting Pot," *The Nation,* 100 (25 February 1915): 212–20, expresses this myth as a fond hope for American society.

3. Nancy Cott, *The Bonds of Womanhood: Women's Sphere in New England, 1780–1835* (New Haven: Yale University Press, 1977), 37–70; Barbara Welter, "The Cult of True Womanhood, 1820–1860," *American Quarterly,* 18 (1966): 151–74.

4. Henry Nash Smith, *Virgin Land: The American West as Symbol and Myth* (Cambridge: Harvard University Press, 1950), 51–61.

5. Ibid., 123–44.

6. Paul Conkin, *Tomorrow a New World: The New Deal Community Program* (Ithaca, N.Y.: Cornell University Press, 1959), 14–15.

7. Smith, *Virgin Land,* 6–7, 169–70, 189–93, 201–6.

8. Frederick Jackson Turner, *Frontier and Section* (Englewood Cliffs, N.J.: Prentice Hall, 1961).

9. John Whiteclay Chambers II, *The Tyranny of Change: America in the Progressive Era, 1900–1917* (New York: St. Martin's Press, 1980), 2–10.

10. Ray Allen Billington, ed., *Frontier and Section;* Selected Essays of Frederick Jackson Turner (Englewood Cliffs: Prentice Hall, 1961), 95, 111, 165.

11. David B. Danborn, *The Resisted Revolution: Urban America and the Industrialization of Agriculture, 1900–1930* (Ames, Iowa: Iowa State University Press, 1979), 24–47; William L. Bowers, *The Country Life Movement in America 1900–1920* (Port Washington, N.Y.: Kennikat Press, 1974), 16–17, 80; Lawrence Cremin, *The Transformation of the School: Progressivism in American Education, 1876–1957* (New York: Alfred A. Knopf, 1961), 75–79.

12. Danborn, *Resisted Revolution,* 61–64.

13. Danborn, *Resisted Revolution,* 55.

14. Danborn, *Resisted Revolution,* 55–56; Conkin, *New World,* 1–5, 17. Quotation from Kenyon L. Butterfield, *Chapters in Rural Progress* (Chicago: University of Chicago, 1908), 122.

15. Bowers, *Country Life,* 80; Cremin, *Transformation of the School,* 75–79.

16. Bowers, *Country Life,* 24–29; Danborn, *Resisted Revolution,* 72–73; Cremin, *Transformation of the School,* 82–84; Michael L. Berger, *The Devil Wagon in God's*

*Country: The Automobile and Social Change in Rural America* (Hamden, Connecticut: Archon Books, 1979), 168.

17. Danborn, *Resisted Revolution,* 81–93; Bowers, *Country Life,* 103–24.

18. Berger, *The Devil Wagon,* 209, 213; Danborn, *Resisted Revolution,* vii–ix.

19. Danborn, *Resisted Revolution,* vii.

20. Allen F. Davis, *Spearheads for Reform: The Social Settlements and the Progressive Movement, 1890–1914* (New York: Oxford University Press, 1967), 10–11, 41–49, 243–44.

21. Davis, *Spearheads,* 41–49, 54–57; R. Allen Lawson, *The Failure of Independent Liberalism, 1930–1941* (New York: G. P. Putnam's Sons, 1971), 25–28; Cremin, *Transformation of the Schools,* 61–63, 69–72.

22. Conkin, *New World,* 3.

23. Cremin, *Transformation of the School,* 106–15.

24. Davis, *Spearheads,* 58–59, 103; Bowers, *Country Life,* 57–61; Cremin, *Transformation of the School,* 117–18.

25. Conkin, *New World,* 4.

26. Lewis S. Feuer, "John Dewey and the Back-to-the-People Movement in American Thought," *Journal of the History of Ideas,* 20 (October–December 1959): 565.

27. Alan Cywar, "John Dewey: Toward Domestic Reconstruction, 1915–1920," *Journal of the History of Ideas,* 30 (July–September 1969): 391.

28. Feuer, "Dewey and the Back-to-the-People Movement," 568.

29. Conkin, *New World,* 3–5.

30. Lawson, *Failure of Independent Liberalism,* 33–34, 62–63, 100–113; Conkin, *New World,* 3–5, 73.

31. Clarke A. Chambers, *Seedtime of Reform: American Social Service and Social Action, 1918–1933* (Minneapolis: University of Minnesota Press, 1963), 88, 95–96, 100–101, 106, argues for a larger element of constructive creativity and a broader continuity between progressivism and the New Deal than has generally been credited.

32. Frank Owsley, "The Pillars of Agrarianism," *American Review,* 4 (1934–35): 529–74.

33. Conkin, *New World,* 45, 56; Elwood Mead, *Helping Men Own Farms: A Practical Discussion of Govenrment Aid in Land Settlement* (New York: Macmillan Co., 1920).

## Chapter Four

1. Charles F. Lummis, *The Land of Poco Tiempo* (Albuquerque: University of New Mexico Press, 1966. Facsimile of 1928 edition by Charles Scribner's Sons, copyright, 1893), 3.

2. Gaither, "A Return to the Village," 2.

3. Keith L. Bryant, "The Atchison, Topeka and Santa Fe Railway and the Development of the Taos and Santa Fe Art Colonies," *Western Historical Quarterly,*

9 (1978): 446; Van Deren Coke, *Taos and Santa Fe: The Artist's Environment, 1882–1942* (Albuquerque: University of New Mexico Press, 1963), 59.

4. Chavez, *The Lost Land,* 87–92; Roland Dickey, *New Mexico Village Arts* (Albuquerque: University of New Mexico Press, 1949), 236; Carey Mc-Williams, *North from Mexico* (Philadelphia: Lippincott, 1949), 39–43; Helen Hunt Jackson, *Ramona: A Story* (n.p.: Roberts Bros., 1884; reprint edition Boston: Little, Brown, & Co., 1919), Chapters 1–2; Bret Harte, "Devotion of Enriquez," in *The Chicano: From Caricature to Self-Portrait* (New York: Mentor Books, 1971), 51–62.

5. McWilliams, *North from Mexico,* 39–43; Dickey, *Village Arts,* 115, 237–305; Gaither, "Return to Village," 90.

6. Bryant, "Santa Fe Railway," 437–42, 446; Coke, *Taos,* 59.

7. Gaither, "Return to Village," 107–15; Edna Robertson and Sarah Nestor, *Artists of the Canyons and Caminos: Santa Fe, the Early Years* (Santa Fe: Peregrine Smith, Inc., 1976); Coke, *Taos.*

8. Ruth Laughlin, "Santa Fe in the 1920's," *New Mexico Quarterly Review* (Spring, 1949): 62; Gaither, "Return to Village," 107, 119–23; Richard H. Frost, "The Romantic Inflation of Pueblo Culture," *American West* (January–February 1980): 5–9, 56–60.

9. *The Land of Sunshine: A Handbook of the Resources, Products, Industries and Climate of New Mexico,* ed. by Max Frost and Paul A. F. Walter (Santa Fe, New Mexico (Ter.) Bureau of Immigration, New Mexico Printing Company, 1906); Bancroft, *History of New Mexico,* 774.

10. *Land of Sunshine,* 9.

11. Gaither, "Return to Village," 18–34, 57; Beatrice Chauvenet, "Paul A. F. Walter," *El Palacio,* 88 (Spring, 1982): 31.

12. Dickey, *New Mexico Village Arts,* 307; Gaither, "Return to Village," 55.

13. Gaither, "Return to Village," 55–58; Marta Weigle, *Santa Fe and Taos: The Writer's Era 1916–1941* (Santa Fe: Ancient City Press, 1982), 11, quotes Ruth Laughlin Barker, a contemporary of the period as follows:

> Even "hard headed businessmen" realized Santa Fe's greatest attraction lay in its atmosphere of remote antiquity. Accordingly, the ancient city . . . pulled a rusty black shawl over her head and posed for the world to come and see her as the oldest capital in the United States, the royal headquarters for the kingdom of Spain for one hundred and fifty years before the Mexican War.

George Kubler, "On the Colonial Extinction of the Motifs of Pre-Columbian Art," in Samuel Lothrop et al., *Essays in Pre-Columbian Art and Archaeology* (Cambridge: Harvard University Press, 1961), 15, comments on the fate of art during periods of cultural conflict. "Enemy" works are generally destroyed and replaced by the art of the conqueror until they cease to correspond with living behavior and become symbolically inert. At that time they are then "safe" to play with as in tourist souvenirs, antiquarian reconstructions, or archaicizing revivals.

14. Marta Weigle, "Publishing in Santa Fe, 1915–40," *El Palacio,* 89 (Summer, 1983): 11.

15. Dickey, *Village Arts,* 239; David Neumann, "Our Architectural Follies," *New Mexican Quarterly Review,* 1 (August 1931): 215–17.

16. Mary Austin, *Earth Horizon* (New York: Houghton-Mifflin, Co., 1932), 359: Gaither, "Return to Village," 79–82; Ruth Laughlin (Barker), *Caballeros* (1st ed., 1931; Caldwell, Idaho: Caxton Printers, 1945), 201–5. Laughlin provides a delightfully graphic description of the 1930s Santa Fe Fiesta and dates its origins to 1712 when the Marques de la Peñuela issued an order commanding the town to commemorate the reconquest by Diego de Vargas in 1692. According to Laughlin, a native fiesta had been in existence prior to the introduction of the Spanish Fiesta. It began as a religious celebration the night before with Vespers, luminarios, and bonfires and continued the next day with Mass, a procession of saints decked out in silk dresses, and strings of gold and pearl beads, and was followed by a "chicken pull," *correr el gallo,* and a *baile* (dance) that lasted far into the night. It generally ended with fist fights and a flash of knives brought on by too much *mula blanca* (whiskey). The Spanish fiesta differed from the native fiesta in reenacting the most dramatic episodes in Spanish-Colonial history and was combined with Indian and Spanish dance performances. The Historical Pageant was followed by the Hysterical Pageant which gave full reign to the artist colony's ingenuity in caricaturing every issue in the life of the village. Upper class Spanish-American society made the most of the opportunity to show off their "pride of racial heritage." Old songs and folk dances were performed in bright, colored costumes in a way reminiscent of the folk dances of Hungary and Russia.

17. *Santa Fe New Mexican,* 3 September 1921. An interesting and insightful discussion of the importance of the Santa Fe Fiesta to Hispanic ethnicity is contained in Ronald L. Grimes, *Symbol and Conquest: Public Ritual and Drama in Santa Fe, New Mexico* (Ithaca, N.Y.: Cornell University Press, 1976).

18. *Santa Fe New Mexican,* 24 July 1924; Gaither, "Return to Village," 82.

19. Dickey, *Village Arts,* 241.

20. Austin, *Earth Horizon,* 359; Thomas M. Pearce, *Mary Hunter Austin* (New York: Twayne Publishers, Inc., 1965), 51. The Carnegie Foundation has no record of Austin's study ever having been done, Sarah Deutsch, personal correspondence, 20 August 1985.

21. Augusta Fink, *I-Mary* (Tucson: University of Arizona Press, 1983), 50–57, 67, 84, 96–100, 153–60, 168, 173; Christopher Lasch, *The New Radicalism in America, 1889–1963: The Intellectual as Social Type* (New York: Alfred A. Knopf, 1966), 104–6; Emily Hahn, *Romantic Rebels* (Cambridge, Massachusetts: Houghton Mifflin, 1967), 217–22; Austin, *Earth Horizon,* 155, 207–8, 251–52, 267, 291, 299, 336, 340; John Collier, *From Every Zenith* (Denver: Sage Books, 1963), 155.

22. Austin, *Earth Horizon,* 359.

23. Mary Austin, "Mexicans and New Mexico," *Survey,* 66 (May 1931): 143.

24. Pearce, *Austin,* 55; William Wroth, "New Hope in Hard Times: Hispanic Crafts Are Revived During Troubled Years," *El Palacio,* 89 (Summer, 1983): 24–25; Mary Austin, "Frank Applegate," *New Mexico Quarterly Review,* 2 (August 1932): 214.

25. Austin, "Frank Applegate," 214.

26. Gaither, "Return to Village," 143.

27. Austin, "Frank Applegate," 214.

28. Charles L. Briggs, *The Wood Carvers of Cordoba, New Mexico: Social Dimensions of an Artistic "Revival"* (Knoxville: University of Tennessee Press, 1980), 6.

29. Ibid., 47.

30. Erna Fergusson, "Mary Austin," in Willard Houghland, ed., *Mary Austin: A Memorial* (Santa Fe: Laboratory of Anthropooogy, September 1944), 25.

31. Dudley Wynn, "Mary Austin," in Houghland, *Austin,* 23; Carey McWilliams, "Mary Austin," obituary in the *Los Angeles Times,* 14 September 1934, Nichol's Collection, MNM-HL.

32. Thomas M. Pearce, "Southwestern Culture: An Artificial or a Natural Growth?" *New Mexico Quarterly Review,* 1 (August 1931): 195–209; Thomas M. Pearce, "Rockefeller Center on the Camino," *New Mexico Quarterly Review,* 5 (1935): 84–87; Gaither, "Return to the Village," 216, sees the beginning of the decline of this cultural movement with Austin's death in 1934.

33. John Collier, *From Every Zenith,* 155; Kenneth Ray Philp, *John Collier's Crusade for Indian Reform, 1920–1954* (Tucson: University of Arizona Press, 1977), 1–3, 9–17; Hahn, *Romantic Rebels,* 67–71; Fink, *I-Mary,* 168.

34. Collier, *Zenith,* 68, 115; Lawrence C. Kelly, "John Collier and the Indian New Deal: An Assessment," in Jane M. Smith and Robert M. Kvasnicka, eds., *Indian-White Relations: A Persistent Paradox* (Washington, D.C.: Howard University Press, 1976), 227–28.

35. Philp, *John Collier's Crusade,* 1–3, 9–17; Kelly, "John Collier," 228; Collier, *Zenith,* 122–26.

36. Philp, *John Collier's Crusade,* ix–xi; Collier, *Zenith,* 158; Kelly, "John Collier," 230.

37. Philp, *John Collier's Crusade,* 29–32; Kelly, *Assault on Assimilation,* 208–11; *Santa Fe New Mexican,* 15 Febraury 1923; Philp, "Albert B. Fall," 238–43.

38. Philp, *John Collier's Crusade,* 69–70; Kelly, "John Collier," 230.

39. Philp, *John Collier's Crusade,* 32–36; Kelly, "John Collier," 230; Philp, "Albert B. Fall," 244–46.

40. "History of the American Indian Defense Association," n.d., Pueblo Lands File, MNM-HL.

41. Philp, "Albert B. Fall," 244–46.

42. David H. Stratton, "Albert B. Fall," in Richard N. Ellis, ed., *New Mexico Past and Present: A Historical Reader* (Albuquerque: University of New Mexico Press, 1971), 212.

43. Philp, *John Collier's Crusade,* 69–70; Philp, "Albert B. Fall," 250–54, argues that this controversy was more influential than the Teapot Dome scandal in Fall's resignation.

44. Kelly, *Assault on Assimilation,* 253, 254; "Pueblo Land Problems," 8–12. Francis Wilson, employed as legal counsel for the Indians by the General Federation of Women's Clubs, together with historian Ralph E. Twitchell, helped to frame the Lenroot bill which proposed a three-person Presidential

Lands Board to determine Pueblo land titles, and a statute of limitations that would allow non-Indians to claim lands on which they had lived continuously for thirty years without title, or with title, for twenty years. Titles to disputed real estate outside these provisions were to be settled by the New Mexico District Court.

45. Hall, "Pueblo Grant Labyrinth," in Briggs and Van Ness, *Land, Water, and Culture,* 119; Philp, *John Collier's Crusade,* 47–53; Kelly, *Assault on Assimilation,* 253–54.

46. Carlson, "El Rancho and Vadito," 29–30, 34, 38; Carlson, "Spanish-American Acquisition," 103–7; Richard Frost, "Fragments of Pueblo History," 23, documents how the lack of a tourist industry caused the decline of Pojoaque Pueblo.

47. *Santa Fe New Mexican,* 8 May 1931; *Albuquerque Journal,* 10 May 1931. Editorials in both newspapers reprimanded Herbert J. Hagerman, commissioner to the Navajos, and a government representative as well as a member of the Pueblo Lands Board, for allowing a conflict of interest to interfere with payment of full compensation to the losing parties. Hagerman defended himself in a speech before the House of Representatives and claimed that the awards made to the Indians by the Pueblo Lands Board were considered so liberal that the courts reversed a number of them (*Santa Fe New Mexican,* 13 February 1931).

48. Hall, "Pueblo Grant Labyrinth," 120.

49. *Santa Fe New Mexican,* 3 September 1923, 18 October 1923, 7 February 1931; 3 May 1931; *Albuquerque Journal,* 24 February 1932.

50. *Santa Fe New Mexican,* 14 February 1931, 17 February 1931.

51. *Santa Fe New Mexican,* 24 April 1931; *Albuquerque Journal,* 3 May 1931.

52. Philp, *John Collier's Crusade,* 105; *Albuquerque Journal,* 5 February 1932, 4 June 1932.

53. *Santa Fe New Mexican,* 15 September 1923.

54. Kelly, *Assault on Asssimilation,* 258–59.

55. Ibid., 319–20.

56. Collier, *Zenith,* 155.

57. Philp, *John Collier's Crusade,* 110–11.

58. Robert Fay Schrader, *The Indian Arts and Crafts Board: An Aspect of New Deal Indian Policy* (Albuquerque: University of New Mexico Press, 1983), 34–37.

59. Diane Thomas, *The Southwestern Indian Detours: The Story of the Fred Harvey/Santa Fe Railway Experiment in Detourism* (Phoenix: Hunter Publishing Company, 1978), 30–36.

60. Thomas, *Indian Detours,* 51.

61. Ibid., 79.

62. Ibid., 156; Weigle, *Brothers of Light, Brothers of Blood,* 114–15. Penitente rituals were a regular stop on the tourist itineraries and a highlight in the regional travelogues. Tourists made such a "Roman Holiday" of Easter Week observances that Judge M. A. Otero, Justice of the First Judicial District Court in Santa Fe was forced to issue a warning that a law would be invoked to protect religious rites from disturbances.

63. Russell, "State Regionalism in New Mexico," 261.

64. Waldo Walker, "Southwest as a Center of a New Civilization," undated, unidentified newspaper clipping from Austin File, MNM-HL; Fink, *I-Mary*, 56–57. In 1927 Austin was appointd by the governor of New Mexico to be a delegate to the Seven States Conference on water resources and the Colorado River. In addition to her mystical vision, she opposed the rape of the natural resources of one state (Arizona) for the advantage of another (California), as well as the creation of international problems, since Mexico also used the water.


## Chapter Five

1. S. P. Nanninga, *The New Mexico School System: A Textbook for "Problems of Education in New Mexico"* (Albuquerque: University of New Mexico Press, 1942), 8–16. Politicos in the Hispano-dominated territorial legislature successfully opposed public education until 1891, in large part because they opposed the Americanizing effect of public schools and preferred parochial schools where lessons would be taught in Spanish and Roman Catholic principles would be transmitted to the next generation. By doing so they not only defended their culture and institutions, they also preserved the privileges of the upper class. David J. Weber, "Editor's Introduction," in David J. Weber, ed., *Foreigners in Their Native Land*, 214.

2. Rupert F. Asplund, "New Mexico's Tax Structure," University of New Mexico Department of Government *Bulletin* (June 1946): 6–7; Deutsch, *No Separate Refuge*, 27.

3. Charles L. Loomis and J. Allan Beagle, *Rural Social Systems: A Textbook in Rural Sociology and Anthropology* (New York: Prentice Hall, 1950), 657–58.

4. Danborn, *Resisted Revolution*, 62–63.

5. L. C. Mersfelder, "A General Survey of Industrial Education in New Mexico," address delivered before the Industrial Section of the New Mexico Education Association, 28 November 1916, Vertical File, Education, MNM-HL.

6. Joan M. Jensen, "Canning Comes to New Mexico: Women and the Agricultural Extension Service," *NMHR*, 57 (October 1982): 361–74; Sarah Deutsch, personal correspondence, 20 August 1985.

7. Edgar Lee Hewett, "New Mexico in the Great War," *NMHR*, 2 (1927): 22; Sanchez, *Forgotten People*, 26.

8. Deutsch, *No Separate Refuge*, 114; Briggs, *The Wood Carvers of Cordoba*, 36.

9. Jensen, "Canning," 367, 373, 381–82.

10. Loomis, *Rural Social Systems*, 663–65.

11. Nanninga, *New Mexico School System*, 107–9.

12. Ibid., 109.

13. Deutsch, *No Separate Refuge*, 117.

14. Wroth, "New Hope," 25.

15. Octavio Paz, *The Labyrinth of Solitude* (New York: The Grove Press,

1961), 153; Michael C. Meyer and William L. Sherman, *The Course of Mexican History* (New York: Oxford University Press, 1979), 561–62. This is not to suggest that the arts revival movement began in Mexico. According to Schrader, *Indian Arts and Crafts Board,* 4–7, the popular arts and crafts movement began in England in the writings of Thomas Carlyle, John Ruskin, and William Morris. Their influence spread to America and blossomed at the Eighth Annual Meeting of the Lake Mohonk Conference of the Friends of the Indians in 1890. As early as 1905 Commissioner of Indian Affairs Francis E. Leupp enunciated the concept of preserving the distinctive features of Indian life. According to Austin, sometime prior to 1909 she and Natalie Curtis, a student and collector of native American music, approached President Theodore Roosevelt to request his help in initiating an arts and crafts revival (Austin interview published 1 November 1933 in unidentified Los Angeles newspaper, Austin File, MNM-HL). Nothing much seems to have come of that effort and in 1919 Austin wrote Secretary of the Interior Franklin K. Lane to request both the preservation of Indian arts and his assistance in marketing them (Schrader, *Indian Arts and Crafts Board,* 12). The first steps taken in the preservation of the Hispanic culture of the Southwest, especially the folklore, were by Aurelio M. Espinosa, born in southern Colorado in 1880, and by Arthur L. Campa, born in Sonora in 1905. Both published the results of their research in the early decades of the twentieth century (Chavez, *The Lost Land,* 98–99).

16. George I. Sanchez, *Mexico: A Revolution by Education* (New York: Viking Press, 1936), 66–67; Moises Saenz, "The School and Culture," *Progressive Education,* 9 (February 1932): 99–111.

17. Richard H. Pells, *Radical Visions and American Dreams: Culture and Social Thought in the Depression Years* (New York: Harper and Row, 1973), 99; Waldo Frank, *America Hispana* (New York: Garden City, 1940), 235, 249–50, 255; Stuart Chase, *Mexico: A Study of Two Americas* (New York: Macmillan Co., 1931), 310, 327; Drewey W. Gunn, *American and British Writers in Mexico, 1556–1973* (Austin: University of Texas Press, 1974), 76.

18. Gunn, *Writers in Mexico,* 77–79.

19. Ibid., 33.

20. Frank, *America Hispana,* 249–50, 255.

21. Chase, *Mexico,* 327; Pells, *Radical Visions,* 99; Robert Redfield, *Tepoztlan, a Mexican Village: A Study of Folklife* (Chicago: University of Chicago Press, 1930); Robert S. Lynd, *Middletown, a Study of Contemporary American Culture* (New York: Harcourt, Brace & Co., 1929). Possibly the happiness and peace of mind were Redfield's own myths since they were not as evident in Oscar Lewis's restudy, *Tepoztlan, a Village in Mexico* (New York: Holt, 1960), Audrey Shalinsky, personal correspondence, August 1985.

22. Gunn, *Writers in Mexico,* 124–25.

23. Gaither, "Return to Village," 87; Wroth, "New Hope," 24–25; *Santa Fe New Mexican,* 12 July 1930.

24. Thomas M. Pearce, "Rockefeller Center on the Camino," *New Mexico Quarterly Review,* 5 (1935): 84–87.

25. *Santa Fe New Mexican,* 23 April 1921; quoted in Gaither, "Return to Village," 95.

26. Austin, "Mexicans and New Mexico," 141–44, 187, 190.

27. Mary Austin, "Education in New Mexico," *New Mexico Quarterly Review,* 3 (1933): 217–21.

28. Lawrence A. Cardoso, "Images of the Mexican and Mexican American in the 1930s: The Emergence of Alternative Viewpoints," paper delivered to Western Historical Association, October 1982, pp. 3–5; Thomas R. Garth, "The Intelligence of Mexican School Children," *School and Society,* 27 (30 June 1928): 791–94.

29. A series of master's theses at the University of New Mexico and the University of Texas examined different aspects of the problem, but, clearly, much more research was necessary before the onus of radical inferiority could be set aside. In 1931 Sanchez was appointed Director of Research at the New Mexico State Department of Education. Fickinger was the Executive Secretary of the New Mexico Educational Association. George I. Sanchez, "Scores of Spanish-Speaking Children on Repeated Tests" (M.A. thesis, University of Texas, 1931); Paul L. Fickinger, "A Study of Certain Phases of the Language Problem of Spanish-American Children" (M.A. thesis, University of New Mexico, 1930); A. Stolz, "A Comparative Study in the Art Judgment of Spanish-Speaking and English-Speaking Children" (M.A. thesis, University of Texas, 1931); *Albuquerque Journal,* 28 March 1932.

30. Lloyd S. Tireman, "San Jose Training School," New Mexico University Training School Series, I (1930); *Santa Fe New Mexican,* 25 January 1930.

31. Lloyd S. Tireman, "The San Jose Project," *New Mexico Quarterly Review,* 3 (1933): 207–16.

32. Saenz, "School and Culture," 99–111; Sanchez, *Revolution by Education,* 79–94.

33. Lloyd S. Tireman, "Some Aspects of Rural Education in New Mexico," New Mexico University Training School Series, II (December 1931): 5–25.

34. Tireman, "San Jose Project," 207–16; Pearce, *Austin,* 59.

35. Mary Austin, "Rural Education in New Mexico," New Mexico University Training School Series, 2 (December 1931): 23–30.

36. Lloyd S. Tireman and Mary Watson, *A Community School in a Spanish-Speaking Village* (Albuquerque: University of New Mexico Press, 1948).

37. *Albuquerque Journal,* 21 February 1935, 20 March 1935; Sanchez, *Revolution by Education;* Sanchez, *Forgotten People.*

38. Brice H. Sewell, "Problems of Vocational Education in New Mexico," Seligman Papers, NMSRCA; Wroth, "New Hope," 25.

39. Wroth, "New Hope," 26.

40. Zeleny, *Relations,* 182, 255, 329, 348, who studied this pattern of social relations in New Mexico in the early 1940s, suggests that Sanchez was one of the few New Mexicans who dared to defy this "gentlemen's agreement" and "conspiracy of silence." When he left the University of New Mexico for Texas some people said it was because his advance in New Mexico had been blocked. In 1935 a psychologist at the University of New Mexico prepared an attitude

test on race and ethnic issues that so antagonized the Hispanos on campus that he had to barricade himself in his home for fear of being mobbed. Shortly thereafter he lost his job at the University.

41. Conkin, *Tomorrow a New World;* Mead, *Helping Men Own Farms;* Owsley, "Pillars of Agrarianism," 529–74; Richard Hofstadter, *Social Darwinism in American Thought* (Revised edition. New York: George Braziller, Inc., 1965); Otis L. Graham, Jr., *An Encore for Reform: The Old Progressives and the New Deal* (New York: Oxford University Press, 1969), material on Ickes; Linda J. Lear, *Harold L. Ickes: The Aggressive Progressive 1874–1933* (New York: Garland Publishers, Inc., 1981); Rexford G. Tugwell, "The Sources of New Deal Reformism," *Ethics,* 64 (July 1954): 249–74; Lawson, *Failure of Independent Liberalism;* Davis, *Spearheads for Reform.*

42. John Collier, "Mexico: A Challenge," *Progressive Education,* 9 (February 1932): 95–98.

43. Stephen J. Kunitz, "The Social Philosophy of John Collier," *Ethnohistory,* 18 (1971): 219–22; Collier, *From Every Zenith,* 195–96, 293–99.

44. A. A. Berle, Jr., "In the Matter of the New Mexico Pueblo Lands— White Claims upon Lands Granted to the Pueblos," Brief printed on behalf of Council of all the New Mexico Pueblos, the Indian Welfare Committee of the Public Welfare Department of the General Federation of Women's Clubs, and the American Indian Defense Association, Pueblo Lands File, MNM-HL.

45. Collier, *Zenith,* 133, 176–77, 285–87; Philp, *John Collier's Crusade,* 39; Lear, *Harold Ickes,* 241–42.

46. Clayton R. Koppes, "From New Deal to Termination: Liberalism and Indian Policy, 1933–1953," *Pacific Historical Review,* 66 (November 1977): 543–66.

47. Philp, *Collier's Crusade,* 122–34; Edward L. Schapsmeier and Frederick H. Schapsmeier, *Henry A. Wallace of Iowa: The Agrarian Years, 1910–1940* (Ames: Iowa State University Press, 1968), 166–95.

48. Collier, *Zenith,* 238–44, 285–87; Richard Lowitt, *The New Deal and the West* (Bloomington: University of Indiana Press, 1984), 136–37, believes that Ickes succeeded in winning the support of Franklin Delano Roosevelt for his Indian policies despite opposition from western members of Congress who worried that they would make the "Americanization" of the Indians impossible.

## Chapter Six

1. U.S., Department of Agriculture, Soil Conservation Service, "Village Dependence on Migratory Labor in the Upper Rio Grande Area," Regional Bulletin 47, Conservation Economics Series 20, July 1937, 4–7; Harper et al., *Man and Resources,* 77.

2. Waite Keeney, State Director, CWA, "New Mexico and Relief before November 15, 1933," Record Group 69, CWA HD 389ON, 6AS, 1934, National Archives, Washington, D.C. (hereafter NARG 69).

3. *Santa Fe New Mexican,* 26 November 1929, 27 November 1929, 19

December 1929; Charles F. Searle, *Minister of Relief: Harry Hopkins and the Depression* (Syracuse: Syracuse University Press, 1963), 10.

4. *Roswell Dispatch*, 13 December 1929; *Santa Fe New Mexican*, 14 December 1929; *Albuquerque Journal*, 19 April 1931, 3 May 1931, 5 August 1931, 29 August 1931.

5. *Santa Fe New Mexican*, 9 December 1930, 27 January 1931; James B. Swayne, "A Survey of the Economic, Political and Legal Aspects of the Labor Problem in New Mexico" (M.A. thesis, University of New Mexico, 1936), 47, 61.

6. *Santa Fe New Mexican*, 6 February 1931; Correspondence relative to relief and public works construction in New Mexico, 9 July 1931, 12 February 1932, Record Group 73, President's Organization for Unemployment Relief, State of New Mexico–Public, National Archives, Washington, D.C.; Gifford Pinchot to Arthur Seligman, telegram, 10 December 1931; Seligman to Pinchot, Governor, Harrisburg, Pennsylvania, telegram, 10 December 1931, Governor Seligman Papers, New Mexico State Records Center and Archives (hereafter NMRSCA); *Albuquerque Journal*, 24 June 1932.

7. *Santa Fe New Mexican*, 6 February 1931, 17 September 1931.

8. Herbert J. Hagerman, "How the Depression Is Affecting New Mexico," *New Mexico Tax Bulletin*, 10 (1932): 121–44.

9. U.S., Department of Agriculture, Soil Conservation Service, "Destruction of Villages at San Marcial," Regional Bulletin 28, Conservation Economics Series 11, May 1937, 2, 9–11; *Santa Fe New Mexican*, 2 October 1929, 10 October 1929, 23 October 1929. Judging from an article in the *Albuquerque Journal*, 14 October 1931, San Marcial residents were probably wise in declining the offer to pick cotton. According to Jay W. Jones, manager of a farm labor office, the pay for picking cotton in New Mexico was forty cents per 100 pounds and only a person accustomed to picking cotton could pick enough to make a living. The pay in Arizona for picking cotton was fifty cents per 100 pounds.

10. C. H. Howell, "The Era of Conservancy" in Robert F. Kelleher, ed., *Resources and Opportunities of the Middle Rio Grande Valley*, University of New Mexico *Bulletin*, Economic Series 2 (1935): 1–17; *Santa Fe New Mexican*, 9 December 1929, 17 February 1930, 10 March 1930; Joseph Karr, "Needs and Opportunities of the Middle Rio Grande Valley," in Kelleher, *Resources and Opportunities*, 44–54; R. G. Hosea, "The Middle Rio Grande Conservancy District," *New Mexico Highway Journal*, 7 (May 1929): 6–9.

11. *Magdalena News*, 12 October 1929.

12. *Santa Fe New Mexican*, 24 April 1930, 5 May 1930, 9 March 1931; *Albuquerque Journal*, 1 January 1931, 17 April 1932, 20 April 1932; SCS, "Destruction of Villages," 9; Supplementary data to "Report on Relief Survey of New Mexico," by State Bureau of Child Welfare, to Reconstruction Finance Corporation, Record Group 234, New Mexico correspondence, National Archives (hereafter NARG 234).

13. U.S., Department of Agriculture, Soil Conservation Service, "The Santa Cruz Irrigation District," Regional Bulletin 45, Conservation Economics Series 18, July 1937, 2–4; Weigle, ed., *Hispanic Villages*, 87, 95.

14. SCS, "Santa Cruz Irrigation District," 5–9; *Santa Fe New Mexican,* 31 March 1931.

15. J. L. Burkholder, "Bringing National Relief to New Mexico," *New Mexico Business Review,* 2 (1933): 6–12; SCS, "Santa Cruz Irrigation District," 9–10; Searle, *Minister of Relief,* 16; *Preliminary Inventory to the Records of the Works Progress Administration, Appendix D,* "Administrative History of the Federal Emergency Relief Administration, the Civil Works Administration, and the Work Projects Administration," 47–54; SCS, "Santa Cruz Irrigation District," 9–11.

16. "Report on Federal Relief Admininstration in the State of New Mexico to the House of Representatives, 11th New Mexico Legislature," by Governor Arthur Seligman, 14 September 1932, Seligman Papers, NMSRCA.

17. Memo, Murray to Reeves, 3 April 1932, 4 April 1932, Correspondence, Seligman Papers, NMSRCA; "Report on Relief Survey of New Mexico by State Bureau of Child Welfare," 22 August 1932, NARG 234.

18. "Report on Relief Survey," NARG 234; Memos Murray to Reeves, 2 April 1932, 6 April 1932; Memo Reeves to County Commissioners, 4 April 1932, Reeves to Dr. H. L. Kent, President, New Mexico College of Agricultural and Mechanical Arts, State College, New Mexico, 5 April 1932; Reeves to Seligman, 20 July 1932; Pineda to Seligman, 22 December 1932, Seligman Papers, NMSCRA.

19. "Report on Relief Survey," NARG 234; Reeves to Croxton, Assistant to Director, RFC, 26 August 1932, NARG 234, New Mexico Correspondence.

20. "Report on Relief Survey of New Mexico," 14 September 1932, and "Supplementary data to report of September 14, 1932," Wayne McMillan to Reeves, 3 March 1933, NARG 234, New Mexico Correspondence. According to William Pickens, "The New Deal in New Mexico" in John Braemon, ed., *The State and Local Levels,* vol. 2 of *The New Deal* (Columbus: Ohio State University Press, 1975), Governor Seligman was bound by the various New Mexico factions and tried fanatically to balance the budget. He was pushed to the right by the Cutting progressives who wanted to return as much money as possible to the taxpayers.

21. Margaret Reeves, "Federal Relief in New Mexico," *New Mexico Tax Bulletin,* 12 (1933): 106–8; Reeves to Seligman, 4 January 1933, "Relief Orders Issued by Bureau of Child Welfare," 17 January 1933; Reeves to Seligman, 7 January 1933, "Report on Federal Relief Administration in New Mexico," 14 January 1933, Seligman Papers, NMSRCA.

22. John A. Salmond, *The Civilian Conservation Corps, 1933–1942: A New Deal Case Study* (Durham: Duke University Press, 1967), 1–8; Paul Conkin, *The New Deal,* 2nd ed. (Arlington Heights, Illinois: Harlan Davidson, Inc., 1967, 1975), 18–19; Robert E. Sherwood, *Roosevelt and Hopkins: An Intimate History* (New York: Harper and Bros., 1948), 31–34.

23. William H. Pickens, "Cutting versus Chavez: Battle of the Patrones," *NMHR,* 46 (January 1971): 10. In 1932 Cutting repudiated the Republican Party because of its conservatism. According to Governor Seligman, "Cutting was a New Dealer before most New Mexican politicians realized it existed";

William H. Pickens, "A Reply to Wolf," *NMHR*, 47 (October 1972): 346.
Cutting was among the minority of Progressive leaders who supported the New
Deal, Robert W. Larson, "The Profile of a New Mexican Progressive," *NMHR*,
45 (July 1970): 233–44. He was not among the 105 Progressive leaders selected
for study by Otis L. Graham for analysis, however, in *An Encore for Reform: The
Old Progressives and the New Deal* (New York: 1967). With Cutting's support,
FDR carried New Mexico with an unprecedented 63.7 percent of the votes;
William H. Pickens, "The New Deal in New Mexico," 311; Lowitt, *The New
Deal and the West,* 4–6.

24. Rexford Guy Tugwell, a member of Roosevelt's "brain trust" and often
considered the architect of the first New Deal, visited Santa Fe in October 1933.
While there he paid tribute to some of its publicizers.

> Spanish-America, as we are all too likely to forget, is even older than English
> America and its impress is just as deep. . . . But the Santa Fe school of writers has
> made this amply evident to those who read books. Miss Cather and Mrs. Austin
> celebrate the land each in her own way and each superbly.

He then went on to express some of his own concerns.

> What no one seems to worry about is the crisis which an outsider can see
> impending. For the land is being wasted, running away into the Rio Grande. . . .
> For the "native" and for the Navajos and Hopis the future is darkened by the
> constant menace of soil exhaustion. (*Santa Fe New Mexican,* 10 October 1933)

The contemporary historian Thomas Donnelly credited the "New Deal of appreciation of the Spanish-American" to Bronson Cutting who, he claimed,
introduced cultural pluralism to New Mexico. Thomas Donnelly, "New Mexico:
An Area of Conflicting Cultures," in Donnelly, ed., *Rocky Mountain Politics*
(Albuquerque: University of New Mexico Press, 1940), 218–51.

25. Chauvenet, "Paul A. F. Walter," 29–34; Walter to John D. DeHuff,
Secretary, Chamber of Commerce, 7 June 1933; Walter to John Collier, Bureau
of Indian Affairs, 5 December 1933; Walter to Dr. Robert O. Brown, Chairman,
Federal Civil Works Administration, Santa Fe, 8 December 1933; Brown to
Walter, 9 December 1933; Walter to Governor A. W. Hockenhull, 24 March
1934; Paul A. F. Walter Collection, Box 123, MNM-HL. Through Walter's
influence the New Mexico Historical Society and the State Museum sponsored
several WPA projects, among them two archaeological field projects, the translation of the Spanish historical archives, and the copying of Spanish-Colonial
ecclesiastical designs, *Santa Fe New Mexican,* 18 December 1935.

26. Alice Corbin Henderson, "E. Dana Johnson," *NMHR*, 13 (January
1938): 120–28. It was Johnson who spread the news nationwide that the famed
Santuario at Chimayo and its historic contents were about to be sold off, piece-
meal. Mary Austin learned about it while lecturing at Yale and used Johnson's
article to interest the anonymous donor who bought and restored the building
to the Catholic Church.

27. *Santa Fe New Mexican,* 10 October 1933, 21 October 1933, 24 October
1933, 21 November 1933, a series of articles written by Rexford Guy Tugwell

to the effect that conservation was good business; letter to the editor from the President of the New Mexico Tourist Development League, 13 February 1935.

28. Preliminary Inventory WPA, Appendix D, NARG 69; Sherwood, *Roosevelt and Hopkins,* 44–45.

29. *Santa Fe New Mexican,* 21 October 1933, 16 December 1933, 14 December 1935; Manual Gamio, "Race Relations in New Mexico," in *Mexican Immigration to the United States: A Study of Human Migration and Adjustment* (New York: Dover Press, 1930, 1971), 210, considered it very significant that two out of three Spanish Americans blamed the federal government for being concerned with the Indians but not the Spanish Americans. This was undoubtedly a reaction brought about by Collier's success in pressing the Indian cause in the Pueblo Indian Lands controversy but it was, as well, objective fact. New Mexico's Hispanos were well aware that the Indians received a good many more benefits than they did. For a fuller discussion of this matter see Chapter Eight, 137–38.

30. "Additional Data Regarding the Relief Situation in the State of New Mexico, 22 September 1932," NARG 234; *Santa Fe New Mexican,* 29 April 1934.

31. *Preliminary Inventory WPA, Appendix D,* 49, NARG 69; Pierce Williams to Harry Hopkins, 16 July 1933, 5 October 1933; L. L. Bondurant to Margaret Reeves, 11 July 1933; Benjamin Glassburg to Aubrey Williams, 5 April 1934, "Summary Data Regarding State and Local Relief Funds, 17 August 1934," Hopkins Collection, Box 58, New Mexico Field Reports, Franklin D. Roosevelt Library (hereafter FDRL); Telephone, J. D. Atwood to Bronson Cutting, 25 January 1934, Bruce McClure, Secretary FERA to Cutting, 1 February 1934, NARG 69, CWA, New Mexico Complaints; *Santa Fe New Mexican,* 1 May 1934, 4 May 1934, 29 January 1935; Rupert F. Asplund, "New Mexico's Tax Structure," University of New Mexico, Department of Government *Bulletin* 4 (June 1946): 6–7.

32. Vernon Northrup to Corrington Gill, 1 November 1933, FERA 406.2; Howard Myers to Mary Perry, 6 April 1934, FERA 401.3, NARG 69.

33. Marie Dresden, Regional Social Worker to Josephine C. Brown, Administrative Assistant, FERA, "Field Trip to New Mexico, October 22–24, 1934"; Dresden to Brown, "Report on New Mexico, December 10, 1934"; Hopkins Collection, Box 58, FDRL. Reeves was not far off. By July 1935, 28 percent of all New Mexicans were on relief, the highest percentage in the nation by far. According to Pickens, "New Deal in New Mexico," the disproportionate assistance was due largely to the effort of Bronson Cutting and Clyde Tingley, although Tingley was never very sympathetic to the needs of Spanish Americans.

34. Alice S. Clements, Regional Social Worker, to Josephine Brown, "Summary of Work from January 4 to January 12," 14 January 1935; Maude Van Kemp, Acting Supervisor, Social Service Division, to Dudley Frank, Acting Administrator, NMERA, 19 April 1935; Van Kemp to Clements, 19 April 1935; Clements to Brown, 29 April 1935; Hopkins Collection, Box 58, FDRL.

35. Clements to Brown, "Summary of Work from January 4–12," 14 January 1935; Clements to Brown, 14 January 1935; Memo Clements to Brown, 31

January 1935; Clements to Brown, 29 April 1935; Hopkins Collection, Box 58, FDRL; Clements to Brown, 20 January 1935; Clements to Aubrey Williams, Assistant Administrator, FERA, 27 April 1935, NARG 69 FERA New Mexico Field Reports; Margaret Reeves, Executive Secretary, State Civil Works Administration, to Aubrey Williams, Assistant Administrator, Federal Civil Works Administration, 5 February 1934, NARG 69, CWA, Administrative Correspondence, February–May 1934.

36. Charles P. Loomis and Glen Grisham, "The New Mexico Experiment in Village Rehabilitation," *Applied Anthropology*, 2 (June 1943): 16–18; Michael Pijoan, "Food Availability and Social Function," *New Mexico Quarterly Review*, 12 (November 1942): 418–23.

37. Stated in "Rules and Regulations in Respect to the Administration of Federal Relief in the State of New Mexico" issued supplementary to the rules and regulations issued 7 October 1932, Seligman Papers, NMSRCA. Reeves also worried a great deal about the problem of tuberculosis and the lack of free hospitals, Lorena Hickok to Harry Hopkins, 6 May 1934, Hopkins Collection, Box 68, Lorena Hickok Reports, FDRL.

38. C. E. Waller, M.D. to Senator Carl A. Hatch, 26 April 1935; S. L. Burton, M.D. to New Mexico FERA, n.d.; NARG 69, FERA 440; E. C. DeMoss to Harry Hopkins, 6 February 1936, NARG 69, FERA 440.

39. In the Tingley administration's efforts to discredit relief administrator Reeves, it was apparently alleged that neoarsphenamine, a medication for the treatment of syphilis, had been misused as a substitute for butter. Earp assured his correspondent that this was most improbable and that any quantity distributed in the state had certainly been used for a very valuable purpose. Rosslyn Earp to William F. Snow, 12 April 1935, NARG 69, FERA 440. Walter Clarke, "Syphilis in New Mexico" (New Mexico Tuberculosis Association, 1934), NARG 69, FERA 440. Lorin F. Jones, Assistant Area Conservationist, Soil Conservation Service, to Ralph R. Will, State Director, Farm Security Administration, 12 August 1941; Will to Jones, 16 August 1941. Record Group 96, Farm Security Administration, Malaria Control, National Archives (hereafter NARG 96).

40. Richard Lowitt and Maurine Beasley, eds., *One Third of a Nation* (Urbana: University of Illinois, 1981), ix.

41. Hickok to Hopkins, 27 April 1934, Hopkins Collection, Box 68, FDRL.

42. Hickok to Hopkins, 4 May 1934, Hopkins Collection, Box 68, FDRL.

43. Ibid.

44. Ibid.

45. Raymond Ryan, Vice Chairman, Bernalillo County CWA to Hatch, 6 January 1934; Paul Dodge to Hatch, 12 January 1934; T. P. Martin, Chairman Taos County CWA to Hatch, 6 January 1934; NARG 69, CWA Administrative Correspondence, New Mexico.

46. Jacob Baker to Hatch, 9 January 1934; Hopkins to Hatch, 17 January 1934, Hopkins to New Mexico CWA, 16 February 1934; *New Mexico Relief Bulletin*, NARG 69, CWA New Mexico Complaints. Carl Hatch urged Hopkins to permit staggering on the basis that men and women were on the verge of

starvation, Hatch to Hopkins, 5 January 1934, NARG 69, FERA, New Mexico, Administrative Correspondence.

47. Telegram, Mrs. W. F. Kirby, National Committeewoman to Mary W. Dawson, National Campaign Committee, 13 October 1936; Mildred H. Andrew, Division Women's Projects, WPA, Santa Fe, to Ellen S. Woodward, Director, Women's Work, WPA, Washington, D.C., 6 August 1936, NARG 69, WPA New Mexico State Files, 661.

48. Ellen S. Woodward to Mary H. Isham, Regional Director Women's Programs, WPA, Salt Lake City, Utah, 20 November 1936; Robert H. Hinckley, Assistant Administrator, WPA, Salt Lake City, to Thad Holt, Assistant Administrator, WPA, Washington, D.C., 11 November 1936, NARG 69, WPA, New Mexico State Files, 661.

49. Swayne, "Labor in New Mexico," 79; Weigle, *Hispanic Villages*, 78, 120–21; Nancie S. Gonzalez, *The Spanish Americans: A Heritage of Pride* (Albuquerque: University of New Mexico Press, 1969), 93; E. E. Maes, "The Labor Movement in New Mexico," *New Mexico Business Review*, 4 (1935): 139; *Santa Fe New Mexican*, 4 August 1934, 2 February 1935, 27 May 1935, 9 August 1935. A petition addressed to Governor Seligman signed by twenty-four Hispanos from Las Vegas, New Mexico, asked for work and seeds because they were on the point of starvation—and threatened trouble if they were not helped; Petition to Seligman, 23 June 1933, Seligman Papers, NMSRCA. The funds allotted to New Mexico in 1935 fell far short of meeting the relief needs due in part to a number of strikes; Pierce Williams to Hopkins, 5 October 1935.

50. Abraham Hoffman, *Unwanted Mexican-Americans in the Great Depression* (Tucson: University of Arizona Press, 1974), 26; Swadesh, *Primeros Pobladores*, 205–6; Maes, "Labor Movement," 139; Swayne, "Labor Problem," 33; Gonzalez, *Spanish Americans*, 93. Jesús Pallares, an organizer of *La Liga Obrera* and chairman of the miners' relief committee which headed a strike movement at Madrid, New Mexico, was accused of being a communist and deported on 29 June 1936; *Santa Fe New Mexican*, 14 May 1934; Acuña, *Occupied America*, 142–43, 158; "Deporting Jesus," *The Nation*, 143 (18 July 1936): 67–69. The WPA crack-down on aliens affected some New Mexican Hispanos who had long considered themselves citizens of the United States. Although some had lived in the country since childhood, they had never been naturalized. Native women who had married aliens prior to 22 September 1922 had, by law, lost their citizenship and so were ineligible for relief. They, along with their United States–born children, were also eligible for deportation; *Albuquerque Journal*, 23 November 1937, 28 November 1937, 3 December 1937.

51. Deutsch, *No Separate Refuge*, 162–64.

52. SCS, "Village Dependence," 26–28; Donnelly, "New Mexico," 223–24.

53. Gladys Meehl, District Supervisor, New Mexico Relief and Security Authority to Presentación Salazar of Questa, 24 February 1936; Salazar to Charles Alspach, Director, Transient Activities, 26 February 1936; Alspach to Salazar, 16 March 1936; Max Martinez of Albuquerque to FERA, 24 February 1936; Alspach to Martinez, 14 March 1936, NARG 69, FERA 421, Transients' Complaints.

54. Deutsch, *No Separate Refuge,* 165. According to Carey McWilliams, *Ill Fares the Land: Migrants and Migratory Labor in the United States* (Boston: Barnes and Noble, 1942), 114–15, Johnson called the blockade on behalf of Colorado's resident Hispanos in order to protect their jobs from imported Mexican labor.

55. Telephone, Tom Jenkins, Chief Inspector, Port of Entry at Tres Piedras to New Mexico Governor Clyde Tingley, 21 April 1936; Juan Vigil, New Mexico State Comptroller to Colorado Governor Edward Johnson, 24 April 1936; W. Wiley Dumm to Tingley, 24 April 1936; Roy S. Shahan to Tingley, 27 April 1936; Governor Tingley Papers, Special Issue: Colorado Embargo, NMSRCA. Two years later *Liga* members in New Mexico urged Hispanic workers to stay out of the Colorado beet fields because their presence would destroy the Colorado Agricultural Workers' Union and bring on a starvation wage policy. *Albuquerque Journal,* 20 March 1938.

56. Hurt, "Manzano," 36, 99; U.S., Department of Agriculture, Soil Conservation Service, "Reconnaissance Survey of Human Dependency on Resources in the Rio Grande Watershed," Regional Bulletin 33, Conservation Economics Series 6, December 1936, 88–95; *Albuquerque Journal,* 1 November 1933; Weigle, *Hispanic Villages,* 68, 83, 86–87, 96.

57. Weigle, *Hispanic Villages,* 175; E. E. Maes, "The World and the People of Cundiyo," *Land Policy Review,* 4 (1941): 9; "Report on San Jose Situation"; Annida Slavens, Field Representative to Seligman, 19 July 1932; Reeves to Seligman, 20 July 1932; Seligman Papers, NMSRCA; *Santa Fe New Mexican,* 10 December 1931, 5 February 1932, 29 April 1932.

58. Paul A. F. Walter, Jr., "The Spanish-Speaking Community in New Mexico," *Sociology and Social Research,* 24 (1939): 150–57.

## Chapter Seven

1. Paul A. F. Walter to John DeHuff, Secretary, Santa Fe Chamber of Commerce, 7 June 1933; Paul A. F. Walter Papers, Box 123, Correspondence 1933–1934, MNM-HL.

2. "Report of the Secretary for the Chamber of Commerce 1933, 1935, 1936, 1937, 1938; Santa Fe Chamber of Commerce Papers, MNM-HL.

3. *Santa Fe New Mexican,* 13 October 1933, 17 November 1933, 25 November 1933; Senator Carl Hatch to Harry L. Hopkins, Administrator, FERA, 19 February 1934, NARG 69, CWA Administrative correspondence, Miscellaneous Projects.

4. Emilie M. Baca, Field Representative, Bureau of Child Welfare, New Mexico, to Jacob Baker, Director, Work Relief and Special Projects, FERA, 6 October 1933, NARG 69, FERA, New Mexico State Files, 450, Work Relief.

5. Telegram from Mrs. George Graham, Chairman, Local CWA, Catron County, to Bronson Cutting, 20 February 1934, concerning the plight of Spanish-American farmers in the region, NARG 69, CWA Administrative Correspondence, New Mexico State Miscellaneous. Petition from 14 Hispanos in Vallecitos, New Mexico, requesting repair of old mail routes in Sandoval County,

29 June 1936, NARG 69, WPA State Files 651.101–651.108; Felipe Tenorio, Anton Chico, New Mexico, to Harry Hopkins, 17 April 1937, NARG 69, WPA, New Mexico State Files, 651.104.

6. *Santa Fe New Mexican,* 16 April 1935; "Minutes of Meeting of the Board of Directors of the Santa Fe Chamber of Commerce held Thursday, April 9, 1935," Santa Fe Chamber of Commerce Papers, MNM-HL.

7. Lea Rowland, Administrator, WPA, Santa Fe, to Frank V. Lanham, Staff Engineer, WPA, Washington, 23 October 1935; Fred G. Healy, Assistant Administrator, WPA, Santa Fe to Frank V. Lanham, 4 October 1935, NARG 69, New Mexico State Files 651.104.

8. *Santa Fe New Mexican* editorial, "Harping on Catron," 7 March 1936; Rowland and Healy to Colonel Lawrence Westbrook, Assistant Administrator, WPA, Washington, 19 March 1936, NARG 69, WPA New Mexico State Files, 651.101–651.108.

9. *Santa Fe New Mexican,* 11 February 1937; Form letter, Santa Fe Chamber of Commerce, President and Field Secretary to community representatives in northern New Mexico, n.d., Santa Fe Chamber of Commerce Papers, MNM-HL. The Santa Fe Chamber held out support for its road program as a primary political consideration in its support for gubernatorial candidates in 1938; Santa Fe Chamber of Commerce President, Ellis Bauer, to Governor John E. Miles, Santa Fe, 13 October 1938, Santa Fe Chamber of Commerce Papers, MNM-HL.

10. Governor Clyde Tingley to Harry Hopkins, 28 April 1938; Captain Conrad P. Hardy to Robert H. Hinckley, Assistant Administrator and Field Representative, WPA, 27 May 1938; Hardy to Colonel F. C. Harrington, Administrator, WPA, Washington, 6 June 1938, NARG 69, WPA New Mexico State Files, 651.101–651.108.

11. Governor Tingley and other leaders of the state Democratic Party carried on a continuing feud with WPA relief administrators, apparently piqued by their independence and refusal to "play politics." His complaints concerning Healy were more likely motivated by a desire to harm him politically than out of any great concern for the efficiency of New Mexico's road building program.

12. *Santa Fe New Mexican,* 23 November 1933, 3 February 1934, 12 March 1935; J. T. Reid, ed., "State Conference on Adult Education, June 28–29, 1935," University of New Mexico *Bulletin,* Education Series, 9 (September 1935): 29–37.

13. Mildred H. Andrew, Director, Division of Women's and Professional Projects, Santa Fe, to Ellen S. Woodward, Assistant Administrator, WPA, Washington, 2 July 1936, NARG 69, WPA New Mexico State Files, 661, May–July 1936.

14. The NYA was established in October 1935 to take over the FERA College student aid program. Director Aubrey Williams gradually expanded the program to include a diversity of projects. Arts and crafts projects in New Mexico were sponsored by the State Department of Vocational Education, "Final Report, National Youth Administration, State of New Mexico"; Thomas L. Popejoy to Aubrey Williams, Director, NYA, New York, 10 October 1935; Richard

Brown, Assistant Director, NYA, New York to Popejoy, 4 August 1936, NARG 119, NYA, Administrative Correspondence, New Mexico.

15. Brice H. Sewell, "A New Type of School," *New Mexico School Review*, 15 (1935): 49–50; Wroth, "New Hope," 26; Reid, "State Conference," 38.

16. Wroth, "New Hope," 27–28.

17. *Albuquerque Journal*, 16 September 1937; Wroth, "New Hope," 29–31; Sewell, "New Type of School," 49; for similar classes in the Hispanic communities of southern Colorado see Stoller, "Spanish-Americans," 48.

18. Reid, "State Conference," 37–39; *Santa Fe New Mexican*, 23 August 1930, 1 December 1930.

19. *Santa Fe New Mexican*, 27 June 1935.

20. Mildred H. Andrew, Director, WPA Women's and Professional Projects, Santa Fe to Ellen S. Woodward, Assistant Administrator, WPA, Washington, 2 July 1936; correspondence relating to school construction; NARG 69, WPA, New Mexico State Files 651.101–651.108; Helen Dail Thomas, Director Women's Work, New Mexico SERA, to Woodward, 14 November 1934; New Mexico Relief *Bulletin*, 20 December 1934, NARG 69, FERA, New Mexico State Files, Director of Women's Work; Reid, "State Conference," 38; Wroth, "New Hope," 28–29.

21. *Santa Fe New Mexican*, 15 May 1935; Tom L. Popejoy, Assistant New Mexico State Director, NYA, to Richard Brown, Assistant Executive Director, NYA, New York, 4 August 1936; "Final Report, NYA, for State of New Mexico," NARG 119, NYA, Administrative Correspondence, New Mexico.

22. Reid, "State Conference," 39.

23. "Statewide Projects in Operation," 26 August 1936, prepared by Division of Women's and Professional Projects, NARG 69, WPA, State Report, New Mexico C to V, W 21.2R32. Nina Otero-Warren, "Experiences and Human Interest Stories," Literacy Division, WPA, Santa Fe, New Mexico, 12 July 1939, NARG 69, WPA, New Mexico State Files, 661, January 1939.

24. Otero-Warren, "Experiences and Human Interest Stories."

25. Ibid.

26. Thomas L. Calkins, "I Heard America Singing at Nambé," January 1940, NARG 69, WPA, New Mexico State Files, 651.314.

27. Margaret Reeves, State Relief Administrator, FERA to Ellen S. Woodward, Director, Women's Work, FERA, Washington, 3 October 1933, 18 September 1934, NARG 69, FERA, New Mexico State Files, Director of Women's Work.

28. Helen Dail Thomas, to Woodward, 27 September 1934, 14 November 1934, NARG 69, FERA, New Mexico State Files, Director of Women's Work.

29. Ivie H. Jones, Home Demonstration Agent, Cooperative Extension Work, New Mexico State College, Las Cruces to G. E. Dalbey, County Administrator, Las Vegas, 21 October 1935; Dalbey to Mary Perry, Director, Women's Work and Public Service, Santa Fe, 21 October 1935; Perry to Woodward, 22 October 1935; Woodward to Lea Rowland, Administrator, WPA, Santa Fe, 4 November 1935; Perry to Woodward, 19 December 1935, NARG 69, WPA, New Mexico State Files, 661, August 1935.

30. R. R. Daughtry, Roswell, New Mexico, to Senator Dennis Chavez, 23 October 1939, NARG 69, WPA, New Mexico State Files, 651.3142; Amy B. Dwelly, Assistant Supervisor Nursery Schools to Isabel Lancaster Eckles, Federal Works Agency, Work Projects Administration, Santa Fe, 18 September 1941, NARG 69, WPA, New Mexico State Files, 651.3144, 1941.

31. "Healthful Living in the Family," prepared by the WPA Adult Education Project and members of the Staff of the State Department of Public Health, Santa Fe, 15 February 1941, NARG 69, WPA, New Mexico State Files, 651.323.

32. Reid, "State Conference," 37–41; Mildred H. Andrews, Director Division of Women's and Professional Projects, WPA, Santa Fe, to Ellen S. Woodward, Assistant Administrator, WPA, 2 July 1936, NARG 69, WPA, New Mexico State Files, 661, May–July 1936; "Statewide Projects in Operation," Division of Women's Work and Professional Projects, WPA, 26 August 1936, NARG 69, State Report, New Mexico, C to V, W 21.2R32; Amy B. Dwelly, State Supervisor, Child Protection, "Narrative Report of the Nursery School Project," 23 July–23 August 1942, NARG 69, WPA, New Mexico State Files, 651.325, 15 February 1942; Richard R. Brown, Assistant Executive Director, NYA, New York, to Thomas L. Popejoy, State Director, NYA, New Mexico, 4 August 1936, NARG 119, NYA, New Mexico Administrative Correspondence.

33. Phyllis Mayne, Supervisor to Santa Fe Headquarters, "Scope of Operations for Housekeeping Aide Project," 16 January 1941; "Narrative Report for Housekeeping Aide Project, New Mexico," October 1942, NARG 69, WPA, New Mexico State Files, 651.3142, January 1941.

34. "Narrative Reports for School Lunch Programs," 16 January 1941; Ruth C. Miller, State Supervisor, School Lunch Project to Isabel Eckles, State Director, Service Division, 14 June 1940; Miller to Eckles, 17 June 1940, NARG 69, WPA, New Mexico State Files, 651.322.

35. "Final Report, NYA, N.M."; Richard Brown, Assistant Executive Director, NYA to Popejoy, 4 August 1936, Popejoy to Brown, 4 August 1936; NARG 119, NYA, New Mexico Administrative correspondence; Popejoy to Dorothy I. Cline, Field Advisor, WPA, in charge of Community Affairs, Washington, 30 June 1936, NARG 69, WPA, New Mexico State Files, 651.363, January–December 1936.

36. WPA Recreation Programs, correspondence and reports, January 1936 to October 1942, NARG 69, WPA, New Mexico State Files, 651.36, 651.361, 651.362, 651.363, 651.3163.

37. Thomas L. Popejoy to John J. Corson, Assistant Director, NYA, Washington, 17 September 1935; Popejoy to Aubrey Williams, Administrator, NYA, Washington, 10 October 1935; "Coordination Project," prepared by Popejoy approximately 10 January 1936, NARG 119, NYA, New Mexico, Administrative Correspondence.

38. David R. Williams, Director, Work Projects, NYA to Popejoy, 28 May 1938; Popejoy to Corson, 20 September 1935; "Final Report, NYA, N.M."; NARG 119, NYA, New Mexico, Administrative Correspondence.

39. Salmond, *CCC*, 1–8, 26, 30; Reeves, "Federal Relief in New Mexico," 108.

40. Salmond, *CCC,* 47–54, 121–26, 129–32; Kenneth E. Hendrickson, Jr., "The Civilian Conservation Corps in the Southwestern States," in Donald W. Whisenhunt, ed., *The Depression in the Southwest* (Port Washington, N.Y.: Kennikat Press, 1980), 15–16; Abad Martinez, personal interview, April 1986; *Albuquerque Journal Magazine,* 6, 25 (April 1983).

41. Salmond, *CCC,* 47–54; Hendrickson, 23; Cremin, *Transformation of the School,* 320–21; CCC Bulletin Number 72, Fort Bliss District Headquarters, Fort Bliss, Texas, 6 August 1936, Tingley Papers, NMSRCA; Abad Martinez, personal interview; Frank Ernest Hill, *The School in the Camp: The Educational Program of the Civilian Conservation Corps* (New York: American Association for Adult Education, 1935), 43–44; *Santa Fe New Mexican,* 14 February 1936; *Albuquerque Journal,* 2 September 1937.

42. Statistical Summaries of States, NARG 35, File 80; "Memorandum for the Press," 16 July 1936, ECW Office, Washington, Tingley Papers, NMSRCA; *Santa Fe New Mexican,* 14 September 1933, 3 November 1933; *Albuquerque Journal,* 9 September 1937, 12 September 1937, 28 October 1937; Grenville Village Council, Union County to Governor Clyde Tingley, 27 March 1937, Tingley Papers, NMSRCA. According to James T. Patterson, *The New Deal and the States: Federalism in Transition* (Princeton: Princeton University Press, 1969), 82, Governor Seligman asked for a list of CCC recruits and their political affiliations. There is no evidence, however, that he ever used this information for political purposes. Seligman Papers, New Deal Agencies, February–September 1933, NMSRCA. In another incident members of the local Democratic Committee of Truchas, New Mexico, complained to Governor Tingley that politics sometimes entered into the CCC selection process which had to go through the county relief agencies. Anastacio L. Romero, J. A. Lucero, Nestor Rael to Tingley, 30 January 1935, Tingley Papers, NMSRCA. CCC camps in New Mexico ranged from a high of forty-four to a low of twenty-two in 1941, Report on the CCC prepared by Governor Miles, Miles Papers, NMSRCA. Hendrickson, "CCC in the Southwest," 14; Salmond, *CCC,* 45.

43. Hendrickson, "The CCC in the Southwest," 20; Monthly Camp and Personnel Reports, Camp F-64, 16 January 1941, NARG 35, File 12; Geneva Short to Jennie M. Kirby, Director New Mexico Department of Public Welfare, 23 April 1941, Tingley Papers, NMSRCA; Abad Martinez, personal interview.

44. Report by Governor John Miles, Miles Papers, NMSRCA; Waite J. Keeney, State Director National Reemployment for New Mexico to Governor Clyde Tingley, 13 May 1935, Tingley Papers, NMSRCA.

45. J. J. McEntee, Acting Director, ECW, Washington, to Tingley, 24 July 1936, Tingley Papers, NMSRCA.

46. Special Report No. 100, 9 August 1936, A. W. Stockman, Special Investigator to J. J. McEntee; McEntee to Tingley, 18 August 1936, Tingley Papers, NMSRCA.

47. A fourth project, the Federal Theater Project was never implemented in New Mexico. William F. McDonald, *Federal Relief Administration and the Arts* (Columbus, Ohio: Ohio State University Press, 1969), 585.

48. The PWAP was set up and supervised by the Treasury Department, one

of the agencies designated to extend relief to unemployed professional people. It was allocated funds for this purpose by the CWA. When the PWAP was terminated in June 1934, its immediate successor was the Treasury Section of Painting and Sculpture, also supervised by the Treasury Department. Its purpose, however, was not so much relief as it was to provide art to decorate federal buildings under construction. Its successor, the Treasury Relief Art Project (TRAP) was initiated in July 1935 and ran concurrently with the Federal Art Project which was set up under Federal Project One of the WPA. Both projects were based primarily upon relief. TRAP art activity in New Mexico centered around Taos and Santa Fe. Emil Bisttram, an area artist, directed the project; William Henry Spurlock II, "Federal Support for the Visual Arts in the State of New Mexico, 1933–1943" (M.A. thesis, University of New Mexico, 1974), 12–38; Arrel Morgan Gibson, *The Santa Fe and Taos Art Colonies: Age of the Muses, 1900–1942* (Norman: University of Oklahoma Press, 1983), 83–84.

49. Spurlock, "Visual Arts in New Mexico," 42–48; McDonald, *Federal Relief and the Arts,* 385, 432; Will Wroth, personal correspondence, 5 February 1985; Gibson, *Santa Fe and Taos,* 174; *Santa Fe New Mexican,* 25 March 1936.

50. Spurlock, "Visual Arts in New Mexico," 48–50; McDonald, *Federal Relief and the Arts,* 442–55, FN 456; Lorin W. Brown, Charles L. Briggs, and Marta Weigle, *Hispano Folklife of New Mexico: The Lorin W. Brown Federal Writers' Project Manuscripts* (Albuquerque: University of New Mexico Press, 1978), 240–42.

51. McDonald, *Federal Relief and the Arts,* 629, 638–39; Brown, *Hispano Folklife,* 241–42; Helen Chandler Ryan, State Director, FMP to Dr. Bruno David Ussher, Assistant to Director, FMP, Washington, 30 April 1936; Major J. A. Chase to Ussher, 16 June 1935, NARG 69, Music Project, 651.311.

52. McDonald, *Federal Relief and the Arts,* 638–39.

53. Henry Putney Beers, *Spanish and Mexican Records of the American Southwest: A Bibliographical Guide to Archives and Manuscript Sources* (Tucson: University of Arizona Press, 1979), 50; Earl E. Watson, Regional Engineer to Tex Goldschmidt, FERA, Washington, 4 January 1935, NARG 69, FERA, New Mexico State Files, 451, Projects; Brown, *Hispano Folklife,* 243.

54. Supervisor (unsigned) of Spanish Translation Project to Ina Sizer Cassidy, Director, State Federal Writers' Project, 26 December 1935, WPA File 5, NMSRCA.

55. McDonald, *Federal Relief and the Arts,* 639; Brown, *Hispano Folklife,* 243.

56. News report to Cassidy, n.d., WPA File 5, NMSRCA. The map, made by don Bernardo de Miera y Pacheco, showed many houses and walls broken out due to "assassinations by the [Comanche and Apache] enemies."

57. McDonald, *Federal Relief and the Arts,* 657–59; Marta Weigle and Mary Powell, "From Alice Corbin's Lines Mumbled in Sleep to Eufemia's Sopapillas: Women and the Federal Writers' Project in New Mexico," *New America: A Journal of American and Southwestern Culture,* 4 (1982): 55–56.

58. Weigle, "Lines Mumbled," 56–57, 61.

59. Brown, *Hispano Folklife,* 245–46; *New Mexico: A Guide to the Colorful State* (New York: Hasting House, 1940, revised edition, 1962), 98–106.

60. McDonald, *Federal Relief and the Arts,* 309–20; Brown, *Hispano Folklife,* 246, 251.

61. Isabel Lancaster Eckles, Director, Professional and Service Division, WPA, to Florence Kerr, Assistant Commissioner, WPA, Washington, 23 January 1942; Amy B. Dwelly, Assistant State Supervisor, Nursery Schools, to Eckles, 18 September 1941; Rebecca Graham, Assistant State Supervisor to Eckles, 19 September 1941; Mamie Meadors, Director, Community Service Projects to Eckles, 19 September 1941; NARG 69, WPA, New Mexico State Files, 651.3144.

62. Nina Otero-Warren to Isabel Lancaster Eckles, 23 January 1942; Florence Kerr, Assistant Commissioner, WPA to Otero-Warren, 17 December 1941; Kerr to Clinton P. Anderson, House of Representatives, 10 April 1941; NARG 69, WPA, New Mexico State Files, 651.314.

63. S. C. Wilson, Jr., District Educational Advisor, CCC Headquarters, Fort Bliss, Texas to Mamie Meadors, 18 September 1941; Violet C. Hoffman, Supervisor, CCC Selection to Donald S. Thornton, State Supervisor, CCC Selection, 9 March 1942; Miles Papers, WPA File, NMSRCA; CCC Letter of Information and Instruction, Number 28, 10 March 1941; Memorandum for Press, CCC, 15 June 1941; Miles Papers, CCC-WPA File, NMSRCA; "Final Report, NYA, N.M.," NARG 119, NYA, New Mexico, Administrative Correspondence. "New Mexico Narrative Report, Literacy, Recreation and National Citizenship Education Program," September 1942; NARG 69, WPA, New Mexico State Files, 651.314. Charles P. Loomis and Nellis N. Loomis, "Skilled Spanish-American War Industry Workers from New Mexico," *Applied Anthropology,* 2 (1942): 33–36

64. "Some Recommendations for the Solution of the Farm Labor Problems of the Southern Great Plains," confidential memorandum from Walter J. Knodel, State Director of Training and Reemployment Division of WPA to Ralph Charles, BAE, Secretary, State Subcommittee on Farm Labor, 26 December 1941; NARG 83, BAE, Records of New Mexico State Representative, Farm Labor Subcommittee.

65. Ibid.; Memorandum Robert F. Black, Arizona BAE Representative to James C. Foster, BAE Representative for Colorado, NARG 83, BAE, Records of New Mexico State Representative, Farm Labor Subcommittee.

66. Minutes of the Meeting of the State Farm Labor Subcommittee, State College New Mexico, 12 May 1942, NARG 83, BAE, Records of the New Mexico State Representative, Farm Labor Subcommittee.

67. Ibid.; John J. McDonough, Director, Division of Training and Reemployment, WPA, to James J. Connelly, State WPA, Santa Fe, 20 May 1942; Walter J. Knodel, State Director Training and Reemployment Division, WPA, to Ralph Charles, Secretary, State Subcommittee on Farm Labor, 26 December 1941; Fred R. Rauch, Assistant Commissioner to Connelly, 15 October 1941; Knodel to H. W. Sinclair, Acting Director Training and Reemployment Di-

vision WPA, 1 October 1941; NARG 69, WPA, New Mexico State Files, 645.25-1942.

68. Florence Kerr, Assistant Commissioner, WPA, to Maggie Alvarado, 18 March 1943; Kerr to Ida B. Hatley, 30 December 1942; NARG 69, WPA, New Mexico State Files, 651.329; Kerr to James J. Connelly, State Work Projects Administration, 25 January 1943; "New Mexico Narrative Report, Service Division," September 1942; "Narrative Report, Defense, Health, and Welfare of New Mexico," October 1942; NARG 69, WPA, New Mexico State Files, 651.325.

## Chapter Eight

1. For information on the Navajo New Deal see Donald L. Parman, *The Navajos and the New Deal* (New Haven: Yale University Press, 1976) and Lawrence C. Kelly, "Anthropology in the Soil Conservation Service," *Agricultural History,* 59 (April 1985).

2. Kelly, "Anthropology in the SCS," 138.

3. Ibid., 137; Parman, *Navajos and the New Deal,* 37–38; Collier, *From Every Zenith,* 238.

4. D. Harper Simms, *The Soil Conservation Service* (New York: Praeger Publications, 1970), 6–10; Kelly, "Anthropology in the SCS," 138; Parman, *Navajos and the New Deal,* 41.

5. Kelly, "Anthropology in the SCS," 138, 140.

6. Kelly, "Anthropology," 140; White, *The Roots of Dependency,* 282; Parman, *Navajos and the New Deal,* 99–100.

7. Kelly, "Anthropology in the SCS," 139; White, *The Roots of Dependency,* 269; Parman, *Navajos and the New Deal,* 43–45; "A Review of the Disagreeable Aspects of the Submarginal Land Program," confidential report, M. M. Kelso, FSA, to Ralph Charles, State Land Planning Specialist, BAE, 23 September 1937, NARG 83, BAE, Records of New Mexico State Representative, "Disagreeable Aspects of Submarginal Land Program," 3066.

8. Eastburn R. Smith, lecture at Rio Grande District Planning Meeting, 7 October 1936, NARG 114, SCS, Region 8, General Records, 1934–39, Meetings and Conferences.

9. M. M. Kelso, "Report Concerning the Comparative Need of Non-Indian Villagers and Indian Villagers for the Ojo del Espiritu Santo Grant in New Mexico," 5 May 1937, NARG 83, BAE, Records of New Mexico State Representative, Kelso Report of Espiritu Santo Grant.

10. Kelso, "Report Concerning Comparative Need"; M. M. Kelso, "Report on the Extent and Character of Desirable Adjustment in Rural Land-Use and the Most Effective Means of Obtaining Such Adjustment," September 1934; "Report on the Extent and Character of Desirable Adjustment in Rural Land Use in New Mexico," May 1935; NARG 83, BAE, Records of Division of Land Economics, Land Utilization Reports, New Mexico, Preliminary L-U 30, National Resources Board.

11. David H. Dinwoodie, "Indians, Hispanos, and Land Reform: A New Deal Struggle in New Mexico," *Western Historical Quarterly* (July 1986): 300–301.

12. Ibid., 301.

13. Ibid., 302, 309; Parman, *Navajos and the New Deal.*

14. "Disagreeable Aspects of Submarginal Land Program."

15. Simms, *Soil Conservation Service,* 11–15; Kelly, "Anthropology in the SCS," 140; "Disagreeable Aspects of Submarginal Land Program."

16. U.S., Department of Agriculture, Soil Conservation Service, "Proposals for the Santa Cruz Area," Regional Bulletin 28, Conservation Economics Series 1, July 1935, 1; George M. Foster, *Applied Anthropology* (Boston: Little, Brown, 1969), 200, writes that the Tewa Basin Study was "the first formal applied anthropological work in the United States"; Weigle, *Hispanic Villages,* 6.

17. "The Availability of Land Resources in the Española Valley," Section of Human Surveys, Soil Conservation Service, December 1936, NARG 83, BAE, Records of the New Mexico State Representative, Kelso Report of Espiritu Santo Grant.

18. Marta Weigle has listed most, if not all, of these studies in the extensive bibliography of sociocultural studies related to Hispanic New Mexico that accompanies her edited reprint of the 1935 Tewa Basin Study entitled *Hispanic Villages of Northern New Mexico.*

19. R. Stewart Ellis, "Santa Cruz: Authority and Community Response in the History of a New Mexican Town" (Ph.D. dissertation, University of Oklahoma, 1980), 152–53; Personal commentary by Myra Ellen Jenkins, former New Mexico State Historian and Chief Archivist, New Mexico State Archives and Records Center, October 1984. These monographs can be found in the libraries of the Colorado Springs Fine Arts Center, Colorado Springs, Colorado; the New Mexico State Records Center and Archives, Santa Fe, New Mexico; the Laboratory of Anthropology of the Museum of New Mexico, Santa Fe, New Mexico, and the Special Collections of the Zimmerman Library at the University of New Mexico.

20. "Introduction" to the Inventory of Record Group 96 pertaining to the Farm Security Administration, NARG 96.

21. Richard S. Kirkendall, *Social Scientists and Farm Politics in the Age of Roosevelt* (Columbia: University of Missouri Press, 1966), 75.

22. Simms, *Soil Conservation Service,* 101; Reid, *It Happened in Taos,* 117–18; Memorandum from Harold Elmendorf, District Water Utilities Supervisor to Homer M. Wells, Water Utilization Section, BAE, n.d., NARG 83, BAE, Water Utilization Section, Water Facilities–New Mexico, General.

23. U.S., Department of Agriculture, Soil Conservation Service, "Organization and Development of the Soil Conservation Service: A Reference for Employees," SCS-CI-13, Revised July 1970, 7; Smith lecture at Rio Grande District Planning Meeting; P.L. 46, 76th Congress 24. SCS, "Soil Conservation Service," 7; Simms, *Soil Conservation Service,* 19–20; P.L. 738, 74th Congress.

25. 50 Stat. 869; SCS, "Soil Conservation Service," 8; Simms, *Soil Conservation Service,* 20.

26. P.L. 210, 75th Congress; SCS, "Soil Conservation Service," 8; Simms, *Soil Conservation Service,* 20.

27. Interdepartmental Rio Grande Committee, "Memorandum on the History of Land Titles in New Mexico," "Comparative Livelihood of Indian and Non-Indian," 26 February 1937, Kelso Report submitted to the U.S. Department of the Interior Land Office, NARG 83, BAE, Records of the New Mexico State Representative, Kelso Report of Espiritu Santo Grant.

28. Smith lecture at Rio Grande District Planning Meeting; Dinwoodie, "Indians, Hispanos and Land Reform," 311–12. Memorandum of the Commissioner of Indian Affairs, 30 December 1936, NARG 83, BAE, Records of the New Mexico State Representative, Specific Problem Data. Government documents repeatedly used the term "subsistence" in referring to the small, family-sized agricultural and pastoral operations of the Indians and Hispanos. Since both groups depended heavily on other sources of income they were hardly "subsistence" peoples in the true sense of the word.

29. Interdepartmental Rio Grande Committee, "Outline of First Point of Attack on the Rio Grande Problem," 24 February 1937, NARG 83, BAE, Records of the New Mexico State Representative, Specific Problem Data.

30. Apparently the Committee had in mind a federal agency comparable in power and function to the Tennessee Valley Authority (TVA) that would assume responsibility for all the developmental problems in the Rio Grande Valley, according to Harper et al., *Man and Resources,* 286–87.

31. Interdepartmental Rio Grande Committee, "Summary of Recommendations," 6 June 1937, NARG 83, BAE, Records of the New Mexico State Representative, Specific Problem Data.

32. Ibid.

33. U.S., Department of Agriculture, Soil Conservation Service, "A Report on the Cuba Valley," by Ernest Maes, Regional Bulletin 36, Conservation Economics Series 9, March 1937, Part I, 1–17; Morris Evans, Acting Chief, Division of Land Economics, BAE to Ralph Charles, State Land Planning Specialist, BAE, "Report on the Cuba–Rio Puerco Project," 17 February 1938, Records of the New Mexico State Representative, Analysis of the Cuba–Rio Puerco Project.

34. SCS, "Report on the Cuba Valley," 24–35. According to Gerald Gwayn Widdison, "Historical Geography of the Middle Rio Puerco Valley, New Mexico," *NMHR,* 34 (October 1959): 248–84, settlers have occupied the Middle Rio Puerco area twice within the last two hundred years—at both times during periods of relatively greater precipitation. In each case a period of drought contributed to the decline and abandonment of the area. Kirk Bryan, "Erosion in the Southwest," *New Mexico Quarterly Review,* 10 (November 1940): 227–32, also argued that cycles of aridity were as much, if not more, responsible for soil erosion than overgrazing of the range. The problem was clearly more complex than that envisioned by the Soil Conservation Service in the mid-1930s.

35. U.S., Department of Agriculture, Soil Conservation Service, "Rural Rehabilitation in the Cuba Valley," by M. L. Fisher, Regional Bulletin 36,

Conservation Economics Series 9, March 1937, Part II, 50–52; "Relief in the Cuba Valley," by M. L. Fisher, Part III.

36. Ralph Will, Assistant Regional Director, FSA to W. W. Alexander, Administrator, FSA, Washington, 5 November 1938; Memorandum from Mastin G. White, Solicitor, to C. B. Baldwin, Administrator, FSA, Washington, 16 October 1940, NARG 96, FSA, Rehabilitation-Relocation, Tenant-Purchase Program, 505; "Introduction" to the Inventory of Record Group 96 pertaining to the Farm Security Administration/Farmers' Home Administration, 3, NARG 96; SCS, "Soil Conservation Service," 7–8; Interdepartmental Rio Grande Board, "Conference Concerning the Rio Puerco," 20 December 1938, NARG 83, BAE, Records of the New Mexico State Representative, Cuba Area Economic Survey; Morris Evans, Acting Chief, Division of Land Economics, BAE, to Ralph Charles, State Land Planning Specialist, BAE, "Report on the Cuba–Rio Puerco Project," 17 February 1938, NARG 83, Records of the New Mexico State Representative, Analysis of Cuba–Rio Puerco Project.

37. "Disagreeable Aspects of the Submarginal Land Program." For specific allocation of land grants see 147.

38. Dinwoodie, "Indians, Hispanos, and Land Reform," 306, 308.

39. Ibid., 306–9; Cyril Luker, Regional Conservator, SCS, to H. H. Bennett, Administrator, SCS, 10 April 1943, Forest Service Office Files, Albuquerque, New Mexico (hereafter FS-Alb).

40. Dinwoodie, "Indians, Hispanos, and Land Reform," 312–14.

41. Ibid., 312–14.

42. Ibid., 314–14.

43. "Creation of the Interdepartmental Rio Grande Board," n.d., Governor Miles Papers, NMSRCA; "Recommendations Concerning the Future Administration of Land Utilization Projects Under the Jurisdiction of the Soil Conservation Service in the State of New Mexico," 11 September 1942, FS-Alb; "Recommendations for a Land Utilization Project Site in the State of New Mexico," 17 March 1938, Ralph Charles, Morris Evans, James C. Foster, Regional Directors, Southern Plains, FSA, NARG 83, BAE, Records of the New Mexico State Representative, Antonio Sedillo Grant; Dinwoodie, "Indians, Hispanos, and Land Reform," 316.

44. "Recommendations Concerning the Future Administration of Land Utilization Projects in New Mexico," "Recommendations for a Land Utilization Project Site in the State of New Mexico."

45. U.S., Department of Agriculture, Soil Conservation Service, "The Rio Grande Watershed in Colorado and New Mexico: A Report on the Condition and Use of the Land and Water Resources Together with a General Program for Soil and Water Conservation," Region 8, Soil Conservation Service, August 1939, 104. In the Upper and Middle Rio Grande and Rio Puerco units together Spanish Americans constituted 76 percent of the total population, Indians 10 percent, and Anglo-Americans 14 percent. According to United States Department of Agriculture, Joseph Gaer, *Toward Farm Security* (Washington, D.C.: U.S. Government Printing Office, 1941), 56, other "starvation group" rural families in the United States had incomes of $480 per year, well above the $100

per year, per family income reported for 31.5 percent of the total New Mexico labor force in 1939 by Helen H. Ellis, *Public Welfare Problems in New Mexico* (Albuquerque: University of New Mexico Department of Government, Division of Research, November 1949), 4–5.

46. SCS, "Rio Grande Watershed," 119–20. In 1935–36 the federal government expended a total of $3,200,000 for rural relief in the Rio Puerco Valley. Rural Rehabilitation loans totaled $450,000 and WPA payments for labor totaled $100,000.

47. SCS, "Rio Grande Watershed," 124–31, 141–42. According to this study the small, resident-owned herds of two hundred cattle or eight hundred sheep composed 90 percent of all operators but only 30 percent of the total cattle units in the grazing district. The remaining 10 percent of commercial operators controlled 70 percent of the cattle units.

48. SCS, "Proposals for the Santa Cruz Valley–Rural Rehabilitation in Santa Cruz," 1–6.

49. SCS, "Proposals for the Santa Cruz Valley–Rural Rehabilitation in Santa Cruz," 2–9; Ibid., 1–15. Shevky seems to have been thinking of an agency with the powers of the TVA.

50. "Proposals for the Santa Cruz Valley," 1–15.

51. Memorandum, Henry A. Wallace, Secretary of Agriculture, 2 February 1939, NARG 96, FSA, Region 12, Records of Office of Director, 500; Harold B. Elmendorf, District Water Utilization Supervisor, BAE, "Preliminary Proposal for a Water Facilities Program in the Española Valley," 29 February 1940; Elmendorf to A. B. Fite, Director of Extension Service, New Mexico State College, 20 April 1940; Elmendorf to Millard C. Peck, Area Leader, Division of Land Economics, BAE, 25 October 1940, NARG 83, BAE, Water Utilization Section, Water Facilities, New Mexico, General. Maes, "The World and the People of Cundiyo," 9; Reid, *It Happened in Taos*, 26–27, 47; Memorandum Ralph Will, Assistant Regional Director, FSA to Jesse B. Gilmer, Executive Assistant, FSA and Regional Staff Specialists, 28 October 1940, NARG 96, FSA, Region 12, Records of the Office of Director, 028–New Mexico Special Area; Kalvero Oberg, "Cultural Factors in Land Use Planning in Cuba Valley, New Mexico," *Rural Sociology,* 5 (December 1940): 438–48, argued that the Spanish-American population was considerably better integrated and more stable than the more recently arrived homesteaders. Since they used their resources more efficiently and lived better for less money their needs should be given priority over both the Anglo homesteaders and the commercial livestock growers.

52. Ralph Will, Assistant Regional Director, FSA, to D. A. Nolan, Floyd, New Mexico. 3 April 1940; Memorandum Ralph Will to members of State FSA Advisory Committee, NARG 96, FSA, Rehabilitation-Relocation, Tenant-Purchase Programs, 505. Governor Clyde Tingley to Jonathan Garst, Regional Director, RA, 28 January 1936; Garst to Tingley, 8 February 1936, Governor Tingley Papers, NMSRCA.

53. "Recommendations Concerning the Future Administration of Land Utilization Projects Under the Jurisdiction of the Soil Conservation Service in the State of New Mexico," 11 September 1942; Cyril Luker, Regional Conservator

to H. H. Bennett, Chief, SCS, Washington, 10 April 1943; Bennett to Senator Dennis Chavez, 24 July 1940; Interdepartmental Rio Grande Committee, "Recommendations for Transfer of Jurisdiction, Allocation of Use-Rights, and Administration of Resettlement Administration Indian Land-Purchase Projects in New Mexico," December 1937; FS-Alb.

54. Wilson Cowen, Regional Director, FSA to C. B. Baldwin, Administrator, FSA, 16 November 1940; Cowen to Baldwin, 15 January 1941, NARG 96, FSA, Region 12, Records of Office of Director, 028–New Mexico Special Area; Charles Loomis and Glen Grisham, "Spanish-Americans: The New Mexico Experiment in Village Rehabilitation," *Applied Anthropology*, 2, 3 (1943): 15, 18, 22; Kelly, "Anthropology in the SCS," 144–47. According to Kelly, the use of anthropologists in the Soil Conservation Service came to an end in 1940 when Congress grew impatient "with the multiplicity of surveys and the absence of results therefrom," and the "absence of direct value" of the surveys to the "determination of conditions pertaining to soil and water losses." However Carl Taylor and M. L. Wilson, both of whom had become convinced of the importance of culture during their years with the Resettlement Administration, used their influence in the USDA to transfer anthropological studies from the SCS to the BAE. John Provinse, an anthropologist who had trained under Radcliffe-Brown at the University of Chicago and later worked with Shevky in the SCS, was brought to Washington where, with other members of the BAE, he participated in the design of what was known as the Culture of a Contemporary Rural Community Project. Studies of six very different rural communities, one of which was the community of El Cerrito, New Mexico, were used to guide policy makers and planners in the USDA in the design of land use programs consonant with the existing social organizations.

55. Ralph Will, State Director, FSA, to A. B. Fite, Director of Extension Service, New Mexico State College, 15 February 1941; Will to State Staff, 10 March 1941; C. B. Baldwin, Administrator, FSA, to Wilson Cowen, Regional Director, FSA, 28 April 1941, NARG 96, FSA, Region 12, Records of Office of Director, 028–New Mexico Special Area.

56. The villages included in the study were Upper Pueblo, Lower Pueblo, Barranca, and Garambujo, in San Miguel County, Loomis and Grisham, "Experiment," 16, 23, 34.

57. Loomis and Grisham, "Experiment," 19–22; Charles L. Loomis and J. Allan Beagle, *Rural Social Systems: A Textbook in Rural Sociology and Anthropology* (New York: Prentice Hall, Inc., 1950), 689–93.

58. Loomis and Grisham, "Experiment," 13–14, 30–32; Loomis and Beagle, *Rural Social Systems,* 693.

59. Reid, *Taos,* 17.

60. Reid, *Taos,* 17–27; J. T. Reid, Director, Taos County Project to Ralph R. Will, State Director, FSA, 3 December 1940; Taos County Wool Growers' Association, Elizardo Quintana, President, to Reid, 19 December 1940; Sophie Aberle, General Superintendent, United Pueblos Agency, Office of Indian Affairs to Ralph Will, 9 December 1940; Will to Aberle, 21 December 1940; Aberle to Will, 28 January 1941; Ray E. Davis, Chief, Community and Family

Service Section, FSA to Will, 1 February 1941; Davis to Will, 20 February 1941; J. Karavas to Wilson Cowen, Regional Director, FSA, 12 March 1941; Memorandum Cowen to Homer R. Robbins, Chief, Tenant Purchase Section, 18 April 1941; Glen Grisham, Special Area Supervisor to Cowen, 23 May 1941; Will to Grisham, 19 June 1941; Will to Reid, 24 June 1941; Cowen to C. B. Baldwin, Administrator, FSA, 2 August 1941; Henry A. Palmer, County Rural Rehabilitation Supervisor to Lionel C. Bolm, Assistant Regional Director, FSA, 7 August 1941; Reid to Will, 9 August 1941; Cowen to Baldwin, 26 November 1941, NARG 96, Region 12, Records of Office of Director, 028–Taos County Project; *Taoseño and Taos Review,* 7 August 1941; Harold B. Elmendorf, District Water Utilization Supervisor, BAE to Reid, 23 September 1940, NARG 83, BAE, Water-Facilities, New Mexico, Taos County; Elmendorf to Ralph Will, Assistant Regional Director, FSA, 21 March 1941, NARG 83, BAE, Water Facilities, New Mexico, Costilla Creek Area; "Minutes of the Meeting of the State Agricultural Planning Committee," 13–14 May 1942, NARG 83, BAE, Water Facilities, New Mexico, State Water Facilities Meetings; Elmendorf to Reid, 23 June 1942; Elmendorf to Jesse B. Gilmer, Executive Assistant, FSA, 21 November 1942, NARG 83, BAE, Water Facilities, New Mexico, Irrigation Survey, Costilla Creek, Taos County; Bruce Johansen and Roberto Maestas, *El Pueblo: The Gallegos Family's American Journey, 1503–1980* (New York: Monthly Review Press, 1983), 78.

61. Reid, *Taos,* 39–45.
62. Ibid., 29–31, 58–66.
63. Ibid., 8.

## Chapter Nine

1. Eldon G. Marr, "Agriculture in New Mexico," *New Mexico Business,* 20, 10 (October 1967): 1–12.

2. A thriving and innovative sheep raising and weaving business based in Tierra Amarilla and Los Ojos is a relatively recent addition to the New Mexico business scene. Its origins date to the 1960s War on Poverty programs and to the community spirit generated by that period of intense Chicano activism. It can be argued, however, that the 1930s Hispanic crafts revival helped to preserve some of the techniques used in dying, spinning, and weaving wool. The employment of women in the WPA workshops may also have stimulated the transition of weaving from an exclusively male profession to one in which women are increasingly active. Interview with Maria Varela, Tierra Amarilla community organizer and planning director for Ganados del Valle, May 1988.

3. Max Bennett and E. Judith Mantlo, *New Mexico Health Resources Registry, Statistical Summary, 1986/1987* (Albuquerque: University of New Mexico Medical Center, 1987), 1–4. The seven poorest counties, according to the 1980 census are, in order: Mora (86.6 percent Hispanic, 38.3 percent living in poverty), McKinley (65.7 percent Indian, 36.8 percent living in poverty), Guadalupe (82.7 percent Hispanic, 30.5 percent living in poverty), San Miguel

(81.4 percent Hispanic, 30.8 percent living in poverty), Rio Arriba (74.4 percent Hispanic, 28.3 percent living in poverty), and Taos (69.1 percent Hispanic, 27.5 percent living in poverty). These figures compare to a 1986 average of 29 percent of Hispanics living in poverty nationally. U.S. Bureau of the Census, Current Population Reports, Series P-60, No. 158, *Poverty in the United States: 1985*, United States Government Printing Office, Washington, D.C., 1987. *New Mexico Statistical Abstract—1984*, Bureau of Business and Economic Research (Albuquerque: University of New Mexico Press, 1984), 95–96.

4. *Albuquerque Journal*, 18 July 1937, 23 November 1937.

5. *Albuquerque Journal*, 18 July 1937, 23 November 1937; "Plan for Development for the Middle Rio Grande Project," Bureau of Reclamation, Washington, D.C., 1947, Governor Miles Papers, NMSRCA.

6. *Albuquerque Journal*, 25 September 1937, 16 November 1937, 25 November 1937, 26 November 1937, 28 November 1937, 29 November 1937, 21 December 1937, 29 December 1937.

7. *Albuquerque Journal*, 16 October 1937, 28 November 1937; *Socorro Chieftain* (editorial), 23 November 1937.

8. *Albuquerque Journal*, 27 November 1937, 28 November 1937, 9 December 1937, 13 December 1937, 13 January 1938.

9. *Albuquerque Journal*, 28 November 1937, 29 November 1937, 1 December 1937.

10. *Albuquerque Journal*, 25 December 1937, 27 December 1937, 13 January 1938.

11. *Albuquerque Journal*, 14 January 1938, 2 February 1938, 8 February 1938, 12 February 1938.

12. "Plan for Development," 19–31.

13. Paul A. F. Walter, Jr., "A Study of Isolation and Social Change in Three Spanish-Speaking Villages of New Mexico" (Ph.D. dissertation, Stanford University, 1938), 154–205.

14. Aristides B. Chavez, "The Use of the Personal Interview to Study the Subjective Impact of Culture Contacts" (M.A. thesis, University of New Mexico, 1948), 49–50.

15. Laura Waggoner, "San Jose: A Study in Urbanization" (M.A. thesis, University of New Mexico, 1941), 41–43, 51, 53, 60, 66–68.

16. Harper et al., *Man and Resources*, 35, 68–69.

17. "Transcript of Record of Investigation Concerning Conditions in the San Luis, Casa Salazar, Cabezon, and Guadalupe Communities in Sandoval County, New Mexico," held at the Office of the Honorable John E. Miles, Governor, 8 March 1941, Governor Miles Papers, NMSRCA.

18. "Recommendations Concerning Future Administration of Land Utilization Projects Under the Jurisdiction of the Soil Conservation Service in the State of New Mexico," 11 September 1942; Cyril Luker, Regional Conservator, SCS to H. H. Bennett, Administrator, SCS, Washington, D.C., 10 August 1943; Forest Service Regional Files, Albuquerque, New Mexico (hereafter FS-Alb).

19. Ibid.

20. Dale R. Shockley, Assistant Agricultural Engineer to Harold B. Elmendorf, District Water Utilization Supervisor, BAE, 20 September 1939; Elmendorf to Paul Berg, Rio Grande Compact Commissioner, 6 November 1940, NARG 83, BAE, Water Utilization Section, Water Facilities–New Mexico, General. Thomas M. McClure, State Engineer to John A. Adams, Executive Officer, Interdepartmental Rio Grande Board, 23 February 1939, Adams to Governor John E. Miles, 17 February 1939, "Petition" from Rio Puerco residents, 7 February 1941, "Transcript of Record," Governor Miles Papers, NMSRCA.

21. "Transcript of Record," "Statement Concerning the Activities and Recommendations of the Interdepartmental Rio Grande Board with Reference to Proposed District Number 8 in the Cuba–Rio Puerco with Exhibits," Governor Miles Papers, NMSRCA.

22. "Recommendations Concerning Future Administration," FS-Alb, recommended the transfer of 53,400 acres of Indian withdrawal land and 104,000 acres of Grazing Service lands, all in the Department of the Interior, to the Department of Agriculture, in exchange for 6,600 acres of Soil Conservation Service lands in the western half of the area.

23. Cyril Luker, Regional Conservator, SCS to H. H. Bennett, Administrator, Washington, D.C., 10 April 1943, FS-Alb.

24. Frank Pooler, Regional Forester, Albuquerque, New Mexico, to Earl Clapp, Assistant Chief, Forest Service, Washington, D.C., 23 February 1943, FS-Alb.

25. Ibid.

26. Ibid.

27. Harper et al., *Man and Resources*, 35, 68–69. The Anglo farmers were correct in arguing that the state was in a cycle of aridity, according to Jerald Gwayne Widdison, "Historical Geography of the Middle Rio Puerco Valley, New Mexico," *NMHR*, 34 (October 1959).

28. Kirkendall, *Social Scientists and Farm Politics*, 195; Sidney Baldwin, *Poverty and Politics: The Rise and Decline of the Farm Security Administration* (Chapel Hill: University of North Carolina Press, 1968), 122; Christiana Campbell, *The Farm Bureau and the New Deal: A Study of the Making of National Farm Policy, 1933–1940* (Urbana: University of Illinois Press, 1962), 165–74.

29. Ben Good, G. R. Vaughan, Stinson Martin, De Baca County Committee, Agricultural Conservation Program, AAA to Governor John Miles, Governor Miles Papers, NMSRCA.

30. Ibid.

31. Covey B. Baker to Arthur Starr, President, Board of Regents, State College, 22 December 1939; Con W. Jacobson, President, New Mexico Cattle Growers Association, A. H. Gerdeman, President State Farm Bureau, A. D. Brownfield, State AAA Land Planning Councilman to John J. Dempsey, House of Representatives, Washington, D.C., 27 December 1939; Belarmino Valdez and others, Park View, New Mexico, to Honorable John E. Miles, 27 December 1939; Adolfo Garcia, Agricultural Conservation Program County Committee,

Rio Arriba County, to Honorable John E. Miles, 27 December 1939; O. E. Pattison, Clovis, New Mexico, to Secretary of Agriculture Henry Wallace and Governor John E. Miles, 9 January 1940; Governor Miles Papers, NMSRCA.

32. "Agreement Between the Bureau of Agricultural Economics of the United States Department of Agriculture and the New Mexico Experiment Station and the New Mexico Extension Service, 1941–1942"; NARG 83, BAE, Records of County Agricultural Planning Project, 217.

33. Harper et al., *Man and Resources*, vii; Weigle, *Hispanic Villages*, 250–53. The last monograph put out under the aegis of the Interdepartmental Rio Grande Board was entitled "Management and Development Program for the Tewa Basin," 9, 68 (17 July 1940). The last monograph in the Soil Conservation Service Conservation Economics Series was entitled "The Relationship of Economic and Cultural Factors to the Land Use Adjustment Program in Cuba Valley," 9, 224 (August 1940). To my knowledge, neither of these two monographs are extant. Notice of abolishment of Interdepartmental Rio Grande Board contained in NARG 69 1–270, FERA–Indian Affairs File and NARG 96, FSA, Allan Harper memorandum, 20 January 1942, Cooperation-Interdepartmental Rio Grande Board File, Region XII, according to Dinwoodie, "Indians, Hispanos, and Land Reform," 320.

34. Ibid., 75–76; Frederick P. Champ, "Our Stake in the Public Lands," *The New Mexico Stockman* (April 1944): 20.

35. Samuel Trask Dana, *Forest and Range Policy: Its Development in the Southwest* (New York: McGraw-Hill, 1956), 260–62.

36. Ibid., 286–87.

37. Jesse B. Gilmer, Regional Director, FSA, to C. B. Baldwin, Administrator, FSA, Washington, D.C., 2 June 1943; George W. Kimball, Acting Regional Forester, for Frank C. W. Pooler, to Chief, Forest Service, Washington, D.C., 26 July 1943, FS-Alb.

38. Forest Service Conference concerning the Lobato Grant of the Abiquiu Project of the FSA, 23 July 1946; Howard V. Campbell, Acting Associate Solicitor to Lamar L. Murdaugh, Special Assistant to Administrator, FSA, 2 July 1946; Memorandum of Understanding Between Charles F. Brannan, Assistant Secretary of Agriculture, Dillard B. Lasseter, Administrator, FSA, and E. W. Loveridge, Acting Chief, Forest Service, 22 October 1946. These properties included the Taos and Gabaldon Grants, transferred to the Forest Service from the FSA in 1938 and the Anton Chico (of which the El Pueblo Project formed a part), the La Majada, Mora, Polvadera, Cañon de San Diego, San Jose, and both the North and South halves of the Juan Jose Lobato Grant. L. F. Kneipp, Assistant Chief, Forest Service to Regional Foresters, 3 August 1938; "Policies Regarding Conservation and Development and Use of Land Utilization Project Lands Administered by the Soil Conservation Service," n.d. (1951 or later); Memorandum, "Application and Scope of Administrative Authorities" to Regional Forester, R-3, 2 May 1983; FS-Alb. Dana, *Forest and Range Policy*, 288.

39. Memorandum, Howard V. Campbell to Lamar L. Murdaugh, 2 July 1946; C. J. McCormick, Acting Secretary, USDA, to the Honorable Secretary

of the Interior, 26 July 1951; Memorandum, James L. Perry, Forest Supervisor to Regional Forester, R-3, "Application and Scope of Administrative Authorities," 2 May 1983; FS-Alb.

40. USDA, "Criteria to Be Used in Determining Whether to Keep U-L Lands in Federal Ownership," 23 August 1954; Memorandum, Richard E. McArdle, Chief, Forest Service, to E. L. Peterson, Assistant Secretary of Agriculture, 12 January 1959; FS-Alb.

41. Malcolm Ebright, "The Juan Jose Lovato Grant: A Victory for Land Grant Research," a paper presented at the annual meeting of the Western Social Science Association, Albuquerque, New Mexico, 25 April 1980. I am particularly indebted to Mr. Ebright for calling this information to my attention since it had been culled from the files of the Forest Service in Albuquerque by the time I did my research. The Lobato Grant is frequently referred to as the Lovato Grant as a result of the frequent transposition of b and v in Spanish orthography. I am indebted for the analogy concerning the Forest Service to Tomás C. Atencio, "The Forest Service and the Spanish Surname American," testimony presented at the Cabinet Committee Hearings on Mexican-American Affairs, El Paso, Texas, 26–28 October 1967, Inter-Agency Committee on Mexican Affairs, Washington, D.C., 35–38.

42. C. Otto Lindh, Regional Forester to Charles Davis, Senator Chavez Office, 27 March 1952; Lyle Watts, Chief (by Howard Hopkins, Acting) to Ed Heringa, President, New Mexico Cattle Growers Association, 23 April 1952.

43. Atencio, "Forest Service," 8; Gonzalez, *The Spanish Americans*, 122; Clark S. Knowlton, "Culture Conflict and Natural Resources," in William R. Burch, Jr., Neil H. Clark, Jr., and Lee Taylor, eds., *Social Behavior, Natural Resources and the Environment* (New York: Harper and Row, 1972), 35–36; *Federal Register*, 18 September 1962, Vol. 27, 9217-8.

44. Johansen and Maestas, *El Pueblo*, 78. Campbell had earlier bought up 318,000 acres of tax delinquent land in Socorro and Valencia Counties that included the La Joya, Belen, San Pedro, and Cañon de Agua Grants. When the Belen Grant Board, consisting of four hundred small Hispanic farmers, realized what had happened to their lands they hired Albuquerque attorney, Gilberto Espinosa, to get it back on the basis that the price paid by Campbell of thirty-five cents per acre was entirely inadequate. The matter was settled when Campbell returned title to twenty thousand acres under irrigation along the Rio Grande to the Belen farmers. Campbell retained title to sixty thousand acres of grazing land in the Belen Grant. Much of Campbell's new land was along the Rio Puerco and he intended to sink wells so as to develop a water supply for farming. Campbell bought the land by paying the back taxes to liquidate the mortgage held by the Bronson Cutting estate. *Albuquerque Journal*, 25 September 1937, 9 October 1937, 8 December 1937.

45. "Minutes of Land Use Planning Meeting, Taos and Sandoval Counties," 20 January 1941; NARG 114, SCS, Records of Santa Fe Office.

46. Johansen and Maestas, *El Pueblo*, 81.

47. Bert N. Corona, "Chicano Scholars and Public Issues in the United States in the Eighties," in Mario Garcia, ed., *History, Culture and Society: Chicano*

*Studies in the 1980s* (Ypsilanti, Michigan: Bilingual Press, 1983), 13; Harper et al., *Man and Resources,* 35, 68–69, 75–76.

48. Gibson, *The Santa Fe and Taos Art Colonies,* 267–71.

49. Johansen and Maestas, *El Pueblo,* 82–85.

50. Atencio, "Forest Service," 4, 5. In 1983 the Forest Service noted that the local residents were not making full use of the El Pueblo grazing allotment of approximately four hundred cattle, and that their actual grazing use for some years had averaged only two hundred fifty cattle. A recent range analysis had indicated a potential grazing capacity of more than six hundred cattle but the existing grazing permittees were neither willing to fully stock the permits they held, nor to accept other forest permittees from over-obligated ranges onto the El Pueblo allotment. Memorandum, "Application and Scope of Administrative Authorities to Regional Forester," R-3, 2 May 1983, FS-Alb.

51. Morris Harry McMichael, "A Case Study of the Taos County, New Mexico Cooperative Health Association" (Ph.D. dissertation, Michigan State University of Agriculture and Applied Science, 1956), 107–11; Charles P. Loomis, "A Cooperative Health Association in a Spanish-Speaking Community, or the Organization of the Taos County Cooperative Health Association," *American Sociological Review,* 10 (1945): 150.

52. McMichael, "Taos County Cooperative Health Association," 98–101.

53. Ibid., 85–86, 116–17, 133–65; Loomis, "Cooperative Health Association," 156–57.

54. Olen E. Leonard and Charles P. Loomis, *Culture of a Contemporary Rural Community: El Cerrito, New Mexico* (Washington, D.C.: Government Printing Office, 1941), 35–36.

55. Ibid.

56. Anacleto Garcia Apodaca, "The Hispano Farmers' Conception of the Federal Agricultural Services in the Tewa Basin of New Mexico" (Ph.D. dissertation, Cornell University, 1951), 1, 74, 99, 111. Apodaca should probably more properly be called by his full patronymic Garcia Apodaca or simply by his father's name, Garcia, in accordance with Hispanic custom, but because he is listed as Apodaca in various bibliographies I have chosen to do the same rather than confuse the reader.

57. Ibid., 12, 154–56.

58. Ibid., 8–9, 21–22, 156, 168–73. According to Apodaca, most federal agencies seemed to work upon the assumption that all low-income farmers would, or should, eventually turn into commercial producers.

59. Ibid., 61, 157, 168.

60. Glen Grisham, Special Area Supervisor, FSA, to Jesse Gilmer, FSA Area Director, 14 April 1942, NARG 96, Region 12, Records of Director.

61. Jesse Gilmer to C. B. Baldwin, Administrator, FSA, 17 April 1942, NARG 96, FSA, Region 12, Records of Director.

62. Briggs, "Our Strength," 241, 255, 277–78. Charles P. Loomis, "Wartime Migration from the Rural Spanish-Speaking Villages of New Mexico," *Rural Sociology,* Vol. 7 (December 1942): 384–95.

63. Marr, "Agriculture in New Mexico," 5–11; Loomis, "Wartime Migra-

tion"; Paul A. F. Walter, Jr., "Rural-Urban Migration in New Mexico," *New Mexico Business Review,* 8 (1939): 136; "Statistical Data Relative to the General Relief Program in New Mexico, 1941–1942"; "Statistical Data on Variable Grants, 1930," Governor Miles Papers, NMSRCA.

64. The war had hardly begun when southwestern growers began once again to lobby vigorously for cheap Mexican labor. They would have preferred to have the government open the borders and allow Mexican workers to come in unencumbered, but the Mexican government would have nothing to do with such a plan. Still smarting over the indignities suffered by Mexican workers during the repatriations of the 1930s, Mexico insisted on protecting her citizens with worker contracts that defined and protected their rights. The first of these guest workers, called *braceros* (helping arms), arrived in 1942. The program continued until 1964 with a gradual erosion of worker guarantees and benefits as the labor shortage eased, the number of migrants rose, and the mechanization of large farms lessened demand. Richard B. Craig, *The Bracero Program* (Austin: University of Texas Press, 1971), 10–11, 36, 54, 58–59, 104–7, 198; Ernesto Galarza, *Merchants of Labor* (Santa Barbara, California: McNally & Loftin, 1964), 47, 66. For a description of working conditions and worker housing see USDA, "Preliminary Report on Migratory Workers in the Cotton Areas of New Mexico," prepared by M. S. Kiston, Labor Division, May 1941, NARG 96, FSA-FHA Preliminary Report O-28, Migratory Workers in New Mexico.

65. Marr, "Agriculture in New Mexico," 5–11; Loomis, "Wartime Migration"; Walter, "Rural-Urban Migration in New Mexico," 136; "Statistical Data Relative to the General Relief Program in New Mexico, 1941–1942"; "Statistical Data on Variable Grants, 1930," Governor Miles Papers, NMSRCA.

66. Ellis W. Hawley, "The New Deal and the Problem of Monopoly," in Alonzo L. Hamby, ed., *The New Deal: Analysis and Interpretation* (New York: Longman, Inc., second edition, 1981), 97–110.

67. Dinwoodie, "Indians, Hispanos, and Land Reform," 322.

68. Deutsch, *No Separate Refuge,* 208–9.

69. Charles P. Loomis and Nellie P. Loomis, "Skilled Spanish-American War-Industry Workers from New Mexico," *Applied Anthroplogy,* 2, 1 (1943): 33–36; John Burma, *Spanish-Speaking Groups in the United States* (Durham: Duke University Press, 1954), 3–34.

70. Tomás C. Atencio, "The Human Dimensions in Land Use and Land Displacement in Northern New Mexico Villages," in C. S. Knowlton, ed., *Indian and Spanish American Adjustments to Arid and Semiarid Environments* (Lubbock: Texas Technological College, 1964), 44–52; Committee on Agriculture, "Effect of Federal Programs on Rural America," Hearings Before the Subcommittee on Rural Development of the Committee on Agriculture, House of Representatives, Ninetieth Congress, First Session, Serial O, 6–8, 12–15, 19–22 June, 10–12 July 1967, especially testimony and paper by Clark S. Knowlton, "The Impact of Social Change upon Certain Selected Social Systems of the Spanish-American Villages of Northern New Mexico," 230–37; Clark S. Knowlton, "Problems and Prospects of the Rural Spanish-American Village of Northern New Mexico," in *The New Mexican American: A New Focus on Opportunity*

(Washington, D.C.: Inter-Agency Committee on Mexican-American Affairs, 1968): 233–38; Clark S. Knowlton, "Recommendations for the Solution of Land Tenure Problems Among the Spanish-Americans"; Rosaldo et al., *Chicano: The Evolution of a People,* 334–39; John Burma, *An Economic, Social and Educational Survey of Rio Arriba and Taos Counties* (El Rito, N.M.: mimeographed report prepared by Northern New Mexico College, 1962); Peter Van Dresser, *Development on a Human Scale: Potentials for Ecologically Guided Growth in Northern New Mexico* (New York: Praeger Publishers, 1972). Daniel Patrick Moynihan, *Maximum Feasible Misunderstanding* (New York: Free Press, 1969), discusses at length the concerns for greater grass roots involvement in the 1960s war on poverty programs.

70. Charles P. Loomis, "Systemic Linkage of El Cerrito," *Rural Sociology,* 24 (1959): 54–57; oral interviews with Connie Coca of Laramie and Eloy Vasquez of Cheyenne, May, June 1984.

# Bibliographic Essay

The single most important work from the standpoint of this study is, by far, Marta Weigle's *Hispanic Villages of Northern New Mexico: With Supplementary Materials, a Reprint of Volume II of the 1935 Tewa Basin Study* (Santa Fe: The Lightning Tree, Jene Lyon Publisher, 1975), with its comprehensive bibliography of sociocultural studies related to Hispanic New Mexico. This bibliography, together with the important reprint of the first of the Soil Conservation Service Human Dependency studies, not only did much to inspire me to make this investigation, but provided me with a checklist of publications with which to begin. The series of monographs put out between 1935 and 1940 by the Soil Conservation Service constitutes the second most important source of material since it gave me an overview of the controversial thinking that lay behind much of the Hispanic New Deal. Without these documents I would have been hard put to understand much of the correspondence contained in the New Deal agency files. Since very few copies of these mimeographed publications have survived, it is important to note that most are in the library of the Colorado Springs Fine Arts Center. Others are in the library of the Laboratory of Anthropology in Santa Fe, in the New Mexico State Records Center and Archives, also in Santa Fe, and in the Special Collections of the Zimmerman Library of the University of New Mexico in Albuquerque. The third, and most extensive, source of information relating to the New Deal in New Mexico is the National Archives in Washington, D.C. It contains the voluminous files of the various federal agencies that operated in New Mexico during the New Deal years. They have been inventoried and subdivided by state or region. However, since no separate category exists for "Mexican" or "Spanish-American," there is no quick or easy way to look up materials relating to the Hispanic

New Deal. To find them virtually every box and folder pertaining to New Mexico had to be surveyed. The Franklin D. Roosevelt Library at Hyde Park, New York, provided materials from the Harry L. Hopkins and Aubrey Williams Papers which included the Lorena Hickok correspondence, various FERA-WPA narrative field reports, and transcripts of telephone conversations. The New Mexico State Records Center and Archives provided a number of documents relating to the New Deal, most of them from the collections of the various New Deal governors; namely, Seligman, Hockenhull, Tingley, and Miles.

Several early studies were extremely useful in providing an overview of conditions in New Mexico during, and immediately following, the Great Depression. Key among these was *Man and Resources in the Middle Rio Grande Valley* by Allen G. Harper, A. R. Cordova, and Kalervo Oberg (Albuquerque: University of New Mexico Press, 1943). This study relates Hispanic distress during the 1930s to the loss of Hispanic grant lands, the devastating damage to the Rio Grande watershed brought about by over irrigation and overgrazing on the adjoining grass lands, the costs in human terms of the Middle Rio Grande Conservancy District, and the loss of wage labor. Based heavily on the findings of the Soil Conservation Service Human Dependency studies conducted by Dr. Eshref Shevky, this study summarizes the material and encapsulates the recommendations contained in the SCS monograph series. Other overviews are contained in John Burma's *Spanish-Speaking Groups in the United States* (Durham: Duke University Press, 1954) and Carey McWilliams's *North from Mexico* (Philadelphia: Lippincott, 1949). Burma stresses the importance of government relief programs in providing the means of preserving Spanish-American village life and the cultural milieu. McWilliams relates the Hispanic Arts Revival of the 1920s and the 1930s with the beginning of many depression programs aimed at New Mexican Hispanics. McWilliams also identifies the discovery of "Spain in America" with the tourist promotion of the 1800s, and the discovery of Hispanic rural poverty with the new sociological interest in regional minorities that followed the passage of the 1924 Immigration Act. Apparently McWilliams also relied heavily upon data generated by the SCS surveys, as did Carolyn Zeleny, whose 1944 doctoral dissertation in anthropology, "Relations Between the Spanish Americans and Anglo Americans in New Mexico" (New York: Arno Press, 1974) constituted a breakthrough study of conflict and accommodation in a dual ethnic society. In it Zeleny challenged the popular myth of tricultural harmony and brilliantly analyzed the nature and origins of New Mexico's accommodative ethnic relationships.

The 1930s saw the beginning of applied anthropology in New Mexico with a number of important studies deriving directly or indirectly from the Human Dependency Surveys begun by Shevky and Hugh Calkins in the Indian Service and carried on later in the Soil Conservation Service. The first of these was the 1935 Tewa Basin Study previously cited. Others used in this study are, in chronological order of publication: United States Department of Agriculture, Soil Conservation Service, "Proposals for the Santa Cruz Area," Regional Bulletin 28, Conservation Economics Series 1, July 1935; "Rural Rehabilitation in New Mexico," Regional Bulletin 50, Conservation Economics Series 23, December 1935; "Reconnaissance Survey of Human Dependence in the Rio Grande Watershed," Regional Bulletin 33, Conservation Economics Series 6, December 1936; "A Report on the Cuba Valley," Regional Bulletin 36, Conservation Economics Series 9, March 1937; "Destruction of Villages at San Marcial," Regional Bulletin 38, Conservation Economics Series 11, May 1937; "Population of the Upper Rio Grande Watershed," Regional Bulletin 43, Conservation Economics Series 16, July 1937; "The Santa Cruz Irrigation District," Regional Bulletin 45, Conservation Economics Series 18, July 1937; "Village Dependence on Migratory Labor in the Upper Rio Grande Area," Regional Bulletin 47, Conservation Economics Series 20, July 1937; "Notes on Community Owned Land Grants in New Mexico," Regional Bulletin 48, Conservation Economics Series 21, August 1937; "Villanueva, a San Miguel County Village," Regional Bulletin 51, Conservation Economics Series 24, February 1938; and "The Rio Grande Watershed in Colorado and New Mexico: A Report on the Condition and Use of the Land and Water Resources Together with a General Program for Soil and Water Conservation," Regional Bulletin 8, August 1939. Another report put out by the Soil Conservation Service under the Section of Human Surveys in December 1936, entitled "The Availability of Land Resources in the Española Valley" was located in National Archives Record Group 83, Bureau of Agriculture Economics, Records of the New Mexico State Office, Kelso Report of Espiritu Santo Grant.

A most important spin-off from the Human Dependency studies was, undoubtedly, George L. Sanchez's *Forgotten People: A Study of New Mexicans* (Albuquerque: University of New Mexico Press, 1940). Conducted by a noted Hispanic educator, this historical and sociological study of

Taos County analyzed the nature and identified many of the causes of Hispanic rural poverty. Unquestionably it played an instrumental role in focusing national attention on the problems of New Mexico's Hispanos. It also launched the Taos Project which is described in detail by J. T. Reid in *It Happened in Taos* (Albuquerque: University of New Mexico Press, 1946). Other more strictly anthropological and sociological reports which grew out of, and in turn influenced, various New Deal Depression programs are: Olen S. Leonard and Charles P. Loomis, *Culture of a Contemporary Rural Community, El Cerrito, New Mexico,* published originally as BAE Rural Life Studies, Number 1, Washington, D.C.: Government Printing Office, November 1941 and reprinted as *The Role of the Land Grant in the Social Organization and Social Processes of a Spanish American Village in New Mexico* (Albuquerque: Calvin Horn Publisher, 1970); Sigurd Johansen, *Rural Social Organization in a Spanish American Culture Area* (Albuquerque: University of New Mexico Press, 1948); Paul A. F. Walter, Jr., "A Study of Isolation and Social Change in Three Spanish-Speaking Villages of New Mexico" (Ph.D. dissertation, Stanford University, 1938); Wesley R. Hurt, "Manzano: A Study of Community Disorganization" (M.A. thesis, University of New Mexico, 1941); and Florence Kluckhohn, "Los Atarqueños, a Study of Patterns and Configurations in a New Mexico Village" (Ph.D. dissertation, Radcliffe College, 1941), which is summarized in Florence L. Kluckhohn and Fred L. Strodtbeck, *Variations in Value Orientations* (Evanston, Illinois: Row, Peterson, 1961). Various studies which followed the effects of the depression and the government programs on the later history of the Hispanic villages are: Paul A. F. Walter, Jr., "Rural-Urban Migration in New Mexico," *New Mexico Business Review,* 8 (1939): 132–37; Charles P. Loomis and Nellie H. Loomis, "Skilled Spanish-American War Industry Workers from New Mexico," *Applied Anthropology,* 2 (1943): 33–36; Charles P. Loomis, "Wartime Migration from the Rural Spanish-Speaking Villages or the Organization of the Taos County Cooperative Health Association," *American Sociological Review,* 10 (1945): 149–57; Charles P. Loomis, "El Cerrito, New Mexico: A Changing Village," *New Mexico Historical Review,* 33 (1958): 53–75; Charles P. Loomis, "Systemic Linkage of El Cerrito," *Rural Sociology,* 24 (1959): 54–57; and Morris Henry McMichael, "A Case Study of the Taos County, New Mexico Cooperative Health Association" (Ph.D. dissertation, Michigan State University of Agriculture and Applied Science, 1956).

These early anthropological studies have been followed by a number of more recent ones which bring an important modern perspective and understanding to the matter of village strength and survival. These are: Charles L. Briggs, "Our Strength Is in the Land: The Expression of Hierarchial and Egalitarian Principles in Hispano Society, 1750–1929" (Ph.D. dissertation, University of Chicago, 1980); Paul Kutsche and John Van Ness, *Cañones: Values, Crises, and Survival in a Northern New Mexico Village* (Albuquerque: University of New Mexico Press, 1981); John Van Ness, "Hispanos in Northern New Mexico: The Development of Corporate Community and Multi Community" (Ph.D. dissertation, University of Pennsylvania, 1979); and Frances Leon Swadesh, *Los Primeros Pobladores: Hispanic Americans of the Ute Frontier* (Notre Dame: University of Notre Dame Press, 1974). A number of excellent minor studies have been compiled in Paul Kutsche, ed., *The Survival of Spanish-American Villages* (Colorado Springs: Colorado College, Spring, 1979). Over the years sociologist Clark S. Knowlton has produced a number of articles bearing on the survival of Hispanic culture and community structure. A few selected titles found useful to this study are: "The Impact of Social Change upon Certain Selected Social Systems of the Spanish-American Villages of Northern New Mexico," in *Effect of Federal Programs on Rural America*, hearings before the Subcommittee on Rural Development of the Committee on Agriculture, House of Representatives, 90th Congress, First Session, (Washington, D.C.: U.S. Government Printing Office, 1967), 230–37; "Problems and Prospects of the Rural Spanish-American Village of Northern New Mexico," in *The Mexican-American: A New Focus on Opportunity* (Washington, D.C.: Inter-Agency Committee on Mexican-American Affairs, 1968), 233–38; "Changing Spanish-American Villages of Northern New Mexico," *Sociology and Social Research*, 53 (1969): 455–74; "Culture Conflict and Natural Resources," in William R. Burch, Jr., Neil H. Cheek, Jr., and Lee Taylor, eds., *Social Behavior, Natural Resources and the Environment* (New York: Harper and Row, 1972); and "Development Theory and the Rural Spanish Americans of San Miguel County, New Mexico," paper presented at the Rural Sociological Society Annual Meeting, Burlington, Vermont, August 24–26, 1979. Nancie S. Gonzalez, *The Spanish Americans: A Heritage of Pride* (Albuquerque: University of New Mexico Press, 1969) and D. W. Meinig, *Southwest: Three Peoples in Geographical Change, 1600–1970* (New York: Oxford University Press, 1971) have given us lucid histories of Hispanic Americans in relation to the development of the West and to their relations with their Anglo and Indian neighbors. Susan

Reyner Kenneson, "Through the Looking Glass: A History of Anglo-
American Attitudes Toward the Spanish Americans and Indians of New
Mexico" (Ph.D. dissertation, Yale University, 1978), has analyzed the
origins and history of Anglo American attitudes toward their two native
minorities. Lawrence Kelly, "Anthropology in the Soil Conservation
Service," traces the origins of applied anthropology to John Collier's and
Eshref Shevky's early investigations of Navajo man-land relationships.
Finally, Alice Reich "Aspects of Ethnicity: The Spanish Americans of
New Mexico" (Ph.D. dissertation, University of Chicago, 1970), iden-
tifies various elements of New Mexican ethnic identity. Anthropological
studies which discuss the development of ethnicity on a broader basis
are: Frederick Barth, ed., *Ethnic Boundaries* (Boston: Little, Brown, 1969);
Anya Peterson Royce, *Ethnic Identity: Strategies of Adversity* (Bloomington, Indiana: Indiana University Press, 1982) and Charles F. Keyes, ed.,
*Ethnic Change* (Seattle: University of Washington Press, 1981).

Several studies which touch marginally on aspects of the New Deal
in New Mexico are Richard Lowitt, *The New Deal in the West* (Bloomington: University of Indiana Press, 1984); William Pickens, "The New
Deal in New Mexico," in John Braemon, ed., *The New Deal* (2 vols.,
Columbus: Ohio State University Press, 1975), Vol. II, *The State and
Local Levels*; James T. Patterson, *The New Deal and the States: Federalism
in Transition* (Princeton: Princeton University Press, 1969); and Paul
Bonnifield, *The Dust Bowl: Men, Dirt and Depression* (Albuquerque: University of New Mexico Press, 1979). However, since all fail to understand
the very special nature of the New Deal experience in relation to New
Mexico's Indians and Hispanos they are useful mainly for comparative
purposes. Of far greater usefulness are several studies dealing with the
social and intellectual history of the New Deal. Without mentioning
New Mexico explicitly, or even apparently being aware of its intellectual
elites and their role in shaping the thought of the period, they provide
a fascinating background to understanding the social and cultural currents of the period. The first and best is Paul Conkin's *Tomorrow a New
World: The New Deal Community Programs* (Ithaca, N.Y.: Cornell University Press, 1959). Others are Richard H. Pells, *Radical Visions and
American Dreams: Culture and Thought in the Depression Years* (New York:
Harper and Row, 1973); and R. Allan Lawson, *The Failure of Independent
Liberalism 1930–1941* (New York: G. P. Putnam's Sons, 1971). Clarke
A. Chambers *Seedtime for Reform: American Social Service and Social Action,
1918–1933* (Minneapolis: University of Minnesota Press, 1963) traces

the continuity of the reform impulse from the Progressive movement to the New Deal. Otis L. Graham, Jr., *An Encore for Reform: The Old Progressives and the New Deal* (New York: Oxford University Press, 1967) does the same but inexplicably fails to include, except in passing, New Mexico's influential progressive Bronson Cutting.

Studies which trace the earlier history of the reform movement, both in the city and in the countryside, are: Allen F. Davis, *Spearheads for Reform: The Social Settlements and the Progressive Movement, 1890–1914* (New York: Oxford University Press, 1967); Christopher Lasch, *The New Radicalism in America, 1899–1963: The Intellectual as Social Type* (New York: Alfred A. Knopf, 1966); David B. Danborn, *The Resisted Revolution: Urban America and the Industrialization of Agriculture, 1900–1930* (Ames, Iowa: Iowa State University Press, 1979); and William L. Bowers, *The Country Life Movement in America, 1900–1920* (Port Washington, N.Y.: National University Publications, Kennikat Press, 1974). Lawrence Cremin, *The Transformation of the School: Progressivism in American Education, 1876–1957* (New York: Alfred A. Knopf, 1961), Lewis S. Feuer, "John Dewey and the Back-to-the-People Movement in American Thought," *Journal of the History of Ideas,* 20 (October–December 1959): 545–68; and Allan Cywar, "John Dewey: Toward Domestic Reconstruction, 1916–1920," *Journal of the History of Ideas,* 30 (July–September 1969): 385–400; discuss the important role of philosopher-educator John Dewey in the development of progressive thought and reform. Although all deal primarily or exclusively with pre–World War I progressivism, there are many striking and thought-provoking parallels with post–World War I New Mexico. The retreat of so many of the old progressives to New Mexico after World War I brought about an almost complete replay of the movement in a western, rural setting. The role of the Santa Fe and Taos artist colonies in attracting intellectuals and providing a regional critique of American culture is ably documented in James Gaither's "A Return to the Village: A Study of Santa Fe and Taos as Cultural Centers, 1900–1934" (Ph.D. dissertation, University of Minnesota, 1957); and in Arrel Morgan Gibson's *The Santa Fe and Taos Art Colonies: Age of the Muses, 1900–1942* (Norman: University of New Mexico Press, 1983), which discusses the particular role of the artists in the movement.

A sampling of 1920s and early 1930s contemporary concerns in New Mexico and among New Mexico's artist/intellectuals is contained in Mary Austin's autobiography *Earth Horizon* (New York: Houghton-Mifflin Co.,

1932); and in her articles "Mexicans and New Mexico," *Survey,* 66 (May 1931): 141–44, 187–90; and "Rural Education in New Mexico," New Mexico Training School Series II, University of New Mexico, Albuquerque, 1931; in Adelina (Nina) Otero's "My People," *Survey,* 66 (May 1931): 149–51; and in Lloyd S. Tireman's "Some Aspects of Rural Education in New Mexico," New Mexico Training School Series II, University of New Mexico, Albuquerque, 1931. The link between the New Mexico intellectual critique of American society and the interest in the cultural revolution in Mexico is contained in George Sanchez's *Mexico: A Revolution by Education* (New York: Viking Press, 1936); John Collier's, "Mexico: A Challenge," *Progressive Education,* 9 (February 1932): 99–111. Its implementation in New Mexico is discussed by Lloyd Tireman and Mary Watson in *A Community School in a Spanish-Speaking Village* (Albuquerque: University of New Mexico Press, 1948). Drewey Gunn, *American and British Writers in Mexico, 1556–1973* (Austin: University of Texas Press, 1974) provides a more recent appraisal of the American intellectual fascination with the Mexican cultural revolution. The links between the intellectual critique of American culture, the Hispanic Art Revival in New Mexico, and the Indian New Deal are documented in John Collier's autobiography *From Every Zenith* (Denver: Sage Books, 1963) and in several perceptive articles, primary among which are: Kenneth R. Philp, "John Collier and the Indians of the Americas: The Dream and the Reality," *Prologue,* 11 (Spring, 1979): 5–21; Lawrence C. Kelly, "John Collier and the Indian New Deal: An Assessment," in Jane M. Smith and Robert M. Kvasnicka, eds., *Indian-White Relations: A Persistent Paradox* (Washington, D.C.: Howard University Press, 1976); and Stephen J. Kunitz, "The Social Philosophy of John Collier," *Ethnohistory,* 18 (1971): 213–29. Longer studies of Collier's entire career also provide useful information concerning his involvement with the Pueblo Lands Controversy. They are Kenneth Ray Philp, *John Collier's Crusade for Indian Reform* (Tucson: University of Arizona Press, 1977) and Lawrence C. Kelly's *Assault on Assimilation* (Albuquerque: University of New Mexico Press, 1983).

Studies describing the New Deal implementation of New Mexico's cultural agenda are William Henry Spurlock, "Federal Support for the Visual Arts in the State of New Mexico, 1933–1943" (Master of Arts thesis, University of New Mexico, 1974); William Wroth, "New Hope in Hard Times: Hispanic Crafts Are Revived During Troubled Years," *El Palacio,* 89 (Summer, 1983): 23–31; Marta Weigle and Mary Powell,

"From Alice Corbin's Lines Mumbled in Sleep to Eufemia's Sopapillas: Women and the Federal Writers Project in New Mexico," *New America: A Journal of American and Southwestern Culture*, 4 (1982): 54–76; Lorin W. Brown, Charles L. Briggs, and Marta Weigle, *Hispano Folklife of New Mexico: The Lorin W. Brown Federal Writers' Project Manuscripts* (Albuquerque: University of New Mexico Press, 1978); and Marta Weigle, *Santa Fe and Taos: The Writers' Era* (Santa Fe: Ancient City Press, 1982). Charles L. Briggs, *The Wood Carvers of Cordoba, New Mexico: Social Dimensions of an Artistic "Revival"* (Knoxville: University of Tennessee Press, 1980), provides a fascinating social history of the efflorescence of the wood carving industry in New Mexico and its role in the Hispanic Arts Revival before and during the New Deal years. William F. McDonald, *Federal Relief Administration and the Arts* (Columbus: Ohio State University Press, 1969), discusses the entire scope of Federal Project One, which included the Art, Music, Writers' and Theater Programs, and provides a number of specific references to its implementation in New Mexico.

Studies describing the New Deal Agricultural programs contain few specific references to New Mexico but several provide a rich background to the social, economic, and political climate in which these programs were conceived and carried out. They are: Sidney Baldwin, *Poverty and Politics: The Rise and Decline of the Farm Security Administration* (Chapel Hill: University of North Carolina Press, 1968); Christiana Campbell, *The Farm Bureau and the New Deal: A Study of the Making of National Farm Policy, 1933–1940* (Urbana: University of Illinois Press, 1962); Richard S. Kirkendall, *Social Scientists and Farm Politics in the Age of Roosevelt* (Columbia, Missouri: University of Missouri Press, 1966); and Samuel Trask Dana, *Forest and Range Policy: Its Development in the Southwest* (New York: McGraw-Hill, 1956). Studies of other New Deal programs which provide useful information and insights into their implementation in New Mexico are: John A. Salmond, *The Civilian Conservation Corps, 1933–1942: A New Deal Case Study* (Durham, N.C.: Duke University Press, 1967); Kenneth E. Hendrickson, Jr., "The Civilian Conservation Corps in the Southwestern States," in Donald W. Whisenhunt, ed., *The Depression in the Southwest* (Port Washington, N.Y.: Kennikat Press, 1980); and Betty and Ernest Lindley's *A New Deal for Youth* (New York: Viking Press, 1938), a study of the National Youth Administration. Studies useful for comparing the implementation of the Hispanic New Deal with the Indian New Deal are: Donald L. Parman, *The Navajos and the New Deal* (New Haven, Conn.: Yale University Press, 1976); and Richard

White, *The Roots of Dependency: Subsistence, Environment and Social Change Among the Choctaws, Pawnees, and Navajos* (Lincoln: University of Nebraska Press, 1983).

Few studies document Hispanic perceptions of the New Deal programs. Three which do are: Anacleto Garcia Apodaca, "The Hispanic Farmers' Conception of the Federal Agricultural Services in the Tewa Basin of New Mexico" (Ph.D. dissertation, Cornell University, 1951); Tomás C. Atencio, "The Human Dimensions of Land Use and Land Displacement," in Clark S. Knowlton, ed., *Indian and Spanish American Adjustments to Arid and Semiarid Environments* (Lubbock: Texas Technological College, 1964); and Tomás Atencio, "The Forest Service and the Spanish Surname American," testimony presented at the Cabinet Committee Hearings on Mexican-American Affairs, El Paso, Texas, October 26–28, 1967, (Washington, D.C.: Inter-Agency Committee on Mexican Affairs, 1967). Two studies which discuss the Hispanic experience in the Southwest from a broader perspective are John Richard Chavez, *The Lost Land: Chicano Images of the Southwest,* (Albuquerque: University of New Mexico Press, 1984) and Rodolfo Acuña, *Occupied America: A History of Chicanos* (New York: Harper and Row, second edition, 1981).

The newspapers from the 1930s and early 1940s provide an extremely useful and revealing, but scattershot, approach to the history of the period. Since none of the New Mexico papers are indexed, information had to be gleaned through a day to day reading. Fortunately, the newspapers from the period are not voluminous. Though tedious and time-consuming, this reading provided much information that could not have been uncovered in any other way. The newspapers most useful for this study were the *Santa Fe New Mexican* and the *Albuquerque Journal.* It was only through reading them that I learned of the local reaction to the Pueblo Indian Lands Controversy and of the long and involved discussions related to the relief of the Hispanic farmers in the Middle Rio Grande Conservancy District.

The New Deal documents contained in the National Archives in Washington, D.C. provided the bulk of the information concerning the implementation of federal programs in New Mexico during the 1930s and 1940s. Working with them was not without some very special problems, however, beside the one noted earlier that there is no special category for "Mexican" or "Spanish American." Since the state files were destroyed sometime after the closing of the state offices, the correspondence is all one-sided. The files, in other words, contain letters and documents sent to Washington but, except for a few copies, none of the letters and documents sent out to the states. The files are also very disorganized. The staff of the National Archives has done an admirable job of inventorying and organizing the overall contents but within each category confusion often reigns. One gets a mental impression of many different people working hastily with files set up haphazardly as programs evolved, were changed and discontinued. One gets the equally strong impression that, when the files were bundled up and packed off to the National Archives some folders may have been spilled and their contents stuffed back into whatever file seemed most appropriate. Finally, because of the way responsibility for programs shifted from agency to agency, and was shared by several agencies simultaneously, one rarely finds all the correspondence pertaining to a certain program within the inventory of one agency alone. Most often it is scattered throughout the files of several different agencies. In sum, it is hard to imagine how a study of this type could have been handled before the availability of copy machines. Only when all apparently pertinent documents were copied and labeled according to original provenance in a record group and file number could they be rearranged chronologically and by subject matter so as to make better sense. The most disappointing and unproductive source of information was the listing of documents printed during the period by the United States Printing Office. As it turned out, most of these documents are not only out of print but copies do not exist even in the Library of Congress.

# Index

AAA. *See* Agricultural Adjustment Administration
Abiquiu Grant, 147
Adams, Birdie, 107
Adams, John, 155
Addams, Jane, 42
Agricultural Adjustment Administration (AAA), 131; and Agricultural Conservation Program, 161–62
Agricultural Conservation Program, 161–62
agricultural employment, seasonal nature of, 14
agriculture: and strain on natural resources, 18; preservation of, 75–76
Albuquerque, 115, 156
*Albuquerque Journal*, 59, 81, 184n39
Alsberg, Henry G., 122–23
Amalia, N. M., 166–67
Amalia Valley, 168–69
American Indian Defense Association, 57, 76
Americanization, 124–25; of immigrants, 42; reaction against, 55
*American Stuff: An Anthology of Prose and Verse*, 123
American West, idealization of, 35–36

Anderson, Clinton, 154, 164
Anglo Americans: and administration of New Deal, viii; cultural domination by, 75; economic domination by, 8–10, 17–25
Anglo-Hispanic relations, xiii, xiv, 26, 33, 65, 75, 148, 172–73, 200n40, 205n29
Anton Chico Land Grant, 148
Apodaca, Anacleto Garcia, 171–73
Appalachia, social reform in, xii, 44
Applegate, Frank, 52–54, 70
architecture, Spanish-Pueblo, revival of, 50–51
archives, translation of, 122, 204n25
art, and assimilation, 194n13
artistic renaissance, in Mexico, 68–70
artist-intellectuals, 47–50, 168
artists, and Santa Fe Railroad, 48–49
arts and crafts, teaching of, 149–50
arts and crafts movement, origins of, 198n15
arts and crafts revival, 70, 72, 74–75
assimilation, of immigrants, 13
Atchison, Topeka & Santa Fe Railroad, 47

250

relief expenditure, congressional
reduction of, 124
Renehan, A. B., 23
repatriation, of Mexican workers,
14–15, 98, 226n64
Republican party, 26, 28, 81
Resettlement Administration (RA):
criticism of, 135; and funding for
village programs, 101; and
grazing lands for Indians, 146;
and loans to rural farmers, 140;
and submarginal land programs,
133–34
resistance: to Country Life
Movement, 40; Hispanic, to
Anglo domination, 25–29
RFC. *See* Reconstruction Finance
Corporation
Rio Abajo area, 52
Rio Arriba County, 3, 27, 86, 107
Rio Grande: and irrigation projects,
30–31; settlement on, 2
Rio Grande Advisory Association,
134
Rio Grande Tri-State Compact, 154
Rio Grande watershed, abuse of, 153
Rio Majada Grant, 164
Rio Puerco area: erosion on, 132;
and failure of New Deal programs,
157; Hispanic concerns in, 133
Rio Puerco Land Use Planning
Committee, 157
road construction programs, 82, 89,
104–7, 209n9
Rockefeller Foundation, 72
Romero, Moises, 110
Roosevelt, Franklin Delano, 76, 87
Roosevelt, Theodore, 39, 44
Rowland, Lea, 97, 105
Rural Recreation projects, and NYA,
115
Rural Rehabilitation programs,
136–37, 145–50
Ruskin, John, 41
Ryan, Helen Chandler, 121

Sanchez, George I., xiv, 74–75,
143, 149, 167
Sanchez, Juan, 120
Sandoval County, 3, 107
*Sandoval* decision, 23–24, 56, 59
Sangre de Cristo Grant, 168
San Jose, N. M., 156–57
San Jose Experimental School, 72–
74, 156
San Jose Grant, 147
San Marcial, N. M., destruction of,
82
San Miguel County, 26, 86
San Pedro Grant, 225n44
Santa Clara Pueblo, 23
Santa Cruz Irrigation District, 84–
85, 100
Santa Cruz Valley, programs in,
139–47
Santa Fe, N. M., 1, 18, 49
Santa Fe Archaeological and
Historical Society, 50
Santa Fe Chamber of Commerce, and
road building programs, 105–6
Santa Fe County, 3; vocational
schools in, 108
Santa Fe Fiesta, 51–53, 70;
described, 195n16
"Santa Fe Indian Detours," 60–61
*Santa Fe New Mexican*, 26, 52, 59,
71, 90–91, 105–6
Santa Fe Planning Board, 51
Santa Fe Railroad, 48, 60, 143
"Santa Fe Ring," 20
Santayana, George, quoted, viii
Santuario de Chimayo, 61; purchase
of, 54, 204n26
school construction program, 109–
10
School of American Research, 50,
51, 53
schools: as community focus, 73–74;
decline of, 12; as focus for
Country Life Movement, 38–39;
funding of, 64, 67; inadequacies